MAKING MODERN FLORIDA

Florida Government and Politics

UNIVERSITY PRESS OF FLORIDA

Florida A&M University, Tallahassee
Florida Atlantic University, Boca Raton
Florida Gulf Coast University, Ft. Myers
Florida International University, Miami
Florida State University, Tallahassee
New College of Florida, Sarasota
University of Central Florida, Orlando
University of Florida, Gainesville
University of North Florida, Jacksonville
University of South Florida, Tampa
University of West Florida, Pensacola

MAKING

MODERN

FLORIDA

How the Spirit of Reform Shaped a New State Constitution

MARY E. ADKINS

Foreword by David R. Colburn and Susan A. MacManus

To Anne Bell,
hope you enjoy this 'journey
through florida.
Mary Adkins Sept 29, 2016

University Press of Florida
Gainesville · Tallahassee · Tampa · Boca Raton
Pensacola · Orlando · Miami · Jacksonville · Ft. Myers · Sarasota

This book may be available in an electronic edition.

21 20 19 18 17 16   6 5 4 3 2 1

A record of cataloging-in-publication data is available from the Library of
Congress.
ISBN 978-0-8130-6285-3

The University Press of Florida is the scholarly publishing agency for the
State University System of Florida, comprising Florida A&M University,
Florida Atlantic University, Florida Gulf Coast University, Florida
International University, Florida State University, New College of Florida,
University of Central Florida, University of Florida, University of North
Florida, University of South Florida, and University of West Florida.

University Press of Florida
15 Northwest 15th Street
Gainesville, FL 32611-2079
http://www.upf.com

For Bob Ervin and Mitchell Prugh

Contents

Illustrations and Tables

Foreword

Florida has held a unique place in the American mind for seven decades. For many retirees, its environment has been like an elixir that allowed them to live longer and more vigorous lives; for other residents, Florida is a place of renewal and new possibilities; and for immigrants, it is a place of political freedom and opportunity. In *Land of Sunshine, State of Dreams*, the historian Gary Mormino describes the state as a "powerful symbol of renewal and regeneration."

During World War II, Americans from all walks of life discovered Florida through military service, and their eyes were opened to the postwar possibilities. The beauty of the landscape and the beaches and the exotic climate and environment led many veterans to describe it to loved ones back home as a paradise. With the end of the war in August 1945, veterans initially returned home, but thoughts of Florida and the opportunities there remained at the forefront of their ambitions. Within months, many were back in the state, soon to be joined by hundreds and then thousands of Americans who embraced a new life in the Sunshine State. In the seventy years between 1945 and 2015, millions moved into the state, increasing the population by more than 18.5 million people, so that the state exceeded 20 million residents by 2015.

Florida's population growth, the settlement patterns of new residents, and their diversity had a profound effect on the state's place in the nation as well as the Floridians' image of themselves. Prior to 1940, Florida was the smallest state in the South and one of the poorest in the nation. Its society and economy were predominantly rural, agricultural, biracial, and segregated. Most residents lived within forty miles of the Georgia border. These demographics and the state's history shaped the public's racial and cultural mind-set and its politics. Florida was essentially a one-party state, controlled by the Democratic Party since the end of Reconstruction in 1876.

All that changed dramatically after World War II. Florida rose from being one of the poorest, most isolated states in the nation, with the smallest population in the South, to the most dynamic state on the east coast and, after California, the most diverse state in the nation. Most Floridians now reside closer to the Caribbean than they do to Georgia, and for most of them, their image of themselves and their state has been significantly influenced by this new geographic orientation. At the onset of the twenty-first century, demographers viewed Florida as a microcosm of the nation, because of its size and its diverse population. Others saw it as a benchmark by which to measure the nation's future.

As Florida changed, so too did its politics. In 1968, voters threw out the Constitution of 1885 in favor of a new document that spoke to the needs of a new state. They then gradually abandoned the racial heritage of the past and the Democratic Party in favor of a dynamic two-party system. By the 1990s, Republicans used their expanding constituency and control of the districting process following the 1990 census to take control of the state legislature and the congressional delegation. These were remarkable developments that reflected the dramatic changes taking place in the state's population. By 2008, Republicans dominated all state offices that were districted, just as Democrats had prior to 1960. The Democratic Party, however, still remained viable in statewide races for governor, U.S. senator, and elected state cabinet positions, as well as in presidential contests that were not affected by districting. Democrats frequently won these races, and they continued to hold a lead of more than 400,000 registered voters over Republicans (4.577 million to 4.172 million), although an increasing number of voters identified themselves as having no party affiliation.

Such a politically and demographically complex and diverse population has made Florida today something other than a unified whole. The maxim that "All politics is local" is truer of Florida than of most other states. For example, those who reside in North Florida share little in common with those living in Central or South Florida, and vice versa. While those in southeast Florida see themselves as part of the "new America," those in North Florida view Miami as a foreign country. Ask a resident what it means to be a Floridian, and few, if any, can answer the question. Ask a Floridian about the state's history, and even fewer can tell you that it has been governed under five different flags, or that its colonial history goes back further than that of New England or Virginia. Perhaps one in ten or twenty residents can tell you who LeRoy Collins was, despite Republican Jeb Bush's recognition of this Democratic governor as the model for all who followed. It is literally a state unknown and indefinable to its people. Such historical ignorance and regional division become major obstacles when state leaders seek to find consensus among voters and solutions that address the needs of all citizens.

An essential purpose of this series is to put Floridians in touch with their rich political history and to enhance their understanding of the political developments that have reshaped the state, region, and nation. This series focuses on the Sunshine State's unique and dynamic political history since 1900 and on public policy issues that have influenced the state and the nation. As part of this series, the University Press of Florida also welcomes book manuscripts on the region that examine critical political and policy developments that impacted Florida.

In this definitive history of the Florida Constitution of 1968, Mary Adkins delineates the constitution revision process in Florida and explains why this particular constitution was so fundamental to the modernization of the state. *Making Modern Florida: How the Spirit of Reform Shaped a New State Constitution* begins with an analysis of the evolution of constitutional reform, commencing with Florida's Constitution of 1838 and culminating with the 1968 Constitution. Adkins posits, "The birth of Florida's modern constitution represented one of the biggest steps forward the state has taken since window screens and air conditioning took hold. The constitution's creators took a backwoods, notoriously manipulative system of government, one actually nicknamed for the prominence of its patronage system, and transformed it into a modern, thoughtful, mostly egalitarian model of efficiency. Its malleability was intentional, a perhaps quixotic effort to put power into the hands of voters, who had never been so entrusted."

The post–World War II population boom and the rise of southeast Florida to political and economic prominence would eventually spark efforts to revise the anti-Reconstruction Constitution of 1885. That constitution underwrote the principle of limited government and served as a bastion for segregation laws, neither of which served the interests or needs of the new residents of South Florida.

Initially, however, these new Floridians showed little interest in changing the political milieu in the state capital of Tallahassee. Former governor and U.S. senator Bob Graham attributed this to what he called the "Cincinnati factor" in Florida politics. The Cincinnati factor explained the behavior of many who continued to identify with political and other loyalties back home. They did not view themselves as Floridians in many respects, Graham observed, choosing instead to subscribe to a Cincinnati newspaper, spend their summers in Cincinnati, send their children back north to schools in Ohio, and eventually have their remains sent to Cincinnati for burial. In many respects, Florida became a way station for them in the passage of life.

As newcomers settled into the state, Adkins notes, they took issue with the state's southern past and its illiberal policies toward blacks and women. Led by Governor LeRoy Collins, South Florida commenced the arduous process of revamping its constitution. Standing in the way, Adkins writes, was the "Pork Chop" delegation, a group of rural politicians in North Florida who fought to retain their region's control of the state legislature, state appropriations, and Florida's future. The struggle became a donnybrook, with representatives of the Pork Chop contingent repeatedly blocking reapportionment of the state legislature to prevent South Floridians from taking direction of state politics. Adkins also highlights the growing divide between South and North Florida over many other important issues, including education, the environment, and race relations. Collins attacked the position of Pork Choppers on apportionment in three ways, according to Adkins: "by encouraging the legislature to reapportion; second, by asking the legislature to create a constitutional advisory commission; and third, by appointing citizens' committees on apportionment and constitution revision." Significantly, Adkins shows, each would fail. Terrell Sessums, who later became Speaker of the House, said he began to feel that reapportionment would never happen "unless it was done by revolution or divine intervention."

Adkins takes us through the tumultuous 1950s and 1960s and the struggle for racial equality and equal representation with great insight and attention to detail. She notes that the struggle unfolded on several levels, with the federal and state courts, the state legislatures, and organizations like the NAACP and the state bar associations weighing in on reapportionment and constitution revision. Finally, in 1965, a constitution revision commission was authorized by the legislature. Adkins identifies two reasons for its creation: "first, the efforts by many to modernize the 1885 'horse-and-buggy' Constitution, efforts that had been tried and stymied time and again; and second, the legislature's own ineffective efforts at reapportioning itself, which gave rise to the federal courts' periodic scoldings."

Adkins's book is a wonderful read and an enormous asset to Floridians who wish to know the past so they can appropriately influence the future.

David R. Colburn
Series Editor

Susan A. MacManus
Series Editor

Preface

I have lived in Florida nearly all my life. As I have watched my state's politics change, I have become increasingly curious about how and why Florida operates the way it does. I read David Colburn's 2007 book *From Yellow Dog Democrats to Red State Republicans: Florida and Its Politics since 1940,* and I was hooked: I read every other book Colburn had written. Then came Buddy MacKay's 2010 book *How Florida Happened: The Political Education of Buddy MacKay.* I began to notice that each of these books about midcentury Florida politics mentioned that in 1968 a new constitution had come into being. That seemed important, but none of the books I had read provided much information about it. The more I tried to delve, the more I realized it was a story untold. I decided it was worth finding out about, and maybe would be worth writing an article about. After all, I am a writing teacher—I teach legal writing at the University of Florida Levin College of Law—and nothing is a better example of legal writing than a constitution.

The first gold mine I found was in a search through the University of Florida's Samuel Proctor Oral History Program (SPOHP) records. SPOHP had sent interviewers to the twentieth anniversary of the 1966 Constitution Revision Commission (CRC) in Tallahassee, and had hundreds of pages of valuable memories available in digital form, easily accessible on the World Wide Web. I saw that Chesterfield Smith had been the chair of the CRC, and I knew that Smith had been a graduate of the University of Florida (now Levin) College of Law. Another online check led me to his collected papers, hundreds of boxes of them, at the University of Florida Smathers Libraries Special Collections. At the beginning of my legal career I had worked in Smith's law firm, Holland and Knight. Although I never worked directly for Smith, he was a legend in the firm, and all new associates were sent to the Lakeland office early in their career for a pep talk from him. It was at Holland and Knight that I learned Smith's twin mantras: Do good. Be somebody.

As I continued my research, the Florida State Archives became for me a kind of second home, as it certainly contained the mother lode of CRC documents. Without the archives and its kind and dedicated professional staff, this book would have been much, much more difficult to research.

After several months of research I began to wonder if any of the CRC members were still living. I began to track them down and ask them for interviews. Doing this quickly was important. After all, most would have been in their forties or fifties during the CRC, which would put them in their eighties or nineties when I was conducting the research. Smith had already passed away, in 2003, and I had just learned of the death of another key member, Thomas Barkdull. I realized I had better get moving. The first person I found was Robert Ervin, who was at that time ninety-three years of age. His kindness and encouragement did much to help me; he made phone calls and vouched for my credibility when I approached others for interviews. Bob's kindness and generosity with his time have led me to dedicate this book to him.

The interviews were, of course, the best part of the research. It was a privilege to sit down with legends of Florida—CRC members, legislators, and former governors alike, those who did their best to lead the state to be the best it could be—and to hear their perspectives over the arc of decades. Losing some of them shortly after speaking with them was the hardest part of creating the book, but I was very fortunate to meet them during their lives.

Another imperative began to become obvious as the years of research continued: the next Constitution Revision Commission will convene within months of the publication of this book. CRCs occur only once every twenty years; because of the time gap, many people are unaware of them at all. Yet Florida's periodic CRCs are unique in the fifty states and provide a powerful opportunity for Florida's citizens to review and revise their constitution. CRCs are made of ordinary citizens and can place recommended changes to the constitution directly on the ballot, without having to go through any other political process first. Floridians need to know the CRC is coming; we need to pay attention to who the members are and what issues are being considered. We need to know where our constitution came from and why it is formed as it is. I have been researching the changes that the CRCs of 1977–78 and 1997–98 brought to the constitution, and I will be watching what the next CRC, which will be formed in February 2017, will do as well. My hope is that this book will inform my fellow Floridians and inspire them to watch and to become involved as well.

Acknowledgments

It is a daunting task to thank everyone who has helped in such a large project as a book, particularly when it is my first book, and I did a fair amount of learning as I researched. For their tireless help, I must start with my colleagues and the administration at the University of Florida Levin College of Law, particularly Jon Mills, who helped me flesh out ideas; the University of Florida Legal Information Center reference librarians; the University of Florida Special Collections librarians, especially Carl Van Ness and James Cusick; the University of Florida Samuel Proctor Oral History Program staff and volunteers, particularly Paul Ortiz, Deborah Hendrix, and Sarah Blanc; and Jack Emerson Davis and the faculty of the University of Florida history department, who have helped a nontraditional graduate student avoid some mistakes. I am sure, however, that many remain; those are my own.

I would also like to thank the committee who awarded me the Patrick Riordan Memorial Fellowship in Florida Studies for 2014. The July I spent at the University of South Florida Special Collections as the Riordan Fellow provided me invaluable time and access to sources; I would especially like to thank Matt Knight and Andy Hues at USF.

Florida-wide research gave me opportunities to visit many of Florida's fine libraries. I would especially like to thank Katie McCormick at Florida State University Special Collections; the staff at the Thomas G. Carpenter Library at the University of North Florida; the excellent and helpful staff at the Richter Library at the University of Miami; the wonderful librarians at the Stetson University College of Law Special Collections; and Teresa Farley of the Florida Supreme Court Law Library, who helped me get started at my very first foray into research for this project.

Perhaps my greatest debt is to Miriam Spalding at the Florida State Archives, who has answered my questions, guided me through oceans of documents, and granted my many requests, and always with a smile. I am thankful that use of the archives remains free and open for citizens.

I am also grateful to those who gave generously of their time to be interviewed. Some of them are no longer living, most remain vitally alive, but all have left their mark on our great state. I have been honored to spend time with them and hear their stories. They are Emerson Allsworth, Reubin O'D. Askew, Martha Barnett, Talbot "Sandy" D'Alemberte, W. Dexter Douglass, Murray Dubbin, Martin A. Dyckman, Robert M. Ervin, Bob Graham, Stephen H. Grimes, Jerome and Gere Johns, Claude R. Kirk Jr., Jon Mills, Jon Moyle Sr., Ben Overton, Dick Pettigrew, Terrell Sessums, Chet Smith, Gene Stearns, and Ralph Turlington.

Deep thanks go to the University Press of Florida, especially series editors David Colburn and Susan MacManus and acquisitions editor Sian Hunter, for believing in the project, and to Marthe Walters, for helping to turn the manuscript into a book. I would also like to thank my copy editor, Jonathan Lawrence, for helping this to come out a much better book than it began. Thank you all for your care and patience.

Thanks seem not nearly enough to describe what I owe to my friends and family for enduring the years of my preoccupation with this project. The Nuñez-Nielsen and Barnett families I especially thank for putting me up in the lovely Tallahassee writers' retreats also known as their guest rooms.

My deepest thanks I reserve for those who have lived through this project with me daily: my beloved Mitchell Prugh, whose moral support and help with research made creating this book both a pleasure and an adventure; and my parents, Flake and Clara Adkins, for waiting for this book patiently and lovingly.

Florida Constitution Timeline

Date	Constitution Action	Reapportionment Action
1887	1885 Constitution is adopted	
1957	Constitutional Advisory Committee ("Sturgis Committee") formed and meets	
1958–59	Special Constitution Advisory Committee ("McRae Committee") formed and meets	
March 26, 1962		U.S. Supreme Court decides *Baker v. Carr*; *Sobel v. Adams* and *Swann v. Adams* are filed in Southern District Court of Florida
July 23, 1962		Southern District Court finds apportionment unconstitutional in *Sobel v. Adams* and *Swann v. Adams* and consolidates them
August 1, 1962		Special legislative session is held to create new apportionment plan
September 5, 1962		Southern District Court approves new apportionment plan
November 6, 1962		Voters reject this apportionment plan
January 29, 1963		Legislature creates new reapportionment plan
January 31, 1963		Florida Supreme Court approves new reapportionment plan

Date	Constitution Action	Reapportionment Action
February 7, 1963		Southern District Court approves plan
June 22, 1964		U.S. Supreme Court reverses *Swann v. Adams* and remands to Southern District Court
June 4, 1965	Legislature passes bill authorizing creation of Constitution Revision Commission (CRC)	
June 30, 1965		Governor Haydon Burns approves legislature's new reapportionment plan
December 1965	Most CRC members are appointed	
December 23, 1965		Southern District Court finds latest reapportionment plan unconstitutional
January 11–12, 1966	Initial CRC meeting held	
January–March, 1966	CRC committee meetings held to determine "certified questions"	
February 25, 1966		U.S. Supreme Court confirms latest reapportionment plan unconstitutional and calls for new plan by next election, May 1966
March 2, 1966		Extraordinary session held to make new apportionment plan
March 18, 1966		Southern District approves new plan
March 25–26, 1966, and April 11, 1966	CRC meets to debate "certified questions"	
May 3, 1966		Primary elections under new apportionment plan
June 30, 1966	Initial draft of proposed constitution is published	

Date	Constitution Action	Reapportionment Action
July 1966	Public hearings held throughout state on draft of constitution	
November 5, 1966		Republican Claude Kirk is elected governor in general election
November 10, 1966	Draft of proposed constitution, incorporating information from public hearings, is finalized	
November 28–December 16, 1966	CRC final debates on proposed constitution	
January 3, 1967		Governor Kirk inaugurated, calls surprise special session on constitution revision
January 7, 1967	CRC signs off on constitution	
January 9, 1967	Special session begins for constitution revision	U.S. Supreme Court invalidates legislature
February 8, 1967		Federal Southern District Court chooses Manning Dauer's reapportionment plan
March 1967		Final elections held under reapportionment plan
April 1967–February 1968	Regular and special legislative sessions reach no agreement on constitution	
July 3, 1968	Legislature agrees on new constitution	
November 5, 1968	Voters approve new constitution (sans Article V)	

Introduction

Florida's 1968 Constitution is sometimes ridiculed for its malleability. Who, after all, would design a document in which pregnant pigs are given explicit rights? And why? Why does it give the state supreme court oversight of legislative apportionment schemes? Why make a state's basic legal document so easy to amend that, after less than fifty years, it already boasts more than one hundred amendments? Should we, as citizens of Florida, be proud of such a beast as it approaches its fiftieth anniversary, or should we hang our blushing heads?

This book argues that the birth of Florida's modern constitution represented one of the biggest steps forward the state has taken since window screens and air-conditioning took hold. The constitution's creators took a backwoods, notoriously manipulative system of government, one actually nicknamed for the prominence of its patronage system, and transformed it into a modern, thoughtful, mostly egalitarian model of efficiency. Its malleability was intentional, a perhaps quixotic effort to put power into the hands of voters, who had never been so entrusted. The authors of the 1968 Constitution represented the leaders of old Florida and new government and private enterprise. As a group they labored to take their state's constitution into the Space Age. They were conscious that they were building the hinge that would connect old Florida to new Florida. They worked together with little regard for political division. Their work shared an electric spark that inspired them to think beyond self-interest. They began the work of making modern Florida.

*   *   *

The written constitution is the quintessential American creation, the explicit collective grant of power from the citizens to a government formed by the citizens' own design. The American penchant for a written constitution likely originated from the written charters governing the colonies prior to the Revolution. The written constitution defines the relationships between different parts of the government and gives citizens certain rights within that government. A written constitution may be well designed or poorly designed; a well-designed constitution defines governmental functions broadly but is flexible enough to allow changes made necessary with time, technology, and population changes. Compared with national constitutions, state constitutions delve more closely into local issues, such as restrictions on taxation, bonding, provisions for education, and control of local governments such as counties and cities. This attention to detail springs from the words of the United States Constitution, which states that all power not specifically given to the federal government remains with the states. Therefore, the individual states are considered to have plenary power; that power must be defined and limited by the terms of their constitutions.[1] The contents of a state constitution can provide a window into the priorities of its citizens.

This book examines the wholesale revision of the Florida state constitution that began in 1966 and was adopted at the polls in 1968. It examines why Florida's previous constitution was poorly designed and why it became so difficult to make that constitution into a better governing document. But to do so we must begin decades earlier, in 1885, when the state had just broken free of Reconstruction. Florida's leaders immediately created a new constitution whose primary characteristic was that it was as different as possible from the constitution the Radical Republicans had drawn up for Florida. The "carpetbaggers," as native-born white southerners called the Radical Republicans, had imposed a constitution that assumed official positions would be occupied by northerners; it provided for a strong executive who could impose the Radical Republican agenda on the vanquished Confederates. The constitution that those vanquished Confederates created in 1885 was crafted for the white citizens of a sparsely populated swampland in which almost all residents lived within fifty miles of Georgia or

Alabama. But the old constitution became rickety fast as Florida experienced the relentless flux of boom after boom of population during the twentieth century, and the constitution's segregationist language, capricious organization, and careless drafting buckled under the weight of an ever-larger and ever-more-sophisticated populace.

To tell the story of the new constitution, this book must also spend time in the decade leading up to its adoption, when the state government was in the thrall of a tight cabal of rural, mostly North Florida, legislators popularly known as the Pork Chop Gang. The Pork Chop Gang controlled everything in state government and, like similar groups of rural legislators in other states, held on to power by resisting the redistricting that would tell the story of the growing urbanization of its state's population. A fair redistricting, or reapportionment, would have dramatically redrawn the legislature. It would have forced the Pork Chop Gang to loosen its fingers from the throat of state power as the balance of that power would move south with the majority of the state's population. It is no surprise, then, that the Gang found ways to make sure this did not happen. But while the Pork Chop Gang resisted change, the rest of Florida embraced it. Florida's Cape Canaveral became the center of the nation's race to the moon; a swampy area of citrus and cattle land near Kissimmee became the home of what would become Walt Disney World. Miami Beach hosted the popular weekly television program *The Jackie Gleason Show*, and a television situation comedy even featured a fictional Cape Canaveral astronaut who lived with a genie.

The leaders of Florida, both old and new, shine through in this book. Many have argued that the legislators of the late 1960s and early 1970s were some of the best in Florida's history. What is certain is that they left the state a much different place than they found it. Legislators such as Reubin Askew, Lawton Chiles, Murray Dubbin, Bob Graham, Beth Johnson, Jack Mathews, Dick Pettigrew, Don Reed, Terrell Sessums, Ralph Turlington, and Bill Young worked hard to transform the state from one in which resources and minorities were exploited to one that protected its environment and its citizens. They provided the necessary political infrastructure for a rapidly growing state and brought transparency to government. Private-sector leaders such as Bill Baggs,

Bob Ervin, and Chesterfield Smith donated thousands of hours to make their state a better place.

The tension of federal involvement in Florida affairs runs throughout this story. Between 1954 and 1966, Florida effectively ceded power to the federal government, particularly the politically progressive decisions of Earl Warren's Supreme Court, by stubbornly resisting racial desegregation and legislative reapportionment.[2] Lawsuits filed to provide rights to blacks, mixed-race couples, non-Christians objecting to prayer in schools, and underrepresented voters always wound up on the losing side in the state supreme court. The inevitable appeal to the federal court would result in a decision in favor of the wronged minority. Thus, Florida progressed mainly by backing itself into laws made by federal courts rather than by state legislators.

But 1966 was the last year the stubbornness held. That year, a constitution revision commission met and proposed a new constitution that, if adopted, would change Florida's government radically. In 1966 and 1967, Florida's legislature achieved a fair reapportionment partly through its own efforts but mostly through the impatience of the federal courts and the patience of one political science professor. The final reapportionment began unexpectedly during the very legislative special session at which Florida's lawmakers were to have taken up their work on the proposed new constitution. Their constitution work would be further delayed by the perceived need to pass new legislation to enable Walt Disney World to set up its infrastructure. In 1968, Florida's legislature finally approved the new constitution, and Floridians reclaimed their state sovereignty by voting it into being. In doing so, they finished the work the Constitution Revision Commission had begun. They made modern Florida.

1

The Old Constitutions

The 1885 Constitution and Its Forerunners

Florida's 1968 Constitution would be the sixth in the state's 123-year history. Although it would formally be called the 1968 Constitution Revision of the 1885 Constitution, because its scope fell one article short of a total revision, it became popularly referred to as the 1968 Constitution; therefore, this book adopts that term. The Territory of Florida created its first constitution in 1838, anticipating statehood, in the tiny Panhandle village of St. Joseph, later to be the Port St. Joe of timber, paper, and land-development fame. After Florida became a state, its constitution was revised in 1861, complete with a declaration of secession from the Union it had joined only sixteen years before. In 1865 a proposed constitution was passed by the legislature but never adopted; in 1868 a Reconstruction constitution, replete with racially evenhanded provisions, was imposed on the people; and in 1885 the people adopted an anti-Reconstruction constitution. That constitution would last more than eighty years, spanning all the way into the years of the civil rights movement, the space race, and glimmers of gender equality.

In 1885, Florida, reacting to the end of Reconstruction as other southern states did, adopted a new constitution intended to weaken state government in favor of local control.[1] The 1885 Constitution enfeebled the governor, devolved power to elected legislators, and continued a legislature that met for only sixty days every two years. Perhaps the most important aspect of the 1885 Constitution is that it was a backlash to the 1868 Radical Republican Reconstruction constitution. The 1868 constitution provided for a strong executive designed to force

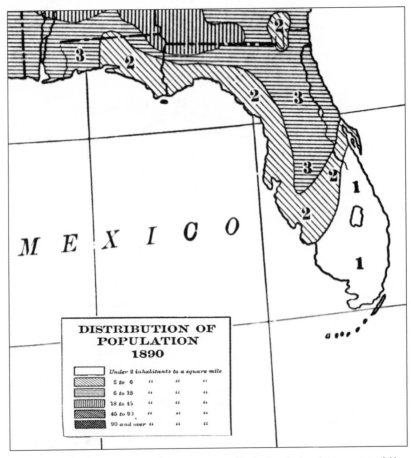

Map 1. Population distribution in Florida in 1890, five years after the Constitution of 1885 was passed. Map produced by Florida Center for Instructional Technology, College of Education, University of South Florida.

the white Floridian southerners, defeated in the Civil War (or, as they preferred to call it, the War of Northern Aggression), to toe the line drawn by the victorious Union. It contained no Jim Crow provisions and assumed that the executive branch would be filled with northern sympathizers. When Reconstruction ended and Floridians were left to govern themselves, they promptly called a constitutional convention and created their own new constitution—the 1885 Constitution that remained in place until 1968.

That constitution was a document of the people of its time—if one counts only white men as "the people." It was intended to create a weak government to prevent resumption of the power held by the carpetbagger Yankee government that had wrestled Florida down during Reconstruction. It provided for a six-member cabinet elected statewide, without term limits, to "assist" a governor who could not succeed himself.[2] Thus the governor was, practically speaking, at most one-seventh of the executive authority of the state. Other southern states had post-Reconstruction constitutions with weak executives, but Florida's system, often referred to as the "plural executive," was uniquely weak. Under Florida's system, it was not unusual for cabinet members to remain in office for decades, building powerful political loyalties and watching, like sunning alligators on a riverbank, impotent governors come and go every four years. Should a governor die or otherwise leave office before his term expired, his powers would transfer to the President of the Senate, another position whose occupant could hoard power.[3]

As a sign of the times, the 1885 Constitution explicitly segregated public schools,[4] even though Florida's public school system was virtually nonexistent; outlawed mixed-race marriages "forever";[5] and provided for a poll tax.[6] There was no home rule for local governments: local cities and counties had to apply to the legislature for any matter other than those that were routine. Article VIII of the 1885 Constitution was littered with amendments pertaining to particular matters in one county or another.[7]

Practically speaking, this was another way of keeping the keys to power and patronage firmly in the fists of legislators rather than in the executive branch. The constitution also contained no provisions designed to protect the environment, contained numerous misspellings, and was curiously organized, having, for example, a lottery ban in Article III, which concerned the legislative branch.[8] It specified the salaries of the governor, legislators, and some judges, and even specified the amount per mile legislators could be reimbursed for travel expenses.[9]

Article III devised a scheme that accurately apportioned the state into nearly equal legislative districts according to the population at that time, using language that the districts be "as nearly equal in population as practicable."[10] Unfortunately, even though it provided that the state reapportion every ten years thereafter, it used a fixed system that could only be modified by constitutional amendment. The article provided for thirty-eight senatorial districts, with one senator per district and counties to not be divided. This meant, in effect, that the best a populous county could do was have one senator not shared with another county.[11] The House of Representatives was limited to sixty-eight members, with at least one member from each county but with no more than three from any county (at the time, Florida had thirty-nine counties, not its current sixty-seven).[12] In 1885, before South Florida's population boomed, it may have been equitable for rural Jefferson County to be guaranteed at least one-third as many representatives as Miami's Dade County—after all, Dade County had a population of only 257 in the 1880 census, and only 861 in the 1890 census, compared to about 16,000 in Jefferson in those censuses—but that rough equity began to vanish in the 1920s as newcomers surged into the southern two-thirds of the state.[13]

In addition, modifying the constitution was difficult. In fact, only the legislature—not any other branch of the government, and certainly no group of mere citizens—could initiate modification of the 1885 Constitution and thus the apportionment plan.[14] Under this sclerotic scheme, reapportionment rarely occurred, because only its victims—legislators—could make it happen, and because the fixed apportionment structure favored those already in power. Florida's straitjacketed constitutional apportionment scheme was far from unique. The various other post-Reconstruction southern state constitutions had a variety of apportionment schemes, with several other states' provisions similar to Florida's.[15]

The limits on legislators per county would cripple attempts at reapportionment; that rigidity presented a major obstacle to fair apportionment. It failed to anticipate that the South Florida counties, which in the late 1800s were full only of alligators, mosquitoes, and choking heat, would grow wildly, while North Florida counties would remain rural. By the 1920s, however, growth in previously empty parts of Florida had outstripped that of the north, and the people coming to the southern half of the state were increasingly not southerners. Railroads opened South Florida to tourism.[16] Florida created twenty-eight new counties, most of them south of Ocala. The still nearly empty peninsula and Gulf coast provided useful land for military bases in World War II.

During World War II, many large military bases holding thousands of soldiers and sailors opened in Florida; at its height, Camp Blanding, carved out of pinewoods and sand in rural Clay County in northeast Florida, was the fourth-largest city in Florida.[17] After the war, many soldiers remembered the beauty of their training grounds and settled in Florida with their families.[18] Sun-seeking retirees and other northern migrants headed south after air-conditioning became commonplace.[19] Midwesterners settled on the southern Gulf coast, and northeasterners moved to the lower Atlantic coast. The Cubans who had long been settled in Tampa were joined across the state by others coming to Miami, although the huge migration to Miami of the Batista and Castro years had not quite begun. Scientists and engineers from all over the nation poured into Brevard County beginning in the 1950s, working on the budding space program.

North Florida, on the other hand, did not grow appreciably. And blacks actually declined as a percentage of the voting-age population statewide.[20] Between 1900 and 1960 the percentage of native-born Floridians living in the state had nose-dived from 67.9 to 38.1, one of the lowest in the South.[21] North Florida residents did not for a moment believe that these newcomers shared their southern values and traditions, and to a large extent they were right. Although almost no one in the state fought for immediate integration, North Floridians held to their traditional southern segregation more tightly than most. Florida had shot from a rural frontier to one of the most urbanized states in the South. It had begun a sprint through rapid change, and the antiquated 1885 Constitution hamstrung it.

Consequences of Failure to Reform the Constitution

The 1885 Constitution endured for more than eight decades, resisting several mid-twentieth-century attempts to revise or replace it. Over and over again, it was amended and tweaked, and sometimes ignored. Over the decades a total of 212 proposed amendments to the 1885 Constitution were submitted to the voters. Of those, 149 passed. Fifty percent of the amendments were passed after World War II, and 25 percent were passed in 1961, 1963, and 1965. The 1965 legislature introduced

111 Joint Resolutions for amendment of 83 separate proposals. Eighteen were approved for submission to the voters in 1965 and 1966.[22] But the 1885 Constitution never received the complete overhaul the growing state needed; instead, what amounted to successive layers of lipstick were administered. As the 1965–66 Speaker of the House E. C. Rowell said: "It makes me wonder if we're as good a state as we're supposed to be if it takes that many amendments to bring our laws up-to-date. . . . [In any given legislative session,] I guarantee you there'll be any kind of bill introduced—most of them for motherhood and against sin."[23]

Florida was far from alone in having a much-amended constitution. Many state constitutions had been amended even more than Florida's; state constitutions tended to contain more detail than the federal one, and more detail meant that the constitution probably dealt with aspects of society subject to change. And as society changed—which it did radically during the twentieth century—the constitutions had to change with them. As a result, many states' constitutions were more patch than pants.[24]

Florida's constitutional rules for apportionment, appropriate when most of the population lived in the rural north, meant that the rural northern population, a substantial minority of the state's population, would keep control. Although few of North Florida's many counties were home to more than a few thousand people, each had a representative, and almost all had a senator. South Florida had relatively few counties, but they tended to cover more territory, and several of them held hundreds of thousands of newly arrived citizens. Because the constitutional restrictions limited the size of the legislature, and most seats were already allocated to rural counties, few seats were left over to accommodate the more heavily populated counties. Additionally, the rural bloc would have been less than eager to share power with urban "Yankees." Although Florida presented an extreme case in its rural power bulge, it was not alone. Not only other southern states, but also states in the West, the Midwest, and New England all shared this characteristic to some degree.[25]

Florida's apportionment problem came to a head in the mid-1950s. By that time, the rural bloc in the Senate had such complete cohesion

Figure 1. The Pork Chop Gang, the group of legislative leaders who controlled the state in the 1950s and into the 1960s, gathered at this fishing camp in Nutall Rise, Florida, for meetings. Photo courtesy of State Archives of Florida, *Florida Memory*, https://floridamemory.com/items/show/147149.

and such a stranglehold on power that it had become known as the "Pork Chop Gang," a sobriquet that referred to its members' "shrewd control of pork barrel spending."[26] By the mid-1950s, the Pork Choppers were as firmly embedded in the legislature as ticks in a dog. They were a true gang, complete with a "blood oath" they took at a North Florida fishing camp in 1955, promising to vote together to preserve the southern way of life: rural values, racial segregation, and minimal government.[27] One critic described them as "smugly and sleepily walking backward into the nineteenth century."[28]

One anecdote may illustrate the state of mind of not only the Pork Choppers but of their ilk, the southern-born rural white segregationists. In the spring of 1965, S. Dilworth Clarke of tiny Monticello, in Jefferson County, the longest-serving member of the Florida Senate and "dean" of the Pork Chop Gang, was stepping down, his district distorted by reapportionment. Some of Clarke's fellow senators were teary-eyed at his retirement. The legislature had just named a short stretch of road in Clarke's honor. Clarke, son of a Confederate veteran, was touched. He blurted: "I have niggers at home with children named after me, but this is the first road."[29]

The last thing the Pork Choppers wanted was to give up power through reapportionment. They liked bringing money to North Florida and found innovative ways to do so. For example, when horse racing began to gain popularity in South Florida, the legislature, led by the Pork Choppers, granted the racing interests the right to have pari-mutuel gambling on condition that the taxes from it be distributed evenly among all counties.[30] This meant that little Liberty County in the Panhandle received just as much revenue from bangtail racing as did the counties hosting it, such as Dade, more than five hundred miles away. This arrangement had the convenient effect of making the sinful gamblers in the south pay for their vice—and provide free revenue to northern residents.

Post–World War II Constitutional Reform

The September 1953 death of Governor Dan McCarty, the first death of a sitting Florida governor under the 1885 Constitution, was the first sign of coming change, setting into motion events that demonstrated to Floridians some of the shortcomings of the 1885 Constitution. McCarty's death shook the system because it brought to the public eye a feature of the 1885 Constitution that had not been tested: succession to the governor's seat. The 1885 Constitution provided for no lieutenant governor. Instead, in the event the governor left office through death or for any other reason, the governor's office would be filled by the President of the Senate.

In September 1953 that meant Charley Johns, a soft-spoken legislator from Starke, in rural northern Bradford County. Johns had grown up poor. His father, the Bradford County sheriff, was killed in the line of duty when Johns was an infant. After a brief stint at the University of Florida, Johns became a railroad worker. Like most legislators of his generation, Johns never served in the military, and his life experiences,

Figure 2. Charley Johns (*center*) was sworn into office after Governor Dan McCarty died less than a year after taking office, in 1953. As President of the Senate, Johns was the constitutional successor to the governor's office, even though his Senate district consisted of only a few thousand voters. Photo courtesy of State Archives of Florida, *Florida Memory*, https://floridamemory.com/items/show/128103.

apart from the railway, were concentrated within Florida's borders. Johns seldom sat still, however: in the 1920s he started an insurance company in Starke, worked the railroad, and ran for the Florida Legislature. His older brother had become Senate President-designate but died of pneumonia before taking that position. Charley Johns set his cap to holding the position his brother had missed. In 1953, he made it.

Soon after Johns became President of the Senate, Governor McCarty died unexpectedly, at age forty-one. Johns "rushed up and took the oath of office"[31] and took charge. Some McCarty supporters nursed hard feelings, saying Johns acted like a governor, not an acting governor.[32] Johns quickly replaced many McCarty appointees, explaining, "I was sitting there at my desk with my hands cupped. Nobody would cooperate with me."[33] The problem from the point of view of Johns's

Figure 3. LeRoy Collins, state senator from Tallahassee, defeated Acting Governor Charley Johns in a special gubernatorial election in 1955 to fill the remainder of the term left by Dan McCarty, who died in 1953. Photo courtesy of State Archives of Florida, *Florida Memory*, https://florida memory.com/items/show/19314.

critics was that the governor's seat was filled by someone who was not elected statewide; a governor attaining the position under this method of succession was unlikely to be well known beyond his district and therefore may not have enjoyed broad support. After all, Johns's district had only a few thousand voters, less than 1 percent of Florida's total.

The acting governorship lasted only until the midpoint of McCarty's original four-year term, then was subject to an election for the remaining two years. Johns ran for the governorship against a fellow Democrat, Senator LeRoy Collins from Leon County. Collins beat Johns badly in the gubernatorial primary and sprinted to victory in the general election, and Johns returned to the Senate. He promptly established the Florida Legislative Investigations Committee (FLIC), which searched for communist infiltrators in civil rights groups such as the NAACP and caused havoc at state universities by attempting to root out gay and lesbian professors. One university particularly badly harassed by the FLIC was the University of South Florida, which Johns's successor and rival, Governor Collins, had established shortly after becoming governor.

Strain on Florida's Environment

The way that environmental protection attempts played out under the old constitution also illustrates the difficulties Florida had under its obsolescing constitution. Cattle, citrus, and timber interests—chiefly located in rural northern and central Florida—went nearly untaxed, and the lucrative phosphate-mining companies, based at that time mostly in rural, inland Polk County, successfully resisted severance taxes. So not only did revenue come into rural parts of Florida from urban areas practically for free, but the rural businesses also got off nearly scot-free from paying taxes. Any fair reapportionment that would actually give the more heavily populated parts of the state their share of representation would end the revelry.

The tension from overpopulation and strained resources was felt acutely in South Florida, and there much of the drive for environmental laws would emerge. In the 1930s, for example, a group of citizens sued a company that had proposed to build a pulp mill in Jacksonville, arguing that the mill would create a public nuisance. The Supreme Court of Florida issued a remarkable opinion denying the claim, stating that although "it is a matter of common knowledge . . . that all wood pulp mills emit noxious and disagreeable odors," a mill could not be a public nuisance as a matter of law because the state had essentially invited pulp mills to Florida by offering a tax exemption for them in a constitutional amendment.[34]

Air- and water-pollution threats from Florida's industries raised environmental awareness statewide by the mid-1950s. Much of the water-pollution problem came from agriculture and dredge-and-fill development, which damaged or destroyed estuaries for the sake of agriculture or the ever-growing desire for waterfront property to house the quickly growing population. From the Everglades drainage to Carl

Fisher's creation of Miami Beach by filling in mangrove swamps with sand from the bottom of Biscayne Bay, Florida developers made fortunes by making and selling new land.

Before 1957, no legislature or governor of Florida had ever opposed or discouraged any practice that could provide growth and money to the state. That year, Governor Collins pitched an epic fight against a massive dredge-and-fill development set to go forward in Boca Ciega Bay, the shallow body of water that separates St. Petersburg, on the Pinellas Peninsula, from the barrier islands along the Gulf of Mexico. Although the project would create many "waterfront" homes, it would also disrupt the bay-bottom ecosystem. Although Collins ultimately lost the fight, and the development was dredged and built, his opposition to the project took government officials and developers by surprise: Collins's battle indicated that development and pollution no longer could assume a friendly nod from Florida government.

Another growing environmental problem in Florida was air pollution. Although pollution from pulp mills caused problems in North Florida, the most concentrated fight over air pollution occurred among the rural commercial titans located in Central Florida: the phosphate-mining companies and the cattle and citrus industries. By the mid-1950s the phosphate industry had caused significant damage to local residents and area businesses. Citrus trees had a characteristic discolored appearance and lower yields where phosphate emissions fouled the air; cattle had deformed bones and swayed backs. Polk County was the largest cattle county, a major citrus county, and one of the two largest phosphate-producing counties in Florida. Citizens, citrus growers, cattle ranchers, and vegetable and flower farmers complained so much that the legislature created a committee in 1955 to address the complaints. As a result of that committee's hearings, the legislature passed an air-pollution-control law, the Florida Air Pollution Control Law, which was touted as the first of its kind in the nation.[35]

But the new law was weak. Responsibility for its enforcement was repeatedly shifted between two agencies, making consistency in administration difficult. It had weak provisions for enforcement and many loopholes, specifically excluding pollution from pulp and paper mills. Worse, the Pork Chop legislature was loath to spend money on a project that was backed by Governor Collins and which could hurt industry. After all, Collins had defeated their comrade, Charley Johns, for the governor's seat just a few years ago. After years of frustration with enforcing the air-pollution law, Collins commissioned a statewide air-pollution study in 1960. Its report was comprehensive and damning—but came out after Collins's term expired.

Collins's successor in the governor's office, C. Farris Bryant, was a North Florida conservative in greater sympathy with the Pork Choppers than Collins had been. The Pork Choppers simply outlasted Governor Collins's term of office; North Florida legislators maintained their chokehold on the state. Florida's phosphate and pulp industries, and their pollution, were safe again. And as late as 1966, air pollution in Jacksonville, a city with more than its share of pulp mills, was bad enough to destroy women's nylon stockings.[36]

Throughout the late 1950s and early 1960s, some legislators attempted to pass laws that would help to clean up the environment, or at least to gather facts that would shed light on causes of environmental problems. The record of environmental legislation and proposed environmental legislation through this period shows that legislation that was primarily local—legislation that would allow a particular local stream or river to be cleaned up, for example, or limit strip mining in a particular county—tended to pass, whereas measures that called for statewide anti-pollution laws or that affected powerful industries such as phosphate or wood pulp tended to either die in committee, come out of committee with unfavorable reports, be tabled, or be withdrawn.

This resistance to statewide environmental reform was only one symptom of Pork Chop conservatism kept in place by the old constitution's apportionment scheme. Combined with their resistance to desegregation, investigation of African American organizations and gays, and willful disregard of the infrastructure the growing parts of the state needed, this resistance demonstrated that the legislature was too entrenched to change. As a result, nongovernmental groups such as the Florida Bar and the League of Women Voters pushed for constitutional reform. They received help from Governor Collins during his six years in office. However, between World War II and 1965, most attempts to redo the constitution that marched across the political landscape marched right off again. One or two would leave an impact, however.

The 1947 Florida Bar Proposal

The first modern attempt to propose an entirely new constitution preceded McCarty's death by six years. In 1947, the Florida State Bar Association, as it was then called, published a pamphlet proposing a new state constitution. In November of that year a committee chaired by attorney D. H. Redfearn printed and distributed a draft constitution.[37] That draft contained progressive elements. First, it proposed lowering the voting age from twenty-one to eighteen, possibly to acknowledge the contributions and sacrifices of thousands of young Floridians who had fought in World War II while they were not yet old enough to vote.[38] But the liberality went farther. In a time of blatant racial discrimination, and before the voting rights and segregation battles that would disrupt the South in the next decade, the section on basic rights provided: "No power, civil or military, shall at any time interfere to prevent the free exercise of the right of suffrage."[39] This provision was modeled on the new Missouri Constitution. Also, the article on the executive branch provided for the creation of a state department of education; the article would also repeal the provision for segregated schools,[40] although later proposed constitutions would revert to providing for segregated schools after the U.S. Supreme Court's 1954 *Brown v. Board of Education* decision reignited white citizens' racial hatred.[41]

Under the bar's proposal, the Senate would remain restricted to thirty-eight members.[42] Only contiguous whole counties would be placed in each Senate district, meaning some counties would be combined within a Senate district;[43] this did not represent a change from the 1885 Constitution. The House would be apportioned based on the same population tiers for small, medium, and large counties as in the 1885 Constitution, but with an additional representative for every 100,000 in population per county.[44] Thus, the number of seats in the House would not be limited and could more closely reflect population growth and shifts—but would be in danger of growing to an unwieldy size in a time of steep growth.

The 1947 draft constitution maintained the weak-governor executive branch by providing for a governor who could not succeed himself, no lieutenant governor, and an elected cabinet with no mention of whether the cabinet members could succeed themselves.[45]

All court rules would be created solely by the Florida Supreme Court, mirroring the Missouri Constitution but not the then-current Florida constitution.[46] The minimum number of circuit judges would be tied to population, with no less than one judge for each 25,000 persons.[47] Additional judges could be added by a county or the legislature. Significantly, the proposal would require for the first time that each judge had been admitted to the Florida Bar.[48] This was congruent with the elimination of the offices of constable and justice of the peace.[49] Likewise, all criminal prosecutions would be performed by a prosecuting officer, and the offices of state's attorney and county solicitor would be eliminated.[50] Transfer of judges from one location to another would be done by the supreme court chief justice and no longer by the governor.[51] However, the draft noted that removing sitting judges would be contentious, and the draft was put forward as a very tentative solution.[52] A judge would have the ability to prevent the formation of a grand jury by court order. Women would be allowed to sit on juries, but if they requested to be excused from a jury, the court was required to grant the request.[53]

The draft still proposed no home rule for counties, which meant that legislators would keep their tight hold over their home areas by having the power to grant or reject their requests for state largesse.[54] A new section dealt with public officers, explicitly banning nepotism.[55] The right to bear arms remained, but a new phrase would restrict "the wearing of concealed weapons."[56] Legislative power to drain lands over the land of another person would continue to require compensation under constitutional eminent domain.[57]

A statewide commission was proposed to equalize tax assessments, especially of property owned by utilities, throughout the state.[58] The excise tax would continue to be equally distributed geographically around the state.[59]

Further ability to revise the constitution remained as already provided in the 1885 Constitution, such that the legislature would control constitutional revision. However, the Bar Association's draft did require a public vote every twenty years on whether the constitution should be rewritten or revised.[60] For all its promise, though, the 1947 proposal never gained traction; the legislature never considered it, and it created no change.

Governmental Attempts to Revise

Then, in 1948, a baby step in the history of the Florida constitution revision happened: an amendment passed that allowed a complete section of the constitution, not just one subject matter within a single section, to be amended.[61] Still, the only way to amend the whole constitution was by a constitutional convention, which sitting legislators did not want to allow because for practical purposes it would mean that the legislature would be reapportioned.

The first major reapportionment battle occurred after the 1954 election of Governor Collins of Tallahassee to the second half of Governor McCarty's original term. Collins, who had campaigned in part on a reapportionment platform, did not carry a majority of counties, but he defeated the acting governor, Charley Johns, by carrying populous South Florida handily. Collins first called for total constitution reform and reapportionment in his first address to the legislature, less than one month after his inauguration. But his efforts were frustrated in the 1955 and 1957 legislative sessions, when the rural legislators saw to it that his reform efforts died a lonely death. No other action by the Florida Legislature more clearly showed the impossibility of reform while malapportionment existed.

As governor, Collins attacked the current manner of apportionment on three levels: first, by encouraging the legislature to reapportion; second, by asking the legislature to create a constitutional advisory commission; and third, by appointing citizens' committees on apportionment and constitution revision. Collins's first method of attempting constitution reform, requesting the legislature to produce a reapportionment plan, was defeated when the legislature failed in its 1955 session to comply with that request. Collins called the legislature back into special session to reapportion, but the legislature, dominated by Pork

Choppers angry with the man who had defeated Charley Johns, did not comply. Representative Reubin Askew recalled that the legislators would thumb their noses at Collins's efforts to get them to reapportion. They "just wouldn't do it. They'd convene, pray, and adjourn."[62] Legislative aide Terrell Sessums said he began to feel that reapportionment would never happen "unless it was done by revolution or divine intervention."[63] The legislature stayed in session, technically, for 520 days, although its members dispersed after just a few days; it still failed—or refused—to reapportion.[64]

The second method by which Collins attacked constitution reform was to ask the legislature to create a constitutional advisory commission. When it did so, that commission nearly was able to put forth the farthest-reaching reform the 1885 Constitution had yet seen. First, though, the Senate resolved to amend the constitution to create a constitution revision commission that would make recommendations to the legislature. Proposed by Senators William Gautier, of New Smyrna Beach in Volusia County, and Verle Pope, of St. Johns County (fondly known as "The Lion of St. Johns"), the resolution stated that an emergency existed requiring the immediate revision of the constitution; it did not state exactly what that emergency was.[65] The resolution proposed to create a thirty-seven-member constitution revision commission appointed by the governor, chief justice, President of the Senate, Speaker of the House, and attorney general. One member was required to be from each U.S. congressional district, and the other members were to be selected at large. The commission was required to submit its proposal to the governor; that proposal would automatically be placed on the ballot for the 1956 general election. The resolution specified that the commission could make no change to sections of the current constitution that dealt with fundamental rights and certain bonding and taxation features.

One day later, on April 13, 1955, twenty-one senators sponsored a bill creating an in-Senate constitution revision commission to study possible revisions and report back to the Senate.[66] Both actions were referred to the Senate Committee on Constitutional Amendments, chaired by Bill Shands of Gainesville. Shands was politically aligned with the Pork Chop Gang, and the committee recommended that neither effort be approved.[67] The second bill, despite having twenty-one sponsoring senators, lacked the additional nine senators to bring the bill to the Senate floor over the committee's disapproval.

Instead, the legislature created the Florida Constitution Advisory Committee (FCAC) that Governor Collins had requested. Among its more than three dozen members, this committee included Mayor Haydon Burns of Jacksonville, former governor Fuller Warren of Blountstown, Stetson College of Law dean Harold "Tom" Sebring, Circuit Judge Hugh Taylor of Quincy, and Senator Elmer Friday of Fort Myers. The FCAC became known colloquially as the Sturgis Committee after its chair, Senator Wallace Sturgis from Ocala.

Accounts differ as to the intent of the members of the FCAC. Historians David Colburn and Richard Scher argued that the FCAC membership was dominated by rural interests without much sympathy for constitution reform.[68] However, a House Committee on Reapportionment report later claimed that "by all accounts, the committee took the job seriously and sought a pragmatic solution."[69] The constitution revision that the FCAC proposed in 1955 was transformed by a joint legislative committee into what became known as the daisy-chain constitution of 1957.

In its draft the FCAC proposed some items on Governor Collins's wish list, including limited home rule and a lieutenant governor to succeed in case of the governor's death,[70] but it completely failed to propose the drastic changes to the "entire so-called Cabinet system" for which Collins had hoped.[71] It did propose that the Florida Supreme Court have the power to reapportion if the legislature could not agree on a scheme.[72]

The FCAC revision was reported to both houses for the 1957 regular session. But it never got out of committee: the respective chamber committees were unable to reconcile their individual proposals. Senator Dewey Johnson of Quincy, west of Tallahassee, introduced a resolution by noting that constitution revision must include reapportionment, an issue that remained unresolved, and that the reapportionment attempt in that session seemed "doomed to failure." He recommended that constitution revision be referred to a joint ten-person committee and requested the governor to call the legislature back into special session no earlier than mid-September 1957.[73]

Neither the Senate committee nor the House committee proposed resolutions for constitutional revision to the full Senate or House. As Senator Johnson had requested, Governor Collins recalled the legislature into an extraordinary session. That session proposed an entirely revised constitution based on the FCAC's proposal, with the exception of Article V, which governed the judicial system and had recently undergone significant amendment. In the proposed constitution, the pledge of paramount allegiance to the federal government in the 1885 Constitution was removed.[74] This omission may have reflected the segregationist majority's fury with the U.S. Supreme Court's recent decision on school desegregration in *Brown v. Board of Education*.

The revision emerging from this session changed the Sturgis Committee's recommendations in three important and telling ways. First, the legislature inserted what became known as the "daisy chain" requirement, which provided that none of the fourteen individual amendments proposed by the Sturgis Committee could take effect unless the public voted to adopt all of them.[75] In his biography of Collins, Thomas Wagy points out that the daisy-chain linkage allowed the legislature to retain control over the constitutional changes this way: its alternative to the daisy chain was to call a constitutional convention, which would be independent and not under its control.[76] Second, the legislature amended the future means to modify the constitution. The Sturgis Committee had recommended that the Florida voters be able to directly propose constitutional revisions by initiative and that any constitutional initiative having signatures of at least 5 percent of at least forty-five counties would be placed on the ballot to be voted upon at the next election. This initiative proposal was unique in Florida's history, and indeed, was more radical than any amendment process proposed or adopted since in Florida. The legislature added to this a brazen provision allowing a three-fourths majority of both houses to override any changes made in the constitutional convention. In diplomatic language perhaps calculated to not jeopardize future legislative funding, the University of Florida Administrative Clearing Service, critiquing the changes, noted this provision was unique and "one which is not paralleled in any of the other forty-seven state constitutions."[77] Third, and finally, the Sturgis Committee had proposed a different apportionment plan; the legislature rejected it, voting to continue to protect its warped apportionment.

In response, Senator Verle Pope and attorney Rafael Rivera-Cruz, who had opposed the legislation, challenged the daisy-chain linkage in court, and before the constitution could be submitted to the people for a vote, the lawsuit was successful. In July 1958 the Florida Supreme Court struck down the proposed constitution, holding that because adoption of each revised article was tied to the others, the proposal violated the constitutional prohibition against revision of more than one article at a time.[78] Prophetically, during the spring legislative session that year, Sturgis Committee member Hugh Taylor had told a reporter, "Should the proposed constitution be rejected, it is my opinion that further efforts for any general revision of the constitution for at least a decade would be absolutely futile."[79]

Collins's third method of attempting to revise the constitution, forming citizens' committees on apportionment and constitution revision, was equally unsuccessful. A citizens' apportionment committee recommended an apportionment plan that lessened but did not eliminate malapportionment; the legislature ignored it.[80] The citizens' committee on constitution revision, Collins's Special Constitution Advisory Committee (SCAC), was formed in the fall of 1958, after the judicial defeat of the daisy-chain proposal. Collins asked Bill McRae to chair it. Not the average small-town southern lawyer, McRae was a Rhodes Scholar who often quoted Latin, Greek, and Shakespeare to the young associates in his law firm. The SCAC consisted of five persons: in addition to McRae, who agreed to serve as chairman, there were Joe Grotegut, chair of the state Road Department; Charles Tom Henderson, an assistant attorney general in charge of statutory revision; Dick Gardner, a Quincy lawyer; and Maxine Baker, a prominent Dade County representative of the League of Women Voters (LWV) with a future in the Florida House.

A series of five letters written by Baker to board members Van Gill and Frances Kilroe of the LWV provide insight into the workings of the McRae Committee. According to Baker, the committee had agreed that they were not a "public body," but just a committee of citizens; therefore they would not hold public meetings or invite the press. She believed this position to be "defensible" even though they might be accused of holding secret meetings. Still, she felt she owed the LWV a report, and wrote the letters to two of its board members, asking them not to tell anyone but members of the board for the time being.[81]

Baker described the first meeting, at which the group discussed its purpose and the scope of its job. Chairman McRae began by explaining, "for the benefit of Mr. Frederick [an out-of-state representative of the Council of State Governments, who was visiting] and Mrs. Baker," the recent history of constitution revision attempts in Florida. Then he asked each member to give an opinion as to what the committee's direction should be—and skipped over Baker. She spoke up and asked how the group was to propose a complete overhaul of the constitution article by article, when that was exactly what the Florida Supreme Court had just rejected. The other members hastened to reassure her that they had been told that such a proposal could legally be made. "Well, who am I, a non-lawyer," she wrote to her LWV colleagues, "to dispute a former president of the Florida Bar [McRae], the Chairman of the State Road Board etc. etc.?" The men assured her that, after all, they weren't actually proposing a complete revision at that point—so, she triumphantly reported to her LWV colleagues, they *were* afraid of getting a complete overhaul attempt thrown out, as she was. But she had earned their respect, and from then on was "just another member of the committee—no more 'explaining' things for my benefit."[82]

Baker also reported, from that first meeting of the committee, that the whole group agreed that what was often euphemistically called "Florida's unique cabinet system"—a plural executive with six cabinet members elected statewide with the ability to succeed themselves without limit, and a governor who could not succeed himself—was so entrenched that "it was entirely utopian to dream about changing *that* at this time."[83]

One thing the SCAC did dream about was provisions for future constitutional amendment. It tentatively settled, in an early meeting, on amendment by citizen initiative and for an automatic referendum on a constitutional convention every twenty years. Baker confessed herself to be "flabbergasted—with delight" at these developments.[84] Although the group ultimately kept the twenty-year convention feature, it did more research on amendment by initiative, found that "the record of states which have initiative provisions is not enviable," and dropped that provision.[85]

Baker's delight was short-lived. The group next tackled the red-hot issue of education—specifically, racial desegregation of public schools. The 1885 Constitution, which was still in effect, provided for separate but equal schools for black and white students.[86] McRae's group came perilously close to agreeing to substitute the word "education" for "schools" in the constitution. The reason, explained by Joe Grotegut, was that under the proposed language, if desegregration were enforced, the legislature could give money to parents who did not want their children in desegregrated schools, so the children could go to private schools. The change was about to be made by acclamation when Baker, "wishing the floor could swallow me," spoke up "in a wee small voice 'No sir, I'm sorry, but I can't agree with that.'" Baker described a lively dialogue featuring herself on one side and all the other members on the other. She added in her letter, "No one admitted it, but I had a feeling that some of my remarks hit a sensitive chord here and there. At any rate, the decision did not go through at that time."[87]

After that meeting, Baker returned to her hotel room in turmoil. She felt she had gone out on a limb and wasn't sure if the other committee members would ostracize her, if she had disgraced the LWV, if she should resign. Then the phone rang. It was McRae, inviting her to dinner. As Baker reported, they had a lovely time, and "talked of many things but kept getting back to The Subject." She assessed McRae to be anti-integration but "not a fire-eating Faubus," a reference to Orval Faubus, the Arkansas governor who in 1957 used the National Guard and in the 1958–59 academic year shut down Little Rock high schools to keep black children from integrating white schools. At the next day's committee meeting, she was treated normally—not "like a red-headed step child." And integration of schools didn't come up again for nearly two months. When it did, Baker was no longer alone in her position, and the plan to sneak a way around integration never became part of the draft.[88]

Home rule was the subject Baker had been assigned in the committee. It was her duty to study and propose language for the revised constitution, and she did a thorough job—perhaps too thorough, she admitted to her correspondents. When it was her turn to lead the committee through the home-rule recommendations at a January 1959 meeting, the discussion was long and technical. Baker noticed that McRae "looked completely at sea" during much of the discussion and that he and Gardner seemed "lost" at times. No decision on home rule was made at that meeting—the group agreed to kick the can along until a later meeting.

Also in January, Governor Collins met with the group, apparently for the first time with any substance. He reminded them that the legislature had just attempted constitution revision and been defeated by the state supreme court. He recommended that "the legislature be made to feel that we are only doing further work on what *they* accomplished in the last session," an attempt to smooth the very sensitive feathers of the powerful Pork Chop Gang.[89]

The draft was completed in late February 1959 and submitted to Governor Collins. In mid-March, the committee—minus its leader, McRae—met with the governor, two senators, Representative Mallory Horne, and the press. Although Horne asked "friendly questions," according to Baker, both senators showed "ill-concealed hostility" to the proposals, especially regarding apportionment.[90] Indeed, after the legislature received the SCAC's proposal, it promptly perverted the apportionment sections into another egregious malapportionment scheme. McRae later said that the SCAC experience was "one of the most frustrating and unsatisfactory experiences that I can remember having."[91]

The League of Women Voters and the Constitution

At a time when women were seldom taken seriously in politics, the League of Women Voters had ignored naysayers and begun studying constitution reform as early as 1939.[92] In 1944 it formally began work on a proposed "New State Constitution for Florida," and in 1947 it started publishing pamphlets on Florida's need for a new constitution. It engaged Maxine Baker to be a lobbyist on constitutional reform in 1949 and organized a citizens' constitutional committee the same year. It adopted what it called a "yardstick for constitutional revision" in 1952. The League had encouraged Governor Collins to form the Sturgis Committee in 1955, and it opposed the doomed "daisy-chain" constitution in 1957. In 1958, of course, Maxine Baker served on the McRae Committee.

The League's 1952 "yardstick for constitutional revision" had some broad and uncontroversial recommendations, such as that a good state constitution should be a simple, understandable, and integrated statement of basic law, free from features that would limit or bind the legislature.[93] It also had some highly controversial recommendations, such as changing from an elected cabinet to an appointed cabinet; it threw in a lieutenant governor to boot. It advocated "self-executing proportionate representation" for the legislature and a uniform system of courts, rather than the hodgepodge of courts that had grown like patches of weeds in Florida's inadequate and dated judicial system. It recommended that a new constitution have provisions by which cities and counties could self-rule, and it advocated free and equal public education.

Later Proposals by the Bar

In 1960 the Florida Bar published another proposed constitution.[94] The bar had undergone a small revolution, or at least an evolution, of its own since its last proposed constitution, in 1947. The Florida State Bar Association had been a voluntary association until 1949. The Florida Supreme Court mandated in 1950 that all attorneys must join the bar, which then became known as the Florida Bar. The Florida State Bar Association had sought such regulation, which resulted in what is called an "integrated" bar. This did not mean a racially integrated bar. Indeed, the first meeting of the 1950 Florida Bar addressed how to prevent black attorneys from attending social functions during bar meetings; the speaker on the subject, pointing out that social functions were not the same as bar functions and therefore need not be racially integrated, was Bill McRae.[95]

Rafael Rivera-Cruz, one of the plaintiffs in the litigation that had killed the daisy-chain constitution revision, was a member of the bar committee that proposed the new constitution, and D. H. Redfearn, chairman of the bar's 1947 Constitution Committee, chaired the bar's committee again. The 1960 proposal reflected its origin as having been largely drafted by lawyers organized under the aegis of the Florida Bar. Organized to mimic the 1885 Constitution, it allowed article-by-article amendments as dictated by the *Rivera-Cruz* court decision. Although in its foreword it claimed to follow the SCAC's 1959 draft, it proposed little in innovative government redesign. Although it eliminated grammatical errors contained in the 1885 Constitution, its wording maintained the turgidity of the 1885 document.

The bar's 1960 draft prohibited all lotteries.[96] It also proposed a feature longed for by Governor Collins's young daughter, a lieutenant governor[97] who would succeed the governor.[98] It retained the elected cabinet.[99] It required the governor to give a two-day warning before he could adjourn the legislature,[100] perhaps a retort to Collins, who had abruptly adjourned the legislature during the 1950s when it had been on the verge of passing a interposition resolution denouncing federal enforcement of the *Brown v. Board of Education* decision.[101]

The proposed constitution allowed the Florida Supreme Court to issue advisory opinions to the governor;[102] kept the voting age at twenty-one;[103] did not provide home rule for counties, instead keeping them dependent on the legislature;[104] and kept the post-Reconstruction provision that schools must remain segregated.[105] The bar's proposal did change the gambling tax distribution, calling for at least 45 percent, rather than 100 percent, of excise taxes from pari-mutuel pools to be distributed in equal parts.[106] This provision would continue Florida's split personality over gambling—allowing it but only if its taxes disproportionately benefited rural counties—while allowing greater distribution to South Florida, where most of the gambling occurred.

The Florida Bar did not let up in its pressure to see a revised constitution. It published a third draft for a proposed constitution in 1961. Its efforts were so steady that a federal judicial opinion in a reapportionment case would state, in 1962, "Since 1946 the Florida Bar has had a Constitution Committee engaged in a study of the Florida Constitution and of proposals for its revision and amendment. On this Committee many distinguished lawyers have served, some of whom are members of the Legislature."[107]

Yet as the 1960s moved forward, none of the bar's efforts at constitution revision nor those of any others had succeeded; Florida's social, business, and legal progress was weighed down with the chains of its old constitution.

2

The U.S. Supreme Court
Reapportionment Cases

By the mid-1950s Florida had become noticeably different from its sister southern states.[1] It was more urban and had more residents who had been born neither in Florida nor anywhere else in the South. Florida had more of a tourist industry as well. But change is seldom comfortable. Many native Floridians and longtime residents of the state viewed the changes with alarm and braced hard against them. That is why, and how, the Pork Chop Gang held on to its power; that is what contributed to Florida's becoming culturally divided (and sometimes opposed) between the "southern" culture in Florida's North and the "northern" culture in Florida's South. Old Florida was still dominated by staunchly Democratic rural white conservatives. As one midcentury Florida legislator, Emory "Red" Cross of Gainesville, recalled in 1978, "a Republican was a curiosity back in those days."[2] And a force that magnified the change and the resistance to change was the prospect of public school desegregation that the U.S. Supreme Court raised when it decided *Brown v. Board of Education* in 1954 and 1955. The story of how Florida's legislators, its white and black citizens, and its governor worked through the "massive resistance" movement has been told in detail elsewhere;[3] this book will concentrate on how the decisions of the Florida Legislature and the supreme courts of both Florida and the United States laid the groundwork for a new Florida constitution.

But Some People Like Pork!

Although many deplored the lopsided nature of the Pork Choppers' governing style, they were not entirely disfavored in Florida. Senator Clarke's retirement comments, in which he recalled (using racist language) having African American babies named after him but never, until then, a road, were quoted in all major Florida newspapers, along with other tasteless racial jokes, and were treated as colorful news. To many throughout Florida, the Pork Chop legislators represented a stable, conservative political force despite their provincialism. After all, Florida was changing and growing very quickly, and not everyone liked the changes. To many Florida voters the Pork Chop bloc represented a necessary bulwark against urban developers' despoliation of Florida. Pork Choppers could be counted on to be stingy with public money outside their own districts, and allergic to raising taxes. And, for the majority of southern whites in Florida, who were opposed to racial integration and appalled by the nascent civil rights movement, the Pork Choppers were a rock of stability and a keeper of the "southern way of life." Florida voters who were caught between their dislike of forced integration and equal distaste of overt bigotry could hide behind stolid Pork Chopper resistance to change. Similarly, Pork Choppers assuaged a nativist feeling for rural Floridians who saw the state being transformed with rapid population growth by midwesterners and northern, "Yankee," ways.

The Pork Chop legislature of 1963, for example, was populated by a comforting mix of men who made a living or spent their leisure time on the land; nearly one-third made their living in cattle, lumber or timber, or farming, including citrus.[4] Fewer than one-fourth were attorneys.[5] Fewer than one in twelve claimed to be in "real estate" or "contracting," which is what a land developer might be expected to call his or her vocation.[6] As recreation, nearly half the 1963 legislators listed hunting or fishing.[7] In contrast, handball, tennis, and golf together were listed by less than 15 percent of legislators.[8] Legislators of the Pork Chop era were intimately involved with the land, usually in ways that used its rural abundance.

Their insistence on keeping the pork in rural Florida wasn't all bad, some argued. In fact, it could be argued that the Pork Choppers' persistence in bringing tax money to poor, rural areas of Florida might reveal a tiny concession to liberal ideas that the government should lift up the disadvantaged. Rural Florida, especially North Florida, was poor, and strict allocation of tax revenues would mean its residents would stay poor forever. Constituents of the Pork Choppers appreciated the fact that a disproportionate amount of tax revenues were spent on North Florida projects. Charley Johns's daughter-in-law defended him fondly on this subject decades after his death: "Papa took good care of his people."[9] Pork Choppers' bald refusal to acknowledge needs outside their rural districts, though, earned them a reputation for being "tyrannical" politicians with a "stranglehold" on Florida.[10] As Senator Louis de la Parte of Tampa mused, "If your frame of reference is a county that's been static for a century, how can you possibly respond to the problems of the growing cities—crime, health, welfare, traffic, water and air pollution and all the rest?"[11]

Florida was not alone, however. By 1955 every state in the Union but one was malapportioned in both houses of its state legislature.[12] Malapportionment occurred when people relocated or grouped somewhere in the state and sufficient legislators were not assigned to represent that area. Typically, people migrated from rural areas to areas in and around cities, and as a result, the newly populous urban areas were underrepresented politically. This led to minority rule, with the now less-populated areas still controlling the state legislatures.

That trend was accentuated in Florida. Florida's legislature was badly malapportioned—among the worst in the nation. In 1955, only about one-seventh of its population could elect a majority in each of the Senate and the House.[13] The problem was not restricted to the South. California's Senate, for example, was dominated by a group known as the Cow County Senators, and Alabama's by a band called the South Black Belt Senators. But underrepresented people across the nation, including in Florida, began to fight back using the courts.

In Florida, underrepresented people lived mainly in South Florida, which had grown much faster than North Florida during most of the twentieth century. The 1960 case *Shiver v. Gray* was Florida's first federal reapportionment case. Miami city councilman Otis Shiver filed suit in federal district court against Florida's long-serving secretary of state, R. A. "Captain" Gray, demanding a fair reapportionment of the Florida Legislature. But the federal court dismissed Shiver's case following prevailing court precedent; it claimed no federal question existed but suggested the plaintiff might try the Florida courts for relief.[14] The Fifth Circuit Court of Appeals upheld the dismissal.[15] The three-judge appellate panel airily wrote:

> Here, with a lengthy brief, arguing the question presented as though it were still an open one, plaintiff insists that the judgment was wrong and must be reversed. The defendants, citing many cases in support of their claim that the so-called constitutional question sought to be raised has been many times determined to be without substance, insist that the district judge's action was right and must be affirmed. We find ourselves in complete agreement with this view. The judgment is affirmed.[16]

One of the three appellate judges was John Minor Wisdom, later lauded for his support for civil rights and the desegregation of public schools. The attorney for Shiver was Richard Swann of Miami, who would later take up the court apportionment battle as the named plaintiff. The mayor of Miami, Robert King High, filed an amicus brief supporting the plaintiff seeking fair apportionment. Assistant Attorney General Joe Jacobs represented the state in the case. He later recalled that he urged his opponent to follow on to the U.S. Supreme Court, but Shiver did not. Jacobs noted if Shiver had continued to the Supreme Court, the landmark reapportionment case might have been *Shiver v. Gray*.[17]

Baker v. Carr

In the early 1960s, *Baker v. Carr*, a case seeking to resolve malapportionment in the Tennessee legislature, had churned through the courts for years and most southern legislators kept one eye on it. There was widespread suspicion that federal courts would intervene in state apportionment just as they had in school segregation. Anticipating the

Baker decision, the Florida Legislature attempted to insulate itself by reapportioning in 1961.[18] At this juncture, the Pork Choppers could have reached a sensible compromise and preserved some power. Instead, they stonewalled with a plan that, when enacted, actually worsened malapportionment. Now, just one-eighth of the population, mostly living in northern Florida, elected a majority in the House and one-eighth elected a majority in the Senate.[19]

Even reform-minded legislators had a hard time voting for reapportionment, much less achieving it, during this period. When Representative Reubin Askew voted for reapportionment in 1961, his fellow representative E. C. Rowell told him he was "going to rip [Askew's] britches."[20] Telling the tale much later, Askew commented, philosophically, "You . . . reapportion [someone] out of politics, and they get downright sensitive about it!"[21] Representative Mallory Horne recalled, "it was terrible to look at a legislator I liked and say, 'I'm going to vote to end your term.'"[22]

Florida was not alone in its failure to heal itself. When the U.S. Supreme Court decided *Baker v. Carr* in 1962, in which it chose for the first time to become involved in apportioning state legislatures to prevent discrimination, not a single southern state had yet reapportioned under the 1960 census.[23] Alabama, Tennessee, and the Oklahoma Senate had failed to reapportion for fifty years.[24] As a result, the South's most urban states saw a sharp drop in the percentage of population able to elect a majority of the legislature.[25] South Florida's population boom ensured that Florida was in the worst shape of all.

Pressure for meaningful state reapportionment was also building within the federal government. The Kennedy administration took office after a close and bitter election in 1960. Kennedy's electoral strength was in urban areas, especially in the southern states where rural voters, historically conservative, were fleeing the Democratic Party based on its position on desegregation and civil rights. Attorney General Robert Kennedy maintained quiet, persistent pressure on Solicitor General Archibald Cox to seek court-ordered reapportionment.[26]

The *Baker* case spanned two critical terms of the Court, in 1960–61 and 1961–62. The first *Baker* conference following oral argument, in November 1960, had been four to four, with Justice Potter Stewart not entering a vote at conference and persuading the Court to delay the case for a year. The second *Baker* opinion was six to two in favor of the courts accepting apportionment cases, with Justice Clark making a belated switch from opposition to support.[27]

The actual ruling in *Baker* was modest, even if its implications were far-ranging. *Baker* simply said the lower federal courts could hear and make rulings on lawsuits alleging unconstitutional legislative apportionment. *Baker* was a limited opinion because the Supreme Court itself was undecided in 1962 regarding how far it would go in prescribing the details of reapportionment. For example, it was widely assumed following the *Baker* decision that "little federal" plans apportioning one legislative house on some basis other than strict population—as, for example, the U.S. Senate is apportioned based on state lines—would be constitutionally acceptable. But the *Baker* decision provoked a vitriolic response nationwide wherever rural-dominated legislatures were threatened.[28] For southerners, *Baker* touched on states' rights and fear of popular domination by anti-majoritarian courts, as had happened in *Brown*. But it was clear that *Baker* was necessary to achieve fair apportionment: without it, malapportioned legislatures could and did vote down any plans challenging the status quo. Like the school-desegregation case of *Brown* in 1954, the reapportionment cases pushed the judiciary into new areas because political and legislative processes had failed.[29] In fact, a U.S. Supreme Court justice—accounts vary as to whether it was William O. Douglas or Hugo Black—later told Governor Collins that the Florida Legislature's recalcitrance in the face of Collins's efforts to reapportion proved the futility of relying on political processes and convinced the Court to hear *Baker v. Carr.*[30] But to many people, *Baker v. Carr* simply proved the Court had again overextended its legitimate reach and usurped power.

The Court's restraint was also evident in areas it identified as "political questions." In these cases the Court voluntarily abstained from exercising authority to decide disputes. For example, the Court has avoided involving itself in questions regarding seating members of Congress: the Constitution provides that each chamber should be the judge of the qualifications of its own members.[31] Constitutional amendments are another area where the Court has been reluctant to intrude. From the turn of the century until *Baker*, the Court had declined to intervene in apportionment decisions, whether for the U.S. Congress or state legislatures. The Court never viewed this as a lack of power; it was simply a discretionary policy it adopted.

Baker raised a number of sensitive points. First, it appeared to interfere with the historical power that legislative bodies had enjoyed since before the United States had become a republic, in England between the death of Cromwell and the restoration of the monarchy, when the Parliament was nearly omnipotent. Second, it interfered with more recent notions, grounded in the U.S. Constitution, limiting federal intervention in a state's internal operations. Third, it raised questions as to whether courts were institutionally capable of making political decisions: the federal courts are anti-majoritarian, being composed of lifetime appointees; they may not have clear standards to follow (as Justice Frankfurter would argue in his *Baker* dissent); and they lack a means to compel compliance. But despite the reasons not to do so, the Warren Court decided to hear the *Baker* case. The U.S. Congress was paralyzed, because its southern constituency could block everything. And because of malapportionment, state legislatures were paralyzed and atrophying. *Baker* came about because of legislative paralysis, just as *Brown* had. It was up to the courts to move society forward.[32]

The *Baker* decision demonstrated Chief Justice Warren's change in opinion on apportionment. State legislative malapportionment was consistent with Warren's position when he was the governor of California, when he had resisted reapportioning the system that had elected him.[33] His thinking had a chance to change, however, as his tenure as chief justice had provided him plenty of opportunities to see how legislatures could suppress minority interests.[34] Warren later stated that he believed *Baker* and *Reynolds* were important because they gave citizens the fundamental ability to elect a representative government.[35] Ironically, Warren's rationale was reminiscent of President Andrew Johnson's belief that a "slavocracy" had dragged white southern yeoman farmers into the Civil War against their will through malapportioned legislatures and voting restrictions.[36] However, a century later the

problem was reversed: whereas the slavocracy had been elites controlling poor farmers, southern malapportionment in the mid-twentieth
century typically involved farmers controlling the elite.

Baker was so intensely debated among the justices that it contributed
to the perhaps premature retirement of two justices from the Court.
Solicitor General Cox recalled hearing about the unexpected retirement
of Justice Charles Evans Whittaker. Cox met Whittaker a few days before Whittaker moved out of the Supreme Court building. Whittaker
told him he had been diagnosed with extreme physical exhaustion; his
doctors told him that continued work would be life-threatening. Whittaker told Cox that it was his inability to reach a conclusion in *Baker*
that had driven him to exhaustion.[37]

Justice Felix Frankfurter too was a casualty of *Baker*. Frankfurter
had long and vigorously opposed any finding that the courts had authority to rule on legislative apportionment. He had written the
Court's opinion in *Colegrove v. Green* sixteen years earlier, which held
that courts should voluntarily abstain from deciding "political questions" such as apportionment.[38] Frankfurter and his law clerk prepared
a sixty-page memorandum arguing Frankfurter's opposition in antici-
pation of the *Baker* case. That memorandum, with a few minor changes,
became Frankfurter's dissenting opinion in *Baker*.[39] One month after
the Court announced the *Baker* decision, rejecting Frankfurter's position, Frankfurter's secretary found the justice unconscious on the floor
of his chambers from a stroke. Frankfurter was carried from his office
to the hospital, complaining that his shoes were being left behind.[40]
Cox visited Frankfurter at the hospital and was led to believe by the
semi-articulate justice that the *Baker* debates had been the cause of the
extreme tension leading to his stroke.[41]

Both Whittaker and Frankfurter retired from the Court following
the 1961–62 term for health reasons. Frankfurter died less than three
years later, having never recovered from his stroke. Justice Frankfurter
eloquently dissented from the majority opinion in *Baker*: his two main
reasons were echoed by southern states'-rights proponents. First,
Frankfurter argued that the Court was overstepping its bounds, thus
endangering the public support that the Court had to depend on, its
authority "possessed of neither the purse nor the sword."[42] Second,

Frankfurter believed the Court should have avoided attempting to decide a political question. Appeals on subjects like reapportionment should not come to the Court, he declared: "In a democratic society like ours, relief must come through an aroused popular conscience that sears the conscience of the people's representatives."[43] But no Pork Chop legislator in Florida intended to be seared. Relief would come only with forced and unwelcome change.

Chief Justice Earl Warren well understood the political significance of the *Baker* decision: in later years, he stated that the racial strife would have been avoided if *Baker* had existed fifty years earlier.[44] U.S. Supreme Court justice Tom Clark, from Texas, opined in the 1962 secret court conference between the justices deciding *Baker* that it was the white power structure in the South that was at stake in *Baker*.[45] Both knew that if the federal courts had become involved in apportionment years earlier, states—particularly those in the South—might have properly apportioned legislatures made up of representative and progressive lawmakers who would have been more likely to integrate schools on their own. The *Baker* opinion caused most states to attempt reapportionment in their next legislative sessions.[46] Lawsuits were filed in a majority of states, whether in state court, federal court, or both.[47] The effect of the *Baker* opinion in Florida was immediate: by 5:00 p.m. on March 26, 1962, the same day the opinion was issued in Washington, two new federal court cases were filed in Miami: *Sobel v. Adams* and *Swann v. Adams*. Tom Adams had replaced "Captain" Gray as Florida's secretary of state. The plaintiff in *Swann* had been the lawyer for Shiver in the earlier *Shiver v. Gray* suit. Both lawsuits were aimed at ending Pork Chop control of the Florida Legislature.

Florida Supreme Court Marginalized

But why did plaintiffs look to the federal courts for relief rather than to their state supreme courts? In Florida, this can be understood by examining the state supreme court's treatment of civil rights cases up to that time. Beginning in the early 1950s, the Florida Supreme Court rapidly became powerless to make reapportionment decisions through a series of defiant, disastrous decisions. It began with that court's long fight with the U.S. Supreme Court over the *Virgil Hawkins v. Board of Control of Florida* case. Virgil Hawkins, a black man, sued in 1949 to attend the University of Florida College of Law. Assisted by NAACP lawyers as well as Daytona Beach lawyer Horace Hill, Hawkins brought suit in state court. Florida senator John Mathews of Duval County issued a radio address sounding an alarm and requesting additional legislative funding for state colleges to maintain separate facilities. Mathews, a staunch segregationist, had been a proponent, in 1947, of the whites-only primary elections; he believed his main political opposition was merely "communists, pinks and negroes."[48]

Darryl Paulson and Paul Hawkes, in a 1984 article on the *Hawkins* case in the *Florida State University Law Review,* contend that the precedent in Hawkins's favor was clear from the Warren Court's *Sweatt v. Painter* decision, in which the U.S. Supreme Court required that a black man be admitted to the University of Texas Law School because the hastily created Texas State University law school, intended for African Americans, did not provide substantial equality in educational opportunities.[49] However, Richard Kluger correctly notes the *Painter* decision was just one of three university segregation cases decided together by the U.S. Supreme Court, and civil rights attorneys, including Thurgood Marshall, considered the rulings a partial failure based on the Court's refusal explicitly to repudiate the *Plessy v. Ferguson* "separate but equal" doctrine.[50] Deliberate segregation was therefore still at issue when the Supreme Court of Florida took up *Hawkins* in 1950.

The state supreme court turned its back on Hawkins's request, both figuratively and literally. Attorney Horace Hill, who argued the case for Hawkins, recalled how some of the justices actually turned their back to him during his oral argument rather than face a black attorney.[51] The court's decision was unanimous, and Justice Sebring, its author, got directly to the point when he denied Hawkins the right to enter the University of Florida law school:

The relator, Virgil D. Hawkins, is a Negro citizen and resident of the State of Florida. He possesses all the scholastic, moral and other qualifications, except as to race and color, prescribed by the laws of Florida and the rules and regulations of the State Board of

Control for admission to the first year class of the College of Law of the University of Florida.[52]

The court ruled that Virgil Hawkins, therefore, because of his race and color, must attend a yet-to-be-created, segregated law school at the historically black state college in Tallahassee, Florida Agricultural and Mechanical College. This was the plainest statement possible: it was because Virgil Hawkins was black, and only because he was black, that he would be denied admission.

This was a risky approach. It can be interpreted as waving the red cape at the federal court and asserting Florida's separate sovereignty. It can also be seen as a subtle split in the court. Justice Sebring was assigned to write the opinion.[53] He drafted an opinion that received the court's unanimous blessing and did not sugarcoat the racist intent. Was Sebring's wording a silent plea by some on the court fearful of more intensive federal involvement, that if lightning was going to strike them down, please do it quickly and mute the more reactionary members of the court?[54] If so, the "quickly" part didn't work. Hawkins waited ten months and filed again, noting that Florida had not yet implemented a functioning "Negro" law school at Florida Agricultural and Mechanical College.[55]

This time, the Florida Supreme Court denied Hawkins's petition but used what must have been a calculated tactic: it ruled that Hawkins could still apply again to the University of Florida College of Law, thereby keeping his petition open. This prevented Hawkins from obtaining certiorari review from the U.S. Supreme Court, because technically the matter remained pending before the Florida court. Hawkins in fact filed a petition for certiorari to the U.S. Supreme Court, which denied it because the matter was still pending before the Florida court. So Hawkins re-filed in the Supreme Court of Florida and requested dismissal of the case so that he could escape state court. This worked, sort of: the U.S. Supreme Court accepted his case but held it for two years until just after its May 1954 decision in *Brown*. It issued its opinion in *Hawkins* one week after *Brown*, reversing the Florida Supreme Court's denial of Hawkins's petition to attend the University of Florida College of Law.[56] The Florida court then copied the example of other states and delayed any action until the U. S. Supreme Court published its second decision in *Brown v. Board of Education*, in May 1955. It then denied his admission request again.

Justice B. K. Roberts wrote the 1955 majority opinion in *Hawkins*, but Justice Glenn Terrell's racist screed in his concurring opinion is what is remembered best.[57] Roberts's majority opinion put off a final decision until a fact-finding commission it had created, led by trial judge John Murphree and known as the Murphree Commission, could publish its findings. Although the majority opinion paid lip service to obeying the U.S. Supreme Court's precedent, implicitly acknowledging that Court as a higher sovereign, it retained some power over what it perceived as the will of its "people" by agreeing to give Hawkins relief at a date it chose, further delaying Hawkins's admission. The majority opinion claimed that admitting Hawkins to the University of Florida College of Law would cause public disruption, and noted with approval an earlier opinion of Justice Terrell, in a different school segregation case, in which he recommended waiting until "segregation comes in the democratic way. . . . If there is anything settled in our democratic theory, it is that there must be a popular yearning for laws that invade settled concepts *before they will be enforced.*"[58] In choosing to borrow this wording, Justice Roberts signaled that the Supreme Court of the United States could tell the Supreme Court of Florida to admit Hawkins all it wanted, but its ruling would not be enforced until there was a "popular yearning" for it. As the institution in Florida with the responsibility to act on directions from the U.S. Supreme Court, the Florida court was in a position to stand in the way of the federal court and protect what it perceived as the "popular yearning" *not* to integrate the University of Florida College of Law.

In his concurring opinion, Justice Terrell first announced he was "expanding" his concurrence because of the "far-reaching effect of *Brown*." He then launched an opinion that invoked psychology, culture, intelligence, voluntary segregation, economics, "innate deficiencies in self restraint [*sic*] and cultural acuteness," popular sovereignty, and God. Terrell's concurrence is notable for how he wove declarations of popular sovereignty into his reasons for weaseling out of obedience to the U.S. Supreme Court's ruling. For example, he noted the heavy fiscal burden caused by carrying two segregated systems when, he asserted, "there is no local agitation for the change."[59] He stated: "In a democracy, law . . . does not precede, but always follows a felt necessity or public demand for it"; otherwise "it is difficult and often almost impossible to enforce. The genius of the people is as resourceful in devising means to evade a law they are not in sympathy with as they are [sic] to enforce one they approve." Perhaps the best-known part of Terrell's concurrence is his invocation of "God's plan" of segregation, in which he waxed poetic:

> The dove and the quail, the turkey and the turkey buzzard, the chicken and the guinea, it matters not where they are found, are segregated; place the horse, the cow, the sheep, the goat and the pig in the same pasture and they instinctively segregate; the fish in the sea segregate into "schools" of their kind; when the goose and duck arise from the Canadian marshes and take off for the Gulf a [sic] Mexico and other points in the south, they are always found segregated; and when God created man, he allotted each race to his own continent according to color, Europe to the white man, Asia to the yellow man, Africa to the black man, and America to the red man, but we are now advised that God's plan was in error and must be reversed.[60]

It is unknown what Terrell thought about occupying, as a white man, the continent assigned to the "red man."[61]

Justice Terrell was saying, in essence, that his court, acting, in his mind, for "the people," was using its "genius" to "evade" the law as handed down in *Brown* and *Hawkins*. Terrell was seventy-four and had already served twenty-seven years on the court when the *Hawkins* opinion was issued; his collected papers reveal a man who seemed to believe fervently in segregation but not in what he probably would have called the "mistreatment" of blacks.[62]

Again, Hawkins took the case to the U.S. Supreme Court, and again that court granted certiorari. Again, in March 1956 the Supreme Court remanded the case, and this time without protracted explaining: the Court tersely stated: "There is no reason for delay."[63] In May 1956, the Murphree Commission's findings and the Board of Control's report were issued, which purported to find that white parents would pull their children from a college that admitted blacks. In fact, that study was inconclusive, finding that a majority of white college students would tolerate black students in their classrooms but might not want to eat at the same cafeteria table with them.[64] And so the Florida court defied the U.S. Supreme Court again in 1957, claiming to rely on the threat of public disruption based on the Murphree Commission's findings.[65] This time the opinion drew two dissents. One of them—from Justice Elwyn Thomas—pointedly noted that if the Florida court expected obedience to its mandates, it had better do some prompt obeying itself.[66] The other was from none other than Justice Sebring, the author of the first *Hawkins* opinion, who reversed course to dissent and call for prompt desegregation. By the time the opinion was published, Sebring had resigned from the court, possibly in disgust, to become dean of the Stetson University College of Law.[67]

The case ended anticlimactically. Hawkins finally stipulated to dismiss his request for admission upon the Board of Control's agreeing to an injunction to not oppose other black candidates for law school. The U.S. District Court for the Northern District of Florida entered an opinion accepting the deal.[68]

Between 1958 and 1963 the Supreme Court of Florida had an opportunity to spar with the Supreme Court of the United States on the subject of the NAACP's supposed links to the Communist Party. In 1958 the notorious Florida Legislative Investigation Committee had subpoenaed Theodore Gibson, Ernest Graham, and several other members of the Miami Branch of the NAACP to appear before it to produce membership lists and answer questions about whether they knew certain people who had allegedly been seen at communism-related meetings. They refused. On the inevitable appeal to the state supreme court, the contempt that the attorney for the FLIC, Mark Hawes, had for the appellant NAACP members was palpable. Defending the FLIC as an equal-opportunity investigator that had also investigated white racist organizations, Hawes's brief seethed, "it is generally conceded by all except Appellants and their beloved Association" that the FLIC had neutralized John Kasper, a race agitator on the "other extreme of the race issue."[69]

The Florida Supreme Court ruled in favor of the FLIC. Justice Campbell Thornal, writing for the majority and clearly ready for a fight, opined for pages on federalism and quoted the Florida constitution's language that "all political power is inherent in the people."[70] The case went to the U.S. Supreme Court, which initially denied review. The case was weaker than similar ones before the Court from other states. But one of Chief Justice Warren's law clerks reasoned that if the Court did not reverse the Florida Supreme Court in this case, "every southern state would seize the opportunity to harass the NAACP under the banner of anti-Communism."[71] The Court reviewed the case and, in March 1963, reversed the Florida Supreme Court again. In its opinion the Court adopted language from its earlier opinion in a Virginia NAACP case: "We cannot close our eyes to the fact that the militant Negro civil rights movement has engendered the intense resentment and opposition of the politically dominant white community."[72] On remand, the Florida Supreme Court was sullen: "Our decision . . . was reversed by the Supreme Court of the United States . . . [and we] now have no alternative to abiding by the decision and judgment of the Supreme Court of the United States."[73]

But it did not give up easily. During the few weeks between the U.S. Supreme Court's *Gibson* opinion and its own reversal on remand, the Florida Supreme Court issued an opinion in a different case, upholding the conviction of a supposedly white woman, Connie Hoffman, and a supposedly black man, Dewey McLaughlin, who were arrested for "habitually liv[ing] in and occupy[ing] in the nighttime the same room," which was then illegal for mixed-race couples under Florida Statute Section 798.05.[74] Interestingly, Ms. Hoffman, who was married to another man, had the maiden name of Gonzalez, and the arresting officer testified that when he approached the house to make the arrest, Mr. McLaughlin spoke to him only in Spanish for the first several minutes, raising the real possibility that the paramours may have been culturally, if not racially, similar. That conviction, too, had to go to the U.S. Supreme Court to get reversed.[75] On remand, the Florida Supreme Court admitted defeat and slunk away. But not without a final snarling opinion written by Justice Millard Caldwell. Caldwell, who had established a strong segregationist record over his career, which included serving as governor of Florida, protested in his written opinion that the court had followed federal precedent in upholding the initial conviction and that on appeal, "the Supreme court [sic] of the United States . . . concluded, notwithstanding its previous holding to the contrary," that the anti-interracial cohabitation statute was discriminatory: "In light of this new and contrary construction of the Constitution," the Florida court must obey "the new Law of the Land."[76]

Justice Caldwell would have further trouble anticipating or adjusting to change. On the subject of reapportionment, in 1962, little more than half a year after *Baker v. Carr*, he wrote an opinion for the Florida Supreme Court that anticipated exactly wrongly the direction the U.S. Supreme Court would take in deciding reapportionment and, in doing so, effectively took from the Florida court the ability or credibility to decide apportionment cases. The case, *Lund v. Mathas*, challenged the discrepancy in population of Florida's twelve congressional districts.[77] Remarkably, the 1960 census showed that Florida should have a 50 percent increase in the number of congressional representatives—from eight to twelve. When the new districts were drawn up, they had a greater than 100 percent discrepancy in population: the smallest district had a population of less than a quarter of a million, and the largest had an even half million. Justice Caldwell, writing for a unanimous court, blithely recited that many factors other than population were legitimate when determining districts, so Florida's new congressional district lines violated neither the federal nor the state constitution. The case was not reversed.

Future plaintiffs were placed on notice: the federal courts, not Florida courts, would be the ones where change might occur; federal, not state, courts would dictate Florida's legislative future.

The *Swann v. Adams* Saga: Running from Slaughter

The next five years saw a game of skill and chance played between the Florida Legislature and the federal courts. The Pork Chop legislators were playing to preserve their own future and, as they saw the situation, the future of Florida as they knew and loved it. The federal courts, and specifically Warren's Supreme Court, played to equalize the size of legislative districts and the power of a vote in all states, but particularly in Florida. Warren's court did not hesitate to involve itself in what had formerly been the inner workings of state government to accomplish the goal of achieving "one man, one vote."

Under its 1885 Constitution, Florida was to reapportion in 1962 using data from the 1960 census. There were two difficulties in reapportioning the state legislature: one from without and one from within. From without, reapportionment efforts were trying to hit a moving target of evolving federal requirements set by the U.S. Supreme Court. From within, Florida legislators continued to try to hold on to their seats, and essentially cheat the system, by proposing only incrementally less egregious malapportionments.

On July 23, 1962, less than four months after the *Swann* and *Sobel* cases had been filed, the federal Southern District Court in Miami ruled Florida's apportionment scheme unconstitutional and consolidated the cases.[78] The district court heard the case as a three-judge panel rather than with the usual single judge. One of those judges was Bill McRae, who had been appointed to the federal bench by President Kennedy two years after McRae's frustrating attempt at constitution revision. The court's opinion did not mince words. It concluded that "the constitutional and statutory provisions of the State of Florida, which provide for the apportionment and reapportionment, are null, void and prospectively inoperative."[79] The court could have forced reapportionment on the state, as federal courts in Alabama[80] and Oklahoma[81] did that year. Instead, it deferred final judgment to allow the legislature time to meet and reapportion itself.[82] If the court approved the new plan, it would dismiss the case; if not, it would take reapportionment into its own hands.[83]

By doing this, the court created a conundrum: it had told Florida to apportion itself, but by nullifying Florida's constitutional and statutory apportionment authority it took away the only source of the government's authority to apportion. Florida was in a legal twilight zone.

The day after the federal court opinion, Governor Farris Bryant called the legislature into extraordinary session to begin the next week, on August 1, 1962. Bryant had come up to the governor's seat as many of his predecessors had, through the legislature. He had been Speaker of the House and had run for governor in 1956, before the incumbent, LeRoy Collins, had declared he would run for reelection. Bryant once recalled that his mother was "a strong woman, and wanted me to be governor."[84] Young Farris did not disappoint, winning the seat on his second try, in 1960. At the outset of the special session, Bryant submitted his reapportionment proposal. But the legislature devised one of its own instead. As a supplemental opinion in *Sobel* later described, in August the legislature withdrew the proposed amendment to the Florida constitution on legislative apportionment that it had submitted at its 1961 session and substituted a new proposal for an apportionment plan in the form of a constitutional amendment, HJR 30X. The proposed amendment would, unless prohibited by judicial decree, be submitted to the voters of Florida at the regular election scheduled for November 1962. The federal district court's opinion described the new proposed plan:

> It would carry on the traditional division of the State into senatorial districts composed of one or more counties and the allocation of one or more representatives to each county. The proposed amendment would give one representative to each of the counties of the State. Provision would be made for representative ratios. A representative ratio is defined as the quotient obtained by dividing the population of the State by the number of counties. Each county would have one additional representative for each representative ratio or major fraction thereof. Any county having more than four representative ratios shall have another representative. The Senate is to consist of forty-six members, each representing a district. Each of the twenty-four most populous counties shall constitute a district. The other twenty-two districts are to be created from the remaining forty-three counties. In 1971 and every ten years thereafter the Legislature is to reapportion itself in accordance with the constitutional requirement.[85]

In a September 5, 1962, supplemental opinion, the Southern District Court approved the August 1962 apportionment plan, even though the court acknowledged it still contained large population variances. For example, Dade County, with 19 percent of the state's population, still had only one senator.[86] In fact, most of the Senate districts remained in the rural north, guarded jealously by the Pork Chop Gang. In approving the plan, the court reasoned that a rational apportionment "may include a number of factors in addition to population."[87] The court noted the problem that another section of Florida's constitution placed counties and municipalities under the legislature's control; the court was concerned that municipalities would lose voice in the legislature if apportionment did not require at least one legislator from each affected area.

The district court was adrift: the U.S. Supreme Court had provided no guidance in *Baker v. Carr* on how to resolve, or even how to think about, reapportionment cases. The Court would eventually demand mathematically exact population distribution for Florida apportionment, and would also eventually back off from that demand in other states' cases. In 1962, however, the entire nation was feeling its way through reapportionment. The district court left the reapportionment plan to the voters in the November 1962 election. If voters approved it, the case was moot; if they rejected it, the case would continue.

Observers of southern politics and law mocked the *Sobel* decision.[88] After all, while Florida's disparities were approved, other states were held to a higher standard. Virginia lost a court case with an apportionment plan in which the disparity between its least populous district and its most populous one was no worse than four to one. Tennessee was in trouble for its plan, in which counties with 43 percent of the population had about one-third of the seats.[89] Florida's plan was approved unanimously by the court, even though 72 percent of its population would have only 24 percent of Senate seats.[90]

Apportionment was not the only crisis in Florida at the time; the Cold War was also heating up only ninety miles south of its border. Just a few weeks after the *Sobel* decision, on October 14, 1962, photos taken from an American U-2 reconnaissance plane flying over Cuba showed evidence of large buildups of nuclear-capable missiles pointed north, toward the United States. The ensuing Cuban Missile Crisis briefly preoccupied the nation. Even before President Kennedy announced the crisis to the nation, on October 22, Floridians on the east coast noticed long military convoys on highways, headed south, and South Florida newspapers reported unusual military exercises offshore.[91] After two long, dread-filled weeks, Kennedy and Nikita Khrushchev, general secretary of the Soviet Union, found a way to defuse the situation, averting both planetary disaster and loss of face.

The 1963 Special Sessions

On the first Tuesday in November 1962, Floridians exercised their right to vote. They rejected the proposed constitutional amendment for reapportionment that the *Sobel* court had approved. In response, the legislature convened twice, for three weeks in November and again at the end of January 1963, and finally passed an apportionment bill—in the form of a statute, not a proposed constitutional amendment—providing for 43 senators and 112 representatives, substantially more legislators than the 1885 Constitution allowed. The Supreme Court of Florida, in an advisory opinion to the governor, green-lighted the unconstitutional apportionment plan. In doing so, it conceded the federal court's power to declare the Florida constitutional provisions on apportionment, including the provision limiting the number of senators and representatives, null and void.[92] The governor signed the bill on February 4 and sent it to the *Sobel* court, which had been holding the reapportionment case in temporary abeyance. That court found that the new apportionment statute complied with the U.S. Constitution and ordered the case dismissed.[93]

In its February 7 opinion the court referred to a *Yale Law Journal* article and a report on apportionment of state legislatures by the Advisory Commission on Intergovernmental Relations. The court's opinion conceded that the principles governing reapportionment might eventually "become better defined and more fully developed,"[94] revealing that it was forced again to feel its way through apportionment law with little formal guidance. Ultimately, the court found that the 1963 apportionment "does not, in any respect, violate the Constitution of the United States."[95] The U.S. Supreme Court would not agree.

For the remainder of 1963, little happened on the reapportionment front. Floridians were free to teach their schoolchildren how to duck under their desks in the event of a nuclear attack; aerospace engineers at NASA worked on the latest stage of the moon race, the Gemini program; and Miami was transformed into a city of busy professional Cuban exiles rather than sleepy retirees occupying park benches. And on November 22, 1963, came an event that would change Florida profoundly. It was not the tragic assassination of President Kennedy. It was the flight over Central Florida of Walt Disney, who saw the crossing of the new Interstate 4 and the new Florida Turnpike among tens of thousands of empty acres, and approved the site as the location of his planned Disneyland East.[96]

The 1964 *Reynolds* Series: Don't Block Up the Hall

In 1964, radio airwaves across the United States began to fill with protest songs heralding changing times. Streets filled with people protesting in favor of civil rights and against the Vietnam War. Times were changing in many ways. Florida politics was also changing, despite what many considered to be the stalling tactics of the Pork Chop legislature. In contrast to the splashy news of Vietnam War protests and the civil rights movement, however, reapportionment was a quiet revolution. Although it had the full attention of many state legislatures and spawned attempts to limit federal power over state legislative apportionment, reapportionment received little public attention.

More than half of the states had attempted reapportionment in the two years after the 1962 *Baker* decision.[97] State legislatures were running scared: lawsuits had been filed in thirty-nine states by June 1964.[98] The U.S. Supreme Court issued a more detailed opinion on apportionment in that month with the *Reynolds v. Sims* cases, a group of six reapportionment cases, including four from the South.[99] These were the cases that brought the phrase "one man, one vote" into common use.

The phrase "one man, one vote" was a slogan of the anticolonial movement in Africa and became a catchword of the civil rights movement.[100] The Court, however, took "one man, one vote" farther in the *Reynolds* cases than almost anyone had expected. At the time of the oral argument, most justices thought that only the lower legislative houses of each state should be apportioned according to population.[101]

The upper houses, like the U.S. Senate, could be apportioned according to other factors, such as geography or political boundaries. Bernard Schwartz reports in his biography of Warren that on the morning of November 22, 1963, the Court was in conference and Warren had just assigned himself the majority opinion when the Court got the news that President Kennedy had been assassinated. At some point after they received the news that day, Warren is reported to have burst into Justice William Brennan's chambers, declaring, "It can't be. It can't be." He was referring to his new conviction that upper-chamber state legislative houses should not be apportionable by anything other than population.[102]

By settling on the "one man, one vote" formula for establishing fair voting apportionment, the U.S. Supreme Court implicitly eschewed other possibilities. First, an electoral system of "winner take all" may itself cause underrepresentation of some groups due to how districts or geographical voting units are formed. For example, modern gerrymandering cases have illustrated how districts may be drawn with equal populations but with the effect of favoring one political party over another.[103] One-man, one-vote supposedly allows a simple majority to prevail, yet does one-man, one-vote require counting every person in a district? Every person eligible to vote? Every person registered to vote? Every person who has actually voted in recent elections?[104] And wouldn't making every legislator electable at large be the truest way to ensure straight majority rule, if that is the aim of one-man, one-vote?

By settling on "one man, one vote" as its mantra, the U.S. Supreme Court also signaled that it was approaching apportionment via the Equal Protection Clause, not the other available constitutional bases of due process or the guarantee of a republican form of government, either of which would have allowed for greater flexibility.[105] And the Court was able, whether intentionally or not, to shift from its explicit rule—districts of equal population—to imply an answer to a very different issue—equal representation. As Robert Dixon, a leading political scientist of the time, pointed out, while the former is objective and verifiable, the latter is "highly subjective . . . connoting a hoped-for result."[106] And as Dixon pointed out, the Court did this without pointing out its shift.[107]

One week after *Reynolds*, the Supreme Court decided nine more apportionment cases. Only two, those from Florida and Oklahoma, were from the South. The Court tersely reversed the district court's *Sobel* (now *Swann v. Adams*) opinion, which had approved Florida's latest reapportionment, and sent it back to the district court to view in light of its one-man, one-vote rule from *Reynolds*.[108] The later 1963 district court opinion, which had dismissed the apportionment litigation, was not before the Supreme Court and was not mentioned. The *Swann* opinion was fractured among three justices, each following a different earlier apportionment opinion. Even now, the Court was divided on how states should reapportion.

The opinion remained technically pending before the Supreme Court until October 12, 1964, when a motion for rehearing was denied along with pending motions in all the *Reynolds* cases. Florida again lacked a constitutional legislature. The Southern District Court again deferred acting and gave the legislature until the end of its next session to come up with another new plan. The deadline was July 1, 1965.[109] The big-county legislators held out little hope for fair apportionment or any other progressive plans before the 1965 regular session.[110]

Florida was an afterthought in the *Reynolds* series. It would take three trips to the U.S. Supreme Court to get Florida a reapportionment plan that passed constitutional muster. That would be the third out in the Pork Choppers' inning.

The 1965 Regular Session

On April 6, 1965, the Florida Legislature began its regularly scheduled biennial session. In his address to the legislature, often called the "state of the state" address, Governor Haydon Burns urged the legislators to "provide for the creation of a Constitutional Revision Commission."[111] One item the legislature considered early on was a proposed joint resolution creating such a commission. Revising the entire constitution was now legally permissible. Unlike the "daisy chain" constitution revision that had been struck down the previous decade, a revision of the entire constitution had been made possible in the previous session in a constitutional amendment.[112] On June 4 the full legislature approved the formation of a constitution revision commission with a nearly unanimous vote and without fanfare. The next day, the first of an extra session, it turned to that intractable problem, apportionment. It attempted reapportionment, but failed. The state had a month to come up with a plan.

The 1966 Constitution Revision Commission

The 1965 bill authorizing the creation of the Constitution Revision Commission (CRC) was a response to two long-running and intertwined sources of tension in Florida government: first, the efforts by many to modernize the 1885 "horse-and-buggy" Constitution,[1] efforts that had been stymied time and again; and second, the legislature's unsuccessful efforts at reapportioning itself, which gave rise to the federal courts' periodic scoldings. As we have seen, the Sturgis Committee's attempt at wholesale constitution revision, through the linked series of amended articles known as the "daisy chain," had failed because the old constitution did not allow itself to be amended more than one article at a time. Much had been said and written about that failure, and it appears that the legislature finally decided to take constitution revision into its own hands and create a law allowing it.

But why now? Did the political, legal, and social changes in Florida and the United States create a "perfect storm"?[2] Did the Pork Choppers agree to humor the relatively few urban reformers (often referred to as "lamb choppers") and allow them to authorize yet another constitution revision group, confident that, once again, no real change would occur because the Pork Choppers would never allow it? How broad was the new commission's mandate?

The people involved in the revision process of the mid-1960s understood that "the rightful place of the states in the federal system had been overwhelmed by central federal power."[3] The federal court decisions in *Brown v. Board of Education* and the reapportionment cases *Baker v. Carr*, *Reynolds v. Sims*, and Florida's *Swann v. Adams* were one probable source of this feeling; the Civil Rights Act and the racial unrest surrounding it was another.

The bill authorizing the Constitution Revision Commission started out as Senate Bill 977. A Florida Bar committee chaired by Dan Redfearn was in charge of drafting it. Redfearn had headed two previous efforts by the Florida Bar to revise the constitution. Robert Ervin drafted the proposed joint resolution at the request of Representative John Crews and Senator Jack Mathews;[4] Chesterfield Smith, who was president of the state bar at the time, recalled having played a role in getting the bill passed.[5] The Senate bill was introduced by William Gautier and eighteen others, including six senators who would be invited to serve on the commission.[6] Although Mallory Horne, Dick Mitchell, and John Crews all proposed House versions, the House ultimately indefinitely postponed its version in favor of the Senate bill.

The Senate bill provided for a thirty-seven-member commission. The only ex officio member would be the attorney general; the others would be chosen by state officials. The chief justice of the Supreme Court of Florida would appoint five members, one of whom was permitted to be a member of the state supreme court. The governor would appoint ten members, one of whom the governor would designate as chairman of the commission. Each chamber of the legislature would have eight members on the commission: eight senators, appointed by the President of the Senate, and eight members of the House, appointed by the Speaker of the House. Finally, the president of the Florida Bar would appoint five members, each of whom had to be confirmed by the bar's Board of Governors, a body with representation from each judicial circuit in the state.[7]

The commission was charged to meet "as soon as practical" after the bill became law and to "invite and consider recommendations from" the governor, cabinet, supreme court, and legislature. In turn, "the several departments of the state government and all other public bodies and officials" were required to "aid and assist" the commission. The commission was required to hold public hearings "as it may deem advisable" at locations and times of its choosing in Florida. In addition to the members, the commission would be staffed with an executive director to handle administrative duties, and two secretaries. The staff would receive salaries for eighteen months; members would receive only reimbursement of travel expenses at regular state rates. The commission's entire budget was $100,000. Finally, the commission was required to submit "reports and recommendations" to the legislature to revise the constitution. Its deadline was sixty days before the 1967 legislature would convene; if one assumes the bill referred to a regular session, this would put the deadline in early February 1967.[8]

The June Special Sessions

Governor Burns recalled the legislature into special session starting on June 5, 1965, for the purpose of passing an acceptable apportionment plan after the summer of 1964 decisions of the U.S. Supreme Court. Like many legislatures before and since, they could not manage to pass a plan, and the governor had to recall them again to start on June 25, less than one week before the court-imposed deadline. At the opening, the House approved a bill that proposed significant reform and sent it to the Senate, where a hardcore group of Pork Choppers voted against everything, including rules for the special session itself. Nearly the same senators opposed each vote, including Charley Johns of the FLIC and Senate "dean" Dilworth Clarke of Jefferson County. Johns and Clarke were senators whose sparsely populated home counties would be swallowed, under the proposed plan, into districts with other counties, where the senators' vote-getting ability was not assured.

The failure to pass a plan was not for want of trying. Many legislators tried to put plans together. A young reform-minded senator, Reubin Askew of Pensacola, got involved and became known for carrying a set of colored pencils around the Senate halls to try to draw up a plan that would produce a fair apportionment. Askew, like many others, would try different reapportionment schemes by grouping adjacent counties into senatorial districts. Senator Verle Pope of St. Augustine teased Askew, telling him the pencils were making everyone nervous. Under the reapportionment pressure, of course, just about anything would have made legislators anxious. To ease the tension, Pope and Askew proposed a reapportionment plan that called for just two senators: one for each county that existed in Florida in 1828. That, of course, would mean just Escambia, Askew's county, home of Pensacola, and St. Johns, Pope's county, home of St. Augustine.[9]

In the heat of the battle, Askew later recalled, he stayed awake for three straight days and nights. Finally, when an apportionment bill that Askew considered acceptable was on its third reading and looked safe, Askew got ready to go get the sleep he knew he needed—but he was too wired up to sleep. One of his colleagues, Senator Beth Johnson of Orlando, gave him a sleeping pill. Askew was dubious—he had never taken one. Finally, he agreed. Within five minutes, the reapportionment bill had come unsewn on a technical issue orchestrated by Pork Choppers, and Askew had to step in to save it. What could he do? He had just taken the first sleeping pill of his life. Not a problem, Senator Johnson said: Here, I have a pill that will keep you awake.[10]

Finally the Senate passed an amended version of the bill, which allowed Pork Choppers who were about to be redrawn out of their districts to stay in the legislature for two years. The House approved it and the governor signed it into law on June 30, one day before the deadline. Askew went home to sleep.

The new law substantially rebalanced both chambers for the upcoming 1966 elections. Now, no less than 41.6 percent of the population could elect a majority of the House, and 44.7 percent could elect a majority of the Senate.[11] This was a vast improvement over the ability of just 26.9 percent of the population to elect a majority of the House and 15.2 percent to elect a majority of Senate in 1963. The new apportionment law returned to the federal district court in Miami to await its fate.

June 1965 in Miami: The *Swann* Litigation Continues

On June 30, 1965, the same day Governor Burns signed the new apportionment bill, University of Florida political science professor Manning Dauer placed a friend-of-the-court brief and a proposed apportionment plan in the mail.[12] Dauer had painstakingly worked out the apportionment plan on his living-room floor, using pencils and adding machines.[13]

Figure 4. University of Florida political science professor Manning J. Dauer created the redistricting plan that the U.S. District Court for the Southern District of Florida would adopt to alter Florida's political face. A friend once wrote to Dauer, "I believe you and I have three things in common. Our hair is rapidly turning white, we both wear glasses, and we are just about as ugly as gentlemen ever get to be." Photo courtesy of the University of Florida.

Born in 1909, Dauer had taught at the University of Florida since 1933 and was the first chairman of the newly independent political science department. He had published many articles and books over his career and had served as a paid CBS analyst for the 1964 Florida election contest. Dauer grew up traveling the country with his mother while she worked in the women's suffrage movement and later supported the move to establish the League of Nations.[14] Four-year-old Manning's first foray into political science, at a suffragist meeting, ended with his wildly erroneous prediction to his mother that "I will vote before you will."[15]

Dauer had served on Governor Collins's 1955 Citizens' Apportionment Committee.[16] He did not participate in or approve of the 1957 daisy-chain draft constitution.[17] Dauer was also involved in constitutional and reapportionment issues at the national level. He met with Solicitor General Archibald Cox just before the oral arguments in *Baker v. Carr*. The two political experts discussed whether the federal fixed allocation of senators by geographic area, as in the U.S. Senate, was applicable to a state.[18] Dauer contended the analogy did not hold, because states can create subdivisions at will. Cox shared his view, but the men agreed that it didn't solve the apportionment problem. The U.S. Supreme Court would come to agree with Dauer's analysis and reject apportionment systems that were based on the federal model.

Dauer had two close friendships that may have influenced the course of the reapportionment saga in Florida. He was a friend of Earl Faircloth, Florida's attorney general. Earl, and sometimes Mrs. Faircloth too, was a frequent guest at Dauer's home either for campaign stops or University of Florida functions years before the apportionment litigation. On at least two occasions Dauer had to ship the attorney general clothes he had left or borrowed while visiting Dauer.[19]

The other close friend of Dauer's was Judge William McRae. Dauer and McRae had known each other since their University of Florida student days in the early 1930s. They had sought to establish a Phi Beta Kappa chapter at the university, and also formed their own "Speculative Club" as a book-reading group.[20] This friendship explains the addendum McRae would add to a personal letter to Dauer in 1966, after Dauer had submitted his amicus brief but before the court ultimately used it in a later round of litigation. The handwritten addendum noted that McRae was enclosing a copy of the latest apportionment decision. "It's close!" remarked McRae, who added, "I certainly hope the U.S.S.C. doesn't throw in a monkey wrench!"[21] Dauer's correspondence files are full of letters from McRae thanking Dauer for his hospitality, proposing joint vacations, asking for the return of forgotten personal items from Dauer's home, and once declaring that he had particularly enjoyed "taking the world apart with you and not bothering to put it back together."[22]

Dauer was a lifelong bachelor, and he vehemently opposed the FLIC legislative investigations into the university faculties at the University of Florida and University of South Florida. Although there is no evidence that the FLIC had investigated Dauer, it is possible that it had taken interest in a bachelor professor as part of its campaign to remove homosexual university professors from state-paid positions.

4

Building a Constitution's Foundation

In 1965 Charles Scribner's Sons published a novel by former safe-cracker, AWOL Navy enlistee, and much-incarcerated Floridian Donn Pearce, titled *Cool Hand Luke*. Like the Pork Chopper legislature, Cool Hand Luke had already escaped the law once. Unlike them, he had been caught, and now he was working on a Florida prison road crew. He was now being given bathroom privacy by the prison road boss in a nearby thicket of scrub bushes. Luke was required to continuously shake a bush to show he was not fleeing. The third time out, Luke tied a string to the bush, left the area while pulling on the string, and successfully absquatulated into an impenetrable thicket of scrub.[1] So too in 1965 the Pork Choppers would escape meaningful reapportionment once again, this time by the skin of their teeth. But, again like Cool Hand Luke, the Pork Choppers could not hold out forever.

October 1965: The Disney Announcement

In just a few weeks in late October and early November 1965, Florida experienced both great chagrin and great glory. In November 1965, the popular nationwide monthly *Harper's Magazine* published Robert Sherrill's article "Florida's Legislature: The Pork Chop State of Mind."[2] In his article, Sherrill skewered Pork Chop legislators as backward, segregationist, allergic to taxes, and jealous of power and patronage. Sherrill remarked that, because of Pork Chopper influence, cattle received more tax revenue than people did. To illustrate what he called the "Pork Chop State of Mind," Sherrill repeated the Dilworth Clarke retirement story without euphemizing Clarke's racist language. This example of thoughtless cronyism, patronage, and racism had circulated in Florida newspapers with little comment and often with sanitized language, but in the national spotlight, using Clarke's racist language, it surely stung.

But overshadowing the embarrassment of the *Harper's* article was the announcement that Walt Disney had chosen Central Florida as the site of his next theme park. Media speculation had been swirling for months, as a "mystery client" had been buying up large tracts of land near Kissimmee. Walt Disney himself had dodged direct questions from an *Orlando Sentinel* reporter about whether he intended to build a new theme park in Florida. But the reporter noticed that Disney "seemed to know a great deal more about Central Florida than someone having no interest in the area."[3] Disney seemed to know about weather, traffic, and tourism in Central Florida. The *Sentinel* reporter, Emily Bavar, put two and two together with some other clues she had gathered, and broke the story. With the secret out and undeniable, Disney officials agreed to let Governor Burns make the official announcement on October 25 in a previously scheduled address to the Florida League of Municipalities in Miami.[4]

The announcement sent a bolt of electricity through the whole state of Florida. Sleepy citrus and cattle towns in the middle of the state, such as Kissimmee, would change like "bab[ies] grown overnight into . . . busy, sprawling giant[s]."[5] The new Disney park promised to transform Florida's economy and tourism.

Behind the scenes, though, the goliath Disney project required special legislation to provide the company control over the infrastructure it needed for such an expansive project.[6] That would end up taking much time, and many billable hours, of a team of lawyers. It would also end up competing with the Florida constitution for the attention of the legislature in 1967.

The CRC's Chair

By December 1965 it was time to start selecting members of the Constitution Revision Commission. Governor Burns started the ball rolling by naming attorney Chesterfield Smith chair of the commission. Smith was fresh off the presidency of the Florida Bar, and he would go on to become the controversial American Bar Association president who denounced President Nixon, embroiled in the Watergate scandal, famously declaring in October 1973 after the Saturday Night Massacre, "No man is above the law."

Smith was a partner with the fast-growing and politically well-connected law firm of Holland, Bevis, McRae and Smith. Forty-eight years old, Smith was competent, confident, and ebullient. Smith was the kind of man who "could strut sitting down" and, a friend remarked, could be heard coming from five blocks away.[7] Smith had never run for elective office and had never been required to curry voters' favor. Although he had considered running for state legislature, he changed his mind when his uncle, also named Chesterfield Smith, ran for, and was elected to, the Florida House. Smith's upbringing was modest; it veered into poverty when his father, the DeSoto County school superintendent, was defeated in an election and the family had to leave the county to find work. Thereafter, he supported the family on the earnings from a variety of odd jobs, including electrical appliance repair, agricultural inspections, and soda-jerk jobs at drug stores. Smith's father was also briefly a member of the House of Representatives in the 1935 session; young Chesterfield, as a legislative page, would accompany him to Tallahassee, and each earned six dollars per day for the sixty days of the legislative session.[8]

Unlike many of the Pork Choppers, Chesterfield Smith was a veteran, having served as an artillery battalion commander in Europe during World War II. Smith displayed his reformist streak as commander by ordering Germans out of their houses and forcing them to trade places with camp prisoners.[9] After his military service, Smith returned home to Florida. Like many other returning vets, he began to question Florida's antiquated racist politics and social order.[10] He returned from World War II with a Purple Heart, a Bronze Star, and several thousand dollars in gambling winnings from the ocean crossing home. Those winnings put him through law school at the University of Florida, where he helped to found the *Law Review*, was president of the law student body, and graduated at the top of his class in 1948. Smith initially practiced law in Arcadia after he graduated, but two years later Bill McRae, then a senior partner in a Bartow law firm, recruited him to join the firm.

Figure 5. Chesterfield Smith chaired the Constitution Revision Commission in 1966. His strong leadership ensured the development of a new constitution that would serve Florida "for a hundred years." Photo courtesy of State Archives of Florida, *Florida Memory*, https://floridamemory. com/items/show/45725.

Smith endeared himself to the firm's clients; when he had been with McRae's firm just four months, one of the biggest clients, a phosphate company, threatened to take its business away from the firm unless Smith did all of the client's work. The next day the firm made Smith a partner.[11] The phosphate industry, which was centered in Polk County, where Smith practiced, was booming. The phosphate industry provided raw material for fertilizer, and the Polk County deposits provided more phosphate to the world market than those from any other location. Extracting that phosphate wrecked the landscape and polluted the air and water, however, damaging not only the area's citizens but also its other major industries, cattle and citrus. Gradually, Smith's representation of the industry led to his being its spokesman and lobbying the legislators from North Florida on behalf of the industry.

Smith had large ambitions for his law firm. Working with both senior and junior partners, he constantly dreamed of strategies that would expand their client base beyond the phosphate companies alone, would cover greater geographical areas, and would increase the number of attorneys in the firm. His son Chet recalled when he was a young boy that Bill McRae would stop by the family home on a weekend morning and go to the kitchen with Smith to discuss the firm's business. There each man would set up a bottle of Scotch and share a large bucket of oysters. Chet was required to shuck enough oysters to start the men eating, then was allowed to play in the yard until he would be recalled to task when the shucked oysters ran out. This process was repeated until the Scotch was finished and, presumably, the firm's future had been discussed thoroughly. Chet also recalled, though, that McRae was the only person his father truly revered.[12]

Smith was at the forefront in his own efforts to give the law firm wider public exposure. He served as chair of the Florida Bar committee that overhauled the Uniform Commercial Code in Florida, and he served a one-year term in 1964–65 as president of the Florida Bar. Even so, Smith hadn't been the governor's first choice for CRC chair. When the governor telephoned Smith and asked him to serve on the commission, Smith, not one to be shy, said he would only serve as chair, and Burns told him he had someone else in mind for that duty. Smith declined the governor's invitation. Several days later, Smith's phone rang again. It was the governor, offering him the chairmanship. Smith was delighted to accept.[13] The governor's appointment letter was mailed to Smith on December 13, 1965.[14] Ten days later, Smith told fellow CRC member Hugh Taylor in a letter, "The chances for the success of our venture at this time appear to me to be particularly bright."[15]

In fact, Smith had already been doing a little planning for the CRC: a letter to him from future CRC member Thomas Barkdull dated December 2, 1965, includes a proposed schedule for CRC meetings, drafts, and final adoption. The commission would ultimately follow a similar schedule.[16]

Who and What Was the CRC?

Who was on the Constitution Revision Commission? Chairman Smith described it in geographical terms at the start of one of its public hearings in the summer of 1966. He pointed out that the thirty-seven members of the CRC represented a very fairly apportioned body, as the nine largest counties, "which of course includes Escambia and my own county of Polk, which represent sixty-seven per-cent of the population,

Table 1. Members of the 1966–1968 Constitution Revision Commission

Thomas Alexander (died in July 1966)
Raymond E. Alley
Emerson Allsworth
Reubin Askew
William C. Baggs
Thomas Barkdull
Lawton Chiles (replaced Thomas Alexander in July 1966)
John J. Crews
S. J. Davis
Richard T. Earle
Robert Ervin
Earl Faircloth
Frank Fee
Elmer Friday
William Gautier
Warren Goodrich
Charlie Harris
George Hollahan
Joseph C. Jacobs
Charley Johns
Beth Johnson
Henry Land
Ralph Marsicano
J. Sidney Martin
Jack Mathews
John M. McCarty
Stephen C. O'Connell
William G. O'Neill
Richard Pettigrew
Donald H. Reed
B. K. Roberts
H. L. "Tom" Sebring
Chesterfield Smith
George Stallings
Hugh M. Taylor
Ralph Turlington
Gordon Vickery
Bill Young

had sixty-five percent of the members of our Commission, yet the rural and smaller areas of our State are represented just as well. We have some great State-wide political thinkers and leaders."[17]

An analysis of those thinkers and leaders must start with Smith. No member of the CRC has said that Smith was anything but forceful in his role as leader. Joseph Jacobs, chief trial counsel in the attorney general's office, recalled that Smith "seldom asked for advice or counsel, he would just tell you what he had in mind for you, and you usually followed that advice."[18] Smith could be brutally candid, friends later recalled, but he also planned, pushed, cajoled, and planted operatives in committees. He kept the meetings on schedule. Thomas Barkdull later told an interviewer that the members often referred to Smith as "Lord Chesterfield."[19] Reubin Askew said: "Bear in mind, there was only one king—and everybody knew who he was and his name was Chesterfield."[20] Smith "made it plain from the beginning that there were going to be no prima-donnas except possibly him," Barkdull said, "and one of the ways he did that was he announced in the beginning that he didn't care what the titles were for everybody that came there, justice, judge, governor, senator, Mr. Speaker or whatever . . . when they were in that mode they were going to be known only as commissioner."[21] But the members also unanimously describe a leader who was committed to the best constitution Florida could make for itself. Smith made sure that every proposal to the commission had both sides researched and argued. That way, Smith reasoned, even aspects of the new constitution that were not controversial would have all their potential weaknesses exposed. Smith had exquisite political sense, but he never sought or held an elected government office. Perhaps as Citizen Smith he was in a position to be most effective as the chairman.

The CRC was unusual in a number of ways. Because appointments came from several sources—the governor, the chief justice, the state bar, each legislative chamber—they could hardly have been made with an intention to blend a commission. The only member who was written into the legislation itself was the attorney general, Earl Faircloth. Robert Ervin, who appointed five commissioners, said that in his appointments as Florida Bar president he attempted to select excellent lawyers and achieve geographical diversity with knowledge of the geographical origins of some of the other members already appointed.[22] It may be happenstance that the CRC ultimately included a diversity of abilities. Legislative experts, local government leaders, a member of the press, a labor leader, judges, a municipal lawyer, a retail executive—all were present. There was also, apparently, no attempt to balance by race or

Figure 6. Senators Beth Johnson and Jack Mathews served on the Constitution Revision Commission; they were two of the members most respected by their peers. Photo courtesy of State Archives of Florida, *Florida Memory*, https://floridamemory.com/items/show/42820.

gender. The year 1965 was still the era of the white man, and the commission had no African American member; it did, however, include one woman, Senator Beth Johnson of Orlando, a longtime member of the League of Women Voters and an appointee of Governor Burns.[23] The choice of Johnson was a testament to her excellent performance in the Senate, where she was the first elected woman. As a matter of fact, Johnson first was elected to the House when Henry Land vacated his House seat to run for an open Senate seat. Johnson succeeded Land in 1958 and was elected to the Senate in 1962.[24] By the time the CRC was formed, Johnson was in the Senate, and Land was back in the House of Representatives.

Johnson's CRC colleagues often called her "the real Beth Johnson," as another woman with the same name had been elected to the Senate in 1965. There is no evidence that the "real" Beth Johnson's sex was a liability, even in that era. Newspaper accounts of her early in her political career did sometimes comment on her looks and demeanor, though always with approval. The *Orlando Evening Star* editorial page approved of her first election to the House, calling her "a young woman with keen vision in governmental affairs."[25] Two years later, Johnson was mentioned in the "For and About Women" section of the *Orlando*

Sentinel: "If there could be just one lady legislator this session, isn't it lucky that she is so photogenic? And smart!"[26] An *Orlando Sentinel* article announcing her Senate candidacy in January 1962 noted that, as she was "very much a lady," if her election were to result "in less secret sessions in smoke filled rooms and in members cleaning up their language somewhat, [it] would be a benefit to the entire state."[27] Johnson was described in a *St. Petersburg Times* article as "superbly poised and controlled. She dresses elegantly. She is in her fifties, grey haired, a Vassar graduate." But Johnson was no softie. She enjoyed boating and fishing.[28] She advised women thinking of entering politics, "Don't run for office if you're apt to burst into tears."[29] Johnson knew better than to push all the available limits in the legislature. She did not try to use the Senate Lounge, insisting that "the wives have a very nice lounge. And for [that] matter, the secretaries have a very nice rest room." Male senators claimed they "loved" having a "lady in the Senate," and one senator noted, "She won't disturb us one bit."[30]

Governor Burns, with ten appointees to the CRC, had the potential for the most influence on the commission. In addition to Smith and Johnson, he appointed Robert Ervin, president of the Florida Bar; Emerson Allsworth, a Fort Lauderdale lawyer and state representative who had campaigned for the governor and who may have been his first pick for chair;[31] Charlie Harris, president of the Florida AFL-CIO; Bill Baggs, editor of the *Miami News,* Vietnam War opponent, and liberal political booster; Sidney Martin, president of the Florida County Commissioners Association; Tom Sebring, Stetson Law School dean and a former Florida Supreme Court justice; Gordon Vickery, an executive with the Jordan Marsh department store chain; and Justice B. K. Roberts of the Florida Supreme Court.

Robert Ervin, like Chesterfield Smith, had never sought or held public office, but his influence as a leader of the bar and as a representative for the construction and development industries in Florida during the boom years of the 1950s and 1960s placed him at the top of everyone's list to help create a new constitution. After serving in the Marines during World War II, eventually becoming a colonel, Ervin returned to Florida, graduated from the University of Florida College of Law, and built his name through hard work in the private sector, leading first the

Tallahassee Bar Association and then the Florida Bar. Ervin modestly noted that his timing as a lawyer for developers was also fortuitous in overlapping with the growth spurt in Florida in post–World War II years: "I caught the growth."[32]

As president of the state bar, Ervin nominated five members to the CRC. One, Joe Jacobs, was an assistant attorney general who had prosecuted the Chillingworth murders, a bizarre case in which a Palm Beach County municipal judge hired a hit man to murder a circuit judge and his wife. Jacobs had also, as assistant attorney general, marched with demonstrators in St. Augustine during its 1964 race riots, "to look after the demonstrators and make sure they were safe," he told a friend at the time.[33] Jacobs, who was Jewish, endured epithets from onlookers, both as to the race of the demonstrators and as to his own religion, as he marched.[34]

Ervin also named Richard Earle, a St. Petersburg lawyer who was a member of the Florida Bar's Board of Governors.[35] Fellow lawyers liked and respected Earle, even though they teased him for his short stature. He was a lifelong Floridian and kept one foot in his past: until the day he died, he never air-conditioned his home.[36]

Another Ervin appointee was Representative Bill O'Neill, a lawyer from Ocala and, like Earle, a colleague of Ervin's on the Board of Governors. O'Neill had served in the House since 1956. Ervin also appointed Bradenton lawyer Warren Goodrich. Goodrich had attended law school with Ervin and Smith, would eventually become Smith's law partner, and was at that time the chair of Florida's Democratic Party. Ervin's fifth appointee was Tampa lawyer Thomas Alexander, another Board of Governors colleague of Ervin's.

President of the Senate James E. Connor appointed eight senators: Reubin Askew of Pensacola; Jack Mathews of Jacksonville; Bill Gautier of New Smyrna Beach; George Hollahan of Miami; Bill Young of Pinellas County; Wilson Carraway of Tallahassee; Robert Williams of Graceville; and Charley Johns of Starke. Before the first CRC meeting in January, two replacements had to be made. Carraway declined his appointment, because he had decided to not seek reelection in 1966.[37] Connor then appointed Senator Elmer Friday of Fort Myers. Robert Williams of

Graceville resigned and was replaced by John McCarty of Fort Pierce; McCarty was the brother of the late governor, Dan McCarty.

From the House, Speaker E. C. Rowell appointed eight representatives. One was Henry Land, from the little town of Tangerine, in Orange County, whom Johnson had succeeded in the House, and who had been the first chair of the FLIC, which later became so closely associated with Charley Johns. Rowell's other appointees were George Stallings of Jacksonville, a conservative Democrat who had served a turn on the FLIC; Ralph Turlington of Gainesville, who would soon succeed Rowell as Speaker; John Crews of Baker County, who was fighting for his political life in the reapportionment wars during this time; Frank Fee of St. Lucie County; Don Reed, a young Republican from Palm Beach County; and S. J. "Joe" Davis of Seminole County.

Rowell's final appointee was startled to be named to the commission. Richard Pettigrew of Coral Gables, a lifelong student of government, recalled feeling "consternation and shock" when he learned that he had been appointed by Speaker Rowell. Pettigrew's relationship with Rowell was "uneasy," he recalled; Rowell was an old-style rural conservative (the northern end of the Florida Turnpike ends in the tiny town of Wildwood largely because it was in Rowell's district), while Pettigrew was an urban, South Florida liberal. Although Pettigrew had badly wanted to serve on the CRC, he had not lobbied a spot and did not expect to be named.[38]

The chief justice of the Florida Supreme Court, E. Harris Drew, appointed five commission members. One was an old colleague, Ralph Marsicano of Tampa, counsel for the Florida League of Cities. Drew had been a city attorney in Palm Beach for decades before taking the bench, and he knew Marsicano from those years.[39] Drew also appointed Thomas Barkdull, who was one of the first judges on Florida's Third District Court of Appeal, in Miami; Hugh Taylor, a North Florida judge; and Raymond Alley, an attorney from Palm Beach who was already a forty-year member of the Florida Bar. The only fellow supreme court justice whom Drew appointed was Stephen C. O'Connell.

However, O'Connell was not the only supreme court justice on the commission. The governor had appointed Justice B. K. Roberts to serve as well. Although having Florida Supreme Court justices helping to form a new constitution may seem logical, it raised questions as to how the supreme court would interpret that constitution when the inevitable litigation over the constitution would come before it. Would the justices who had not served on the CRC defer to Roberts and O'Connell in deciding cases under the new constitution?

The vast majority of the commissioners were white men, but they were far from politically homogeneous. The CRC included Republicans as well as Democrats, liberals as well as conservatives and moderates, urban representatives and rural Pork Choppers. But, aside from a desire for constitutional reform, all had one more thing in common, according to CRC member Bill O'Neill: every one of them was outspoken; none was shy.[40] Although "there were not any fistfights,"[41] the constitution revision process promised to be a full-throated debate.

Although politicking and horse trading were kept to a minimum in the CRC's work, according to Robert Ervin (and as a former lobbyist, he should know) it was not entirely absent. For example, Florida Supreme Court justice Millard Caldwell, who had been governor twenty years earlier, saw fit to try to influence, or at least advise, the commission. He wrote to Smith on supreme court letterhead: "I hope your Commission will not undertake the writing of a new constitution—that it will content itself with the correction of deficiencies. Unnecessary new language will be productive of confusion and litigation."[42] Nor was deal making absent within the commission. Smith dictated a memorandum to his file that CRC member George Hollahan requested to be appointed to the Local Government Committee or the Steering and Rules Committee because Dick Pettigrew was (the two were on opposite sides in litigation between Dade County and Southern Bell).[43] Hollahan and Pettigrew both ended up serving on the Local Government Committee.[44]

Although the commissioners had the benefit of nearly two decades of constitution revision attempts to draw from in their work, memories differed as to the extent they were influenced by their predecessors' work. Richard Earle would later dismiss the previous revision attempts, declaring that "there is no use looking at a mess that came to nothing."[45] In contrast, William O'Neill spoke more respectfully of the previous committees' work but did not remember the CRC using it extensively.[46]

Swann v. Adams, December 1965

On December 23, 1965, the U.S. District Court for the Southern District of Florida found the 1965 Florida legislative apportionment inconsistent with equal protection as interpreted by *Reynolds*.[47] The court noted that even Florida's attorney general, Earl Faircloth, had acknowledged that the 1965 apportionment failed the one-man, one-vote test. But the court, perhaps aware of the pun, stated that the attorney general had requested "the State of Florida, acting through its legislature, [to have] an opportunity to put its legislative house in order."[48] The court rejected the provision that would have allowed the "leftover" Pork Choppers to stay in the legislature to the next election. The court gave the reapportioning task back to the Florida Legislature, stating that the legislature would be better equipped than the court to make apportionment decisions that might require isolating economically different areas. Showing a sensitivity to nuance in reading the political situation, the court opined that without the carryover Pork Choppers, the legislature might have "the will" to reapportion itself.[49] The generous opinion therefore allowed the legislature to meet to reapportion itself in the 1967 regular session—the next one the biennial legislature would have—and gave it until sixty days after that session's end, in the event a later special session of the 1967 regular session failed to create a valid reapportionment scheme.[50] The court had given the Pork Choppers nearly a year and a half to strategize.

As the U.S. Supreme Court had done in *Brown v. Board of Education*, the Southern District Court in its opinion blended a finding that a current situation was unconstitutional with advice as to how quickly compliance should be achieved, without setting an absolute deadline.

It seemed that the CRC, which was slated to do the bulk of its work in 1966, would be able to meet in comparative peace to create a new constitution deliberated and proposed and submitted to the public.

5

Putting It Together, Part I

Chesterfield Smith and his Steering and Rules Committee had put into place mechanisms that would provide that the public could observe the CRC's work; that would ensure completion of the redraft; and that would produce a politically palatable document. Although Florida did not yet have a law requiring public meetings to be open, Smith made sure that every CRC meeting was open to the public and that the entire process could be seen, watched, or read about by any citizen who was interested.

Based on the previous constitution revision attempts, it appeared that three potential pitfalls faced the 1966 constitution revision. First, the commission could succumb to internal squabbles or propose a politically unacceptable revision for legislative approval. Second, the legislature could reject or substantially alter the CRC's proposals before putting them on the popular ballot. Finally, the public could reject the proposal at the polls. The commission in general, and Smith in particular, using his skills as lobbyist and litigator, would try to avoid all three pitfalls.

According to Thomas Barkdull, the first organizational discussions about the CRC occurred during a December 1965 University of Florida football weekend.[1] At that meeting were Chesterfield Smith, Bill O'Neill, Richard Earle, John Crews, Barkdull, and possibly John McCarty and Jack Mathews. The CRC's Steering and Rules Committee would take its membership almost exclusively from this group. After this meeting Barkdull roughed out a schedule and organizational ideas.[2]

Once appointed, CRC members had to sign an oath of office and pay a ten-dollar administrative fee. They were issued identification cards and cardboard telephone credit cards as well. E. C. Rowell, at Smith's request, allowed the CRC to use the House Rules Committee room and adjoining offices when the legislature was not in session. The offices opened in early January 1966 in rooms 240–42 and borrowed Dene Nichols from the Secretary of the Senate to act as the CRC's executive director and assist it through its organizational meeting. Betty Sparks acted as the CRC's secretary, and Rogers Turner acted as its staff counsel.

On January 11 and 12, 1966, three weeks after the *Swann v. Adams* court found the latest apportionment plan only partly constitutional, the CRC held its first meeting in the Senate chamber of the capitol.[3] Smith divided the CRC into ten committees, including two governing committees and eight committees assigned to substantive areas of the constitution. The governing committees were the Steering and Rules Committee and the Style and Drafting Committee. The substantive committees were Executive Branch, Legislative Branch, Judicial Branch, State Finance, Local Government, Human Rights, Education and Welfare, and Suffrage and Elections.

After Chesterfield Smith, the commissioner most often mentioned as crucial to the CRC's success was Hugh Taylor, an appointee of Chief Justice Drew. Smith named Taylor chair of the Style and Drafting Committee. Taylor, a longtime circuit judge from Quincy in Gadsden County, near Tallahassee, whom Smith described as "a brilliant, old, savvy, wise trial judge," was widely acknowledged as one of Florida's foremost constitutional experts.[4] As a trial judge in the judicial circuit of the state capital, he regularly heard questions of Florida constitutional law. As chair of the Style and Drafting Committee, Taylor's task was to write the constitution so that, as a fellow CRC member said, "the boy behind the plow could understand" it.[5] His fellow commissioners would refer to him as the "father" of the new constitution. But Taylor was no mere amanuensis for his fellow members. Representative Maxine Baker, longtime League of Women Voters spokeswoman, cautioned (without naming names) that the Style and Drafting Committee tended to "edit and polish [certain provisions] right out of existence."[6] Reubin Askew has stated that Taylor would regularly change not just the style but also the substance of what the Judicial Committee would

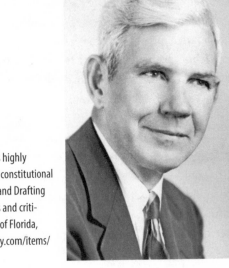

Figure 7. Circuit Judge Hugh Taylor was highly respected for his knowledge of Florida constitutional issues. His efforts as chair of the Style and Drafting Committee earned him both accolades and criticism. Photo courtesy of State Archives of Florida, *Florida Memory*, https://floridamemory.com/items/show/10321.

present to him, because he strongly opposed certain parts of it.[7] Smith gave an alternative reason for the substantive changes, however. At one of the public hearings the CRC held around the state before the final draft was completed, he explained that he had charged the Style and Drafting Committee to make substantive changes to the text if necessary for the document to read as a cohesive whole. Even those who criticized Taylor's substantive changes had great respect for him, though; Askew's opinion was typical when he called Taylor "one of the truly outstanding jurists of our time."[8]

At that first meeting, Taylor addressed the full commission and informed members that he believed the 1955 revision attempt had failed for four reasons: poor attendance, protracted debate of minute wording matters, recurring debates over the same issues, and an attempt to complete the revised articles in numerical order.[9] The Steering and Rules Committee would try to prevent all four problems from occurring again.

Throughout the process, Smith made it clear he expected commission members to take their task seriously. He repeatedly reminded members to attend CRC meetings, committee meetings, and the public hearings. At one meeting he baldly told CRC members: "If you cannot

Table 2. Committees of the 1966–1968 Constitution Revision Commission

Chesterfield Smith, chair

GOVERNING COMMITTEES

STEERING AND RULES	STYLE AND DRAFTING
Chesterfield Smith, chair	Hugh Taylor, chair
Thomas Barkdull, vice-chair	Thomas Barkdull
Bill O'Neill	Jack Mathews
John Crews	
Richard Earle	

SUBSTANTIVE COMMITTEES

EXECUTIVE BRANCH	LEGISLATIVE BRANCH
Earl Faircloth, chair	Emerson Allsworth, chair
Charley Johns, vice-chair	Henry Land, vice-chair
Hugh Taylor	Robert Ervin
Warren Goodrich	John McCarty
Bill O'Neill	Jack Mathews
George Stallings	Bill Young

JUDICIAL BRANCH	STATE FINANCE
Reubin Askew, chair	Frank Fee, chair
Stephen O'Connell, vice-chair	Thomas Alexander, vice-chair (died in July 1966; replaced by Lawton Chiles)
Bill Baggs	Elmer Friday
S. J. Davis Jr.	George Hollahan
John Crews	Thomas Barkdull

LOCAL GOVERNMENT	HUMAN RIGHTS
William Gautier, chair	B. K. Roberts, chair
Ralph Marsicano, vice-chair	Charlie Harris, vice-chair
Joseph Jacobs	Donald Reed
Sidney Martin	Raymond Alley
John Crews	Richard Earle
Dick Pettigrew	
George Hollahan	
H. L. "Tom" Sebring	

EDUCATION AND WELFARE	SUFFRAGE AND ELECTIONS
Ralph Turlington, chair	George Stallings, chair
Beth Johnson, vice-chair	Bill Young, vice-chair
H. L. "Tom" Sebring	Dick Pettigrew
Gordon Vickery	Warren Goodrich
William O'Neill	Richard Earle

serve, I personally don't want you."[10] To head off the other three potential problems that Taylor had identified, the Steering and Rules Committee assigned each substantive committee a particular part of the new constitution to draft, indicating for each committee which portion of the 1885 Constitution to consider when drafting their portion. Because the 1885 Constitution was so disorganized and heavily amended, some of its sections were assigned to multiple committees if they affected more than one area. For example, regarding whether the legislature should consider passing local laws affecting only one part of the state or certain people, both the Legislative Branch Committee and the Local Government Committee would address relevant provisions from the 1885 Constitution.[11]

The division of the CRC into committees had three significant impacts. First and most important, it strongly influenced the shape of the new constitution. Each committee was to meet and develop broad philosophical questions on its area, such as whether the new constitution should propose an elective cabinet. Division would help to concentrate expertise in each committee. Because each committee drafted a section of the constitution, the new constitution's form was already largely fixed. This structure ensured from the outset that the CRC's work was to be a new constitution and not a rewrite of the old constitution, as had happened in earlier efforts.

Second, the division of work into substantive committees organized the job of drafting the constitution and kept it to manageable proportions. Each committee could do a thorough and cohesive job organizing its portion of the constitution. Third, for each part of the constitution, this structure created a group within the CRC that could later definitively speak to the full commission on why certain items were included or omitted in a particular section, and why certain language was used.

Smith maintained control of the substantive committees through the two governing committees. The Steering and Rules Committee, which Smith chaired, scheduled meetings, hired experts, and established the rules governing the commission and its committees. Smith later admitted to having placed only his most trustworthy allies with him on this committee, namely, Barkdull, vice-chair; Bill O'Neill; John Crews; and Richard Earle.[12] The Style and Drafting Committee was also peopled only with men whom Smith wholly trusted. This small committee consisted of Taylor, chair; Barkdull; and Jack Mathews. Taylor's experience on earlier constitution revision efforts and with adjudicating constitutional challenges in Florida made him an ideal chair of the committee. Barkdull, too, had served on earlier constitution revision efforts. Mathews, a World War II sailor who had survived a kamikaze attack, was widely acknowledged to be one of the most able statesmen in Florida.[13] His contemporaries considered him a consummate legislator, able to find consensus and "achieve the possible" like few others.[14] He had run for governor once, and many expected him to run again.

Because of his commitment to the success of the CRC, Smith kept track of members who might challenge the process or his own influence. In particular, he had CRC members bird-dog B. K. Roberts, a sitting Florida Supreme Court justice.[15] Roberts, who had been serving on the court since 1949 and had already served two terms as chief justice, understood power: two of his close friends were former governor Fuller Warren, who had appointed him to the court in 1949, and Edward Ball, who controlled the vast du Pont and St. Joe Paper Company empires, which also included the Florida National Banks and the Florida East Coast Line Railroad.[16]

Although the January meetings were intended to be primarily organizational, with the new substantive committees meeting briefly to organize and adjourn to the Governor's Mansion for cocktails on the final evening, the Legislative Branch Committee wasted no time getting to work.[17] It announced on January 12 that it had already decided two matters: the legislature would remain bicameral and would meet in annual sessions.[18] The decision to continue the bicameral legislature had not been a foregone conclusion; some favored a unicameral legislature, such as Nebraska had recently adopted. Ralph Turlington, though not a member of the Legislative Branch Committee, remarked later that he personally favored a one-house legislature but realized it would never go over: "We are conditioned in this country to a bicameral situation. We think that must have been ordained by the Lord, or at least some of the angels."[19] Upon motion of Barkdull, the Legislative Branch Committee agreed to put off any decisions until a later meeting.[20]

Between mid-January and the next CRC meeting, on March 25, the committees were to develop a few broad, disputed philosophical issues in their area and send these to the Steering and Rules Committee so that they could be addressed at the convention in March. But before the CRC could reconvene as a whole, the U.S. Supreme Court again reversed the district court on February 25, invalidated the latest reapportionment plan, and sent the legislature—including, of course, the nineteen legislators who were CRC members—into another scramble. This time the Supreme Court reasoned that because everyone involved admitted that the latest plan failed to pass constitutional muster, there was no good reason to allow it to stand even on an interim basis.[21] The Court struck down the plan partially on the basis that its eighteen-month implementation calendar was unacceptable, and instructed that a valid plan "be made" in time for the 1966 elections. The Court refrained from saying which body—the district court or the legislature—should make the plan.

This latest Court decision came at an exquisitely inopportune time. The deadline to qualify for candidacy for a legislative seat had been set for March 1, just four days later. Hundreds of candidates statewide had already qualified for seats in what they thought would be the apportionment plan governing the 1966 elections. The primary elections were to be held barely two months later, but now there were no seats to which to be elected. The Court's last-minute decision could throw Florida into "a state of political chaos."[22]

On February 26, Governor Burns called a special legislative session to begin on March 2, even though even-numbered years were usually not years in which the biennial legislature met. Burns sounded the warning that the state must take control or invite the federal government to do so: "It now clearly appears," he declared, "that the Florida Legislature must adopt an acceptable plan at the earliest possible date or relinquish to the Federal Courts this portion of our state sovereignty."[23]

The March 2, 1966, Extraordinary Session

Florida's latest apportionment recommendation from the legislature, Joint Resolution HB-19XX(65), had not actually been considered on its merits by the U.S. Supreme Court. Nor was the Court was likely to do so. It had taken the Southern District Court's opinion at face value that the apportionment scheme was unconstitutional, a level of deference it had never given when the district court had approved apportionment plans. Instead, the Court directed its attention to the district court's provision allowing the legislature eighteen months to create a new plan. That, after all, was what the plaintiffs' appeal requested. However, the legislature did not need the Supreme Court to identify the plan's frailties. It already knew it had better come up with a plan that came closer yet to creating equally populated legislative districts for both houses.

The March 2 session began with Governor Burns imploring the legislators to "prevent what well could be a complete breakdown in the legislative branch of our state Government."[24] He understood how gargantuan the legislature's task was: they must, he pointed out, accomplish in ten days what they had not accomplished in the preceding ten years. Remarkably, he claimed to hope that "the terms 'pork choppers' and 'lamb choppers' have been buried forever."[25] He proposed mapping state districting onto the just-approved congressional districting, reasoning that if the federal apportionment passed constitutional muster, a state apportionment allocating representatives within congressional districts in the same proportions must also be constitutional. Burns went so far as to indicate the desired number of legislators in each chamber, and suggested that they all run at large. Then he threw down the gauntlet: the legislature need not match his plan exactly, but he would not accept any plan less equitable than his. And, even though this address was to the legislature, he recommended to the nascent CRC that the new constitution provide that the Supreme Court of Florida be the final body to apportion Florida in the event the legislature failed to do so.[26] This would keep the federal courts out of Florida's internal legislative apportionment decisions.

House Speaker Rowell gave a rousing speech to his troops. "We are assembled here today under totally unexpected circumstances," he began. He invoked the banner of states' rights but acknowledged that if a state failed to assume its governmental responsibilities, the federal government would fill the vacuum. The task before the legislature was an example of such a situation. "If we fail to do this job, and promptly," he said, "we might as well resign ourselves to a reapportionment plan handed to us by judicial decree."[27]

In the opposite wing of the capitol, Senate President James Connor was rallying his members as well. It was, he proclaimed, "our last opportunity, the very last chance" for Floridians to take their legislative future into their own hands. Echoing Governor Burns, he said that the successful plan would neither be a "pork chop" formula nor an urban formula, but "everyone's formula."[28] Connor would not want to adjourn "other than for the purpose of eating and sleeping" until an acceptable plan had been formed.[29]

The ensuing week saw a flurry of proposals, proposed amendments, and votes on related issues. For example, the House voted to allow itself to decide an issue other than reapportionment, but that issue was simply to appoint a group of legislators to present population statistics to the federal courts if needed during the reapportionment litigation.[30] Representative Don Reed proposed an amendment that would provide for keeping the legislature's present composition in place until the November general election could be held under whatever new plan the legislature could come up with.[31] The proposal was defeated. Imagine the legal no-man's-land in which the legislature was operating: the U.S. Supreme Court had rejected the current apportionment of the House and the Senate, which after all complied with Florida's 1885 Constitution. This legislature, though illegally apportioned, had to figure out what new formation the Supreme Court would approve. It was anyone's guess what types of apportionment plans would comply with the Court's evolving jurisprudence.

On Saturday, March 5, the House passed a plan that provided for 48 senators and 117 representatives, and certified it to the Senate. While awaiting the Senate's action, House members got busy passing a raft of local bills: funding to build schools in DeSoto County, courthouse and jail funds for Sumter County, and statewide distribution of racetrack funds. On March 8 the Senate passed the House's version of the reapportionment bill with several amendments; the plan passed later that day with the Senate's amendments intact. The governor signed it and sent it to the court.

The new apportionment had some unusual features. For Pork Choppers in less heavily populated counties it carried potential doom, and the fact that this plan had passed showed that their hold on the legislature had already begun to slip. The most extreme example of how the new plan affected Pork Choppers was the twenty-four-county district that included the homes of Charley Johns, John Crews, and B. C. Pearce, a Pork Chopper from Putnam County. The counties stretched from Jackson in the west to Nassau on the northeastern shoreline, a distance of well over two hundred miles. Though the giant district would elect four senators, candidates would have to travel much more widely in campaigning than they had done under earlier plans. There were two more unfavorable features in this redrawn district for small-county Pork Choppers. First, because the district did not include Jacksonville in the northeast, its population was clustered predominantly in west Florida, around Tallahassee. Second, all four senators would be elected at large. This meant that out of all the twenty-four counties, the few that had the majority of the population could elect all four senators. Johns's old district of Bradford and Union Counties was lumped into this goliath Senate district. His old district would likely be voiceless in the Senate. The process of some Pork Choppers gobbling others was about to begin.

On March 18 the Southern District Court found the legislature's reapportionment plan was acceptable for the purpose of "selecting members for the 1967 session of the Florida Legislature."[32] Candidates went forward with campaigning in the spring 1966 primary election season. But Richard Swann quickly appealed to Washington for a third time, alleging the plan still did not fairly apportion Florida's voters. One thing was obvious to Pork Chopper and Lamb Chopper alike: hog-slaughtering day was approaching for the Pork Chop Gang.

Early Spring 1966: The Substantive Committees Meet

During late February and March, while many of the CRC's legislator members were busy figuring out which new districts they needed to run for reelection in, the CRC's substantive committees began meeting to determine their broad, philosophical questions, which the commission called "certified questions," to submit to the full CRC for debate in March and April. The March and April meetings would provide a sense of the group's feeling about the topics of the certified questions. After those meetings, each committee would propose a draft of its section for the full constitution by May or June. The Style and Drafting Committee would then coordinate all committee submissions and produce a proposed draft, in June, and this would be followed by public hearings that the CRC would hold across the state in the second half of July. Each committee would then submit a final draft following the public hearings, presumably incorporating suggestions the public set forth in those hearings. The Style and Drafting Committee then would issue a final proposed constitution in November. That document would be the working draft for the final constitutional debates in November and December. CRC members would debate the language of the working draft, propose and debate amendments to it, and finalize their draft to send to the legislature. At least that was the plan.

But in the spring of 1966, when the substantive committees were to meet, many CRC members in the legislature had to worry about getting reelected. As of March 21, Reubin Askew was the only CRC member in the Senate who would be unopposed; Senators Johns, Mathews, Friday, and Young had opponents, so their attention would be divided. In the House, Representatives Pettigrew, Stallings, and Turlington had no opponents, but Representatives Fee and Allsworth did.

Executive Branch

The Executive Branch Committee was composed of Attorney General Earl Faircloth, chair; Charley Johns, vice-chair; Hugh Taylor (also the chair of the Style and Drafting Committee); Warren Goodrich; Bill O'Neill; and George Stallings.

A few issues vied for the attention of this committee, but perhaps the hottest political potato was whether the cabinet should be appointed by the governor or elected statewide. Many political theorists believed that the system in which cabinet members were elected statewide without term limits, and in which cabinet members served on more than one hundred governmental committees along with the governor, contributed to the government's being convoluted and not motivated to work together as a team. On the other hand, those who feared a strong government believed that having all members of the cabinet elected independently helped to ensure a government that did not have an overly strong center; if the chief executive appointed the cabinet, as in the federal system, the governor would have far too much power. Many in positions of authority in Florida's government, including those on the CRC, probably remembered the tales they had heard of the repressive carpetbagger government of Reconstruction days. The Yankees had forced a strong government of outsiders on the Floridians after the Civil War. Fear of a strong executive was in the blood of these Floridians. Also, experienced (some would say entrenched) politicians often were friendly with cabinet members or had reason to fear their regulatory power, and could be counted on to vote to keep the cabinet elected out of loyalty, respect, or fear.

But the idea of an appointed cabinet also had powerful supporters, among them serious students of government. Both Chesterfield Smith and Dick Pettigrew favored an appointed cabinet. So did the League of Women Voters. But the majority of the CRC, the legislature, and the public did not. The cabinet, after all, was where legislators had always gone to learn about the substantive content of proposed bills.[33]

The 1885 Constitution divided executive power among an elected governor and six other elected officials. These officeholders acted both through their own elected offices and through a labyrinth of boards, committees, and executive agencies composed of some or all cabinet members. There were so many interlocking agencies in 1966 involving cabinet members that their actual number was unknown. The Institute of Governmental Research at Florida State University estimated that there were about 150 in 1966.[34] And because cabinet members could succeed themselves without limit, this web of executive agencies, built carefully over decades, was as thick, strong, and impenetrable as elephant hide.

Hot potato though this issue was, it appears not to have generated much debate in the Executive Branch Committee meeting. The committee simply added the issue to its list of certified questions to be debated at the March and April meetings by the full CRC.[35] The committee also proposed debating whether a lieutenant governor position should be created.

Legislative Branch

The Legislative Branch Committee was composed of Emerson Allsworth, chair; Henry Land, vice-chair; Robert Ervin; John McCarty; Jack Mathews; and Bill Young. It proposed several questions that, if answered in the affirmative, would add fundamental and permanent improvements to Florida government. The Legislative Committee decided early on to propose questions debating whether the legislature should remain bicameral, move to annual sessions, provide for longer terms for members, provide for a minimum and maximum number of members, provide for automatic apportionment in the event of the legislature's failure to apportion, and be empowered with a legislative auditor to track appropriations.[36]

The Legislative Committee had a fatalistic attitude regarding apportionment. Although the committee would provide for apportionment in its proposal, it knew that the federal court would probably decide Florida's future in this regard. The legislature had tried and failed to reapportion so many times that the committee, like the legislature, realized that a successful apportionment would require not only the cooperation of the CRC's Legislative Committee and the state legislature but also the approval of the federal courts.

The Legislative Committee's proposed certified question regarding apportionment reflected the pain of the lawsuits and special sessions of recent years. The committee proposed to ask whether the constitution should provide for an automatic reapportionment process in the event the legislature failed to reapportion. The state legislature had, since Florida's first constitution in 1838, been under a constitutional mandate to reapportion every ten years. The problem was that it had simply failed to accomplish an accurate reapportionment since the 1920s. Florida was like many other states in this regard. Until *Baker v. Carr* there had been no reapportionment fire built under any state legislature, and without a motivated legislature, reapportionment just would not happen. After all, the turkey cannot be expected to vote in favor of Thanksgiving. Avoiding the elimination of existing seats may sound expedient from the distance of decades, but at the time it was a sensitive issue. After all, each seat was occupied by a human being, probably one with long-standing ties to other legislators.

Philosophies differed as to placing a cap on the number of legislators. On the one hand, the greater the number, the easier it would be to avoid eliminating existing seats and throwing out sitting legislators. On the other hand, the larger the legislative body, the more unwieldy the decision-making process would be. Under the 1885 Constitution, reapportionment was accomplished by the legislature's passing a bill establishing the representatives' districts, subject to veto by the governor.[37] The public had no say in reapportionment unless a constitutional change in the formula was sought.

The debate within the committee on annual sessions was halfhearted, with a general sense that annual sessions should be adopted. Robert Ervin joked that although the legislature met for sixty days every two years, it would be better as two days every sixty years.[38] However, the tremendous growth Florida was experiencing during the 1960s made it clear that the state's needs were growing and changing far too quickly to be handled adequately in biennial sessions.

The committee also proposed to eliminate the legislative election of United States senators, finally conforming Florida's constitution to the U.S. Constitution's Seventeenth Amendment, which had been passed in 1913, providing for popularly elected senators.

Judicial Branch

The Judicial Branch Committee was composed of Reubin Askew, chair; Justice Stephen O'Connell, vice-chair; Bill Baggs; S. J. Davis; and John Crews. Askew was in his seventh year as a state legislator. Although born in Oklahoma, Askew moved with his mother to Pensacola as a young child. When he was appointed to the CRC in 1965 he was thirty-seven years of age and still looked very young. Askew had served in both the Army, as a paratrooper, and in the Air Force, in military intelligence during the Korean conflict. He was a teetotaler and later became notable for drinking an orange-juice toast at his first inauguration as governor. Many of the stories that circulate around Askew have to do with his lifelong sobriety. His friend Dexter Douglass used to tease (accurately) that Askew "didn't drink, he didn't smoke, and all his children were adopted."[39] At Florida State University, where Askew was student body president, one of his classmates and friends was Dempsey Barron. Barron recalled that a group of them used to buy a bottle of liquor and a six-pack of Coca-Cola and drive around the Leon County backroads on weekend evenings for entertainment. According to Barron, Askew went along, never drank any of the liquor, but always paid his share.[40] Barron used to tell another story about Askew, when Askew was governor and Barron was President of the Senate. Barron was reluctant to pass the new judicial article of the constitution, which Askew cared deeply about. In an attempt to persuade Barron, Askew and his wife invited Barron to spend the weekend with them at the Governor's Mansion. Barron later said that, with no alcohol served in the Mansion, he was not a houseguest so much as a political prisoner.[41]

Askew became known in his legislative career as a man of unassailable integrity and uncompromising principle. Chesterfield Smith later said of Askew that the latter quality made Askew better suited to be a governor than a legislator.[42] Askew also had a lifelong interest in judicial reform, and he chaired the CRC's Judicial Committee.

The committee proposed questions that, if adopted, would radically rework Florida's sprawling court system. The 1885 Constitution provided for an elected supreme court, seven trial circuit courts, and additional criminal courts. Judges of these courts were required to be attorneys.[43] Additionally, the constitution provided for one county court for each Florida county and at least two justices of the peace in each county.[44] Holders of these positions were not required to be attorneys.

Over time, the Florida court system under the 1885 Constitution had expanded into additional courts. Since 1885 the legislature had tied the number of circuit judges to one for every fifty thousand persons living in a judicial circuit. This ratio was too small to keep pace with Florida's rapidly expanding population.[45] Other courts were added to meet the overflow. A large chart created for the CRC in 1966 by the attorney general's office listed, in addition to the supreme court and district courts of appeal, all the types of trial courts in the state: circuit court, civil and criminal court, civil court of record, court of record, criminal court of record, felony court of record, claims court, county judges court, county court, juvenile court, special juvenile court, juvenile and domestic relations court, traffic court, J. P. (presumably justice of the peace) court, small claims court, and magistrate's court.[46] These courts were added on a local basis, so their creation and distribution were not uniform throughout the state. For example, Volusia, Dade, and Escambia Counties had markedly different court systems, many of which had overlapping jurisdictions. Astute practitioners were able to shop for the court most favorable to their cause. Many lawyers complained, though, that understanding the various jurisdictions of the courts in one's own county meant little when a case had to be filed in another county: the jurisdictions of the local courts were inconsistent throughout the state. Cities and counties drew revenue from payment of fines in these lower courts, so there was a fear that the local courts were practicing "cash-register justice."

Almost all of these courts were headed by elected officeholders who were fiercely protective of their status and salaries. Prior to 1965, efforts to comprehensively reform the Florida court system had failed when the sitting judges and other officials who appointed the positions opposed the reforms. As Askew has observed, local judges were a nearly impossible group to overcome because they were all grass-roots politicians close to their particular voters and to other local officials.[47] Also, many CRC members and legislators were attorneys who would return to practice before the judges who opposed the changes; they may justly have feared the judges might retaliate against anyone voting for the modifications.[48] In North Florida, in particular, the judges were an integral part of the informally recognized "courthouse clique" that effectively ran each county.[49]

The proposal would make all probate and juvenile judges into circuit judges, greatly increasing the number of circuit judges. Likewise, justices of the peace, the various courts of record, and most magistrate courts would be abolished. It was unclear whether these judges would be transferred to county court or simply left unemployed. CRC member Elmer Friday said that court revision was "so filled with barbs, hooks, and sandspurs that even if you wore long sleeves and heavy shoes you were still going to get hurt walking through those fields."[50]

Even with the mess the court system was in in 1965, it was better than it had once been. Some incremental court reforms were accomplished before 1965. The Florida Bar, composed of all licensed attorneys, had proposed systematic reform beginning in the 1940s. A legislatively created Florida Judicial Council also proposed judicial system changes to the legislature. The CRC's Judicial Committee merged the recommendations of the Judicial Council and the Florida Bar proposals for its draft.[51]

The Judicial Committee's proposal simplified the court system into a uniform four-tier court structure: the supreme court, intermediate appellate courts called the district courts of appeal, and two levels of trial court: the senior-level circuit court and the county court. County courts were retained to overcome the perceived political problem of either removing many non-attorney county judges or elevating the non-attorney judges to the circuit court. While the committee discussed the idea of a single tier of trial courts, a two-level trial court emerged because the large majority of cases would be heard in traffic, small claims, and misdemeanor offenses and there was no easy solution to whether appeals from these cases would swamp the district appeals courts. By having two levels of trial courts, the circuit court also would hear appeals from the county courts. A magistrate's court would be permitted to remain if authorized by law.[52] The circuit court could now have specialized divisions, such as probate or juvenile cases. The specialized divisions, however, would be established by law—by the legislature— and not through the state supreme court's administrative powers. The supreme court maintained its sole authority to establish rules of procedure for all courts.

Most significantly, the Judicial Committee proposed that justices and judges would not participate in elections but instead would be subject to an up-or-down vote every six years by the public on whether to retain them.[53] This merit retention system would be nonpartisan; that is, no political party affiliation would be listed on the ballot.

Removing judges from popular election has always been controversial; many feel that judges should be answerable to the people whose justice they are dispensing. However, difficulties can arise when judges must raise campaign money: the money typically comes from lawyers, who have the most knowledge of the sitting judges and some of whom aspire to be judges. Judges who accept money from the lawyers who appear before them are subject to at least a perception of bias. In addition, justice frequently does not square with popular sentiment. For example, Justice Glenn Terrell, who sat on the Florida Supreme Court from 1923 to 1964, once had campaign help through the Florida Police Chiefs Association; the executive secretary of that organization attached a note to fund-raising letters noting that, because "a statewide Negro political organization" had endorsed Terrell's opponent, the reader should return Terrell to the court. The letter closed, "Let's not be complacent. Consider this matter very seriously."[54] Regardless of whether Justice Terrell himself approved of the sentiment in the letter, it serves as an example of how campaigning can, at the least, lead to the appearance that a judge is taking a position contrary to what is constitutional. The Judicial Committee's proposal would have removed judges and justices from the awkwardness of taking, or seeming to take, political positions to garner campaign support.

The committee further attempted to distance judges and justices from controversy and politics by proposing to require them to retire at age seventy;[55] by proposing to provide that the state, and not the individual counties, would now pay the judges' salaries; and by proposing to provide that any vacancy in a judicial position would be filled by the governor selecting from one of three candidates proposed by a judicial nominating commission. The supreme court would make the choice should the governor fail to act within thirty days.[56] The composition of the judicial nominating commissions would be provided for by general law.[57]

Finally, the Judicial Committee proposed the creation of a judicial qualifications commission that would investigate and, if necessary, discipline or remove from office those judges who were accused of violating the law or ethical canons, or those who were prevented by disability from continuing in office.[58] The composition of the commission would be specified in the constitution itself. The draft detailed an appeals process through the Florida Supreme Court.

These three features—merit retention, merit selection by a judicial nominating commission, and discipline administered by a judicial qualification commission—were all bold departures by the Judicial Committee. The revamping of the court structure was also a far-reaching proposal.

State Finance

The State Finance Committee takes our story into the absorbing area of Florida taxation and bonds. One member of the committee, Elmer Friday, has stated that he believed the State Finance Committee was the guts of the entire CRC.[59] Because finance and taxation is so central, people who hold money—taxpayers—and the governmental units wanting that money—such as schools and law enforcement—both tend to develop a laser-tight focus on the issue of taxes. Thus the committee members—Frank Fee, chair; Thomas Alexander, vice-chair; Friday; George Hollahan; and Thomas Barkdull—could expect scrutiny of their work.

The article on tax and bonding in the Florida constitution was one of limitation. The legislature, as an arm of the state, has broad power to tax and borrow within the limits of the U.S. Constitution; the Florida constitution limits that power. It is easy to understand, therefore, how influential, and how sensitive politically, work on the taxation provisions of the state constitution could be.

In 1966 the hot issues were property-tax assessments for agricultural land such as timberland; severance taxes for the mining of phosphates; and issuing bonds to build new roads. Agricultural land was perennially undertaxed, and Florida had no tax at all for mining, at a time when Central Florida was the source of 75 percent of the nation's phosphate and 25 percent of the world's.[60] Huge swaths of land in Polk, Hillsborough, and Manatee Counties had been rendered virtual moonscapes by phosphate mining. Cattle and citrus downwind and downstream from phosphate mines were sick and deformed. Yet Florida had no severance tax. And a network of good roads was critical, of course, to Florida's growth. A state that is more than eight hundred miles from tip to tip could not function without good roads, and roads had to be paid for. Presently, Florida taxed gasoline purchases to cover that road construction.

George Stallings has said that Florida's tax system was one of the most crazy-quilt systems anywhere in the nation, and he may have been right.[61] In 1966, Florida's tax system had two main components: ad valorem taxes imposed by the counties or municipalities, and non–ad valorem taxes imposed by the state (an "ad valorem tax" is a tax based on the value of land or personal property). Before 1940 the constitution provided for payment of ad valorem property tax to the state. A constitutional amendment ended that, and in 1966, ad valorem taxes were used at local levels for education and other local needs. Local ad valorem taxes were not capped under the 1885 Constitution.[62] Local ad valorem taxes were used to fund counties' education systems; there were no separate school district taxes.[63] A growing state obviously would need more money for education. In fact, the 1885 Constitution required the legislature to support public education liberally,[64] but it never had done so.

The rub in Florida's ad valorem system was the appraisal process. The 1885 Constitution provided that property must be assessed at "a just valuation."[65] However, in largely rural and agricultural Florida, agriculture had a special and privileged taxation classification. This favored the citrus and cattle barons in Florida's interior. It also favored the du Pont estate's million acres of piney-wood timberland in the northernmost band of Florida, the land controlled by the powerful du Pont manager, Edward Ball. The fact was that if all of Florida's land were assessed at its "just value" for tax purposes, Florida's government would be rich. But tax assessments at "just value" almost never happened.

Another way in which Florida failed to maximize its tax base was by having no state income tax. The absence of a provision that would result in a state tax on personal income was, and remains, a sacred cow of Florida's tax system. There is no indication that the State Finance Committee ever considered creating one for the new constitution.

Florida also historically had an inheritance tax, which occasionally was a big component of the state's tax revenue. For example, when multimillionaire Alfred du Pont died in 1935, the tax revenue from his estate paid for years of unpaid bills for school supplies.[66] To cover expenditures, the state taxed gasoline for road construction; it also taxed cigarettes and liquor. Under this tax scheme, joked Manning Dauer, if one drank liquor, drove fast, and then "cracked up on the highway and killed yourself," that would cover all of Florida's state taxes.[67] However, in 1966 the state no longer had the inheritance tax, leading B. K. Roberts to quip, "Our prohibition of a state inheritance tax has brought thousands of fine citizens to our state who find it not only a good place to live, but a cheaper state in which to die."[68]

By far the largest portion of non–ad valorem taxes the state collected was from the sales and use tax. It had been added in 1949 to accommodate the needs of the state as it began its post–World War II boom. Farris Bryant, a legislator at the time, recalled that getting a state sales tax passed required a "bloody" fight, as it was opposed by nearly all state businesses,[69] but was ultimately passed by a legislature that realized it was necessary. The state also collected tax on pari-mutuel gambling revenues from horse and dog racing, with the twist that the revenues, most originating from South Florida, were distributed equally to each county.

No other portion of the constitution required such careful drafting to limit the power of the legislature, concerning not only the types and amounts of taxes capable of collection but also the types of financing permitted to the state and local governments.[70] And the committee did not have an easy time deciding what its part of the constitution should say. After the spring CRC meeting, Chairman Fee wrote Hugh Taylor, "Frankly, I am not happy over the accomplishments of the committee to date nor the general direction in which the committee seems to be headed."[71]

The committee proposed maintaining the balanced budget provision from the 1885 Constitution but omitting its restrictions on issuing bonds. The 1885 Constitution allowed the legislature to issue debt only to repel invasion or insurrection, and allowed it to redeem existing bonds only at lower interest rates.[72] Also, committee members discussed state and local bifurcation of tax collection. For instance, if a city imposed a cigarette tax, then those taxes were collected on behalf of the state, but the state refunded them to the city.

Local Government

The Local Government Committee had eight members, more than any other on the commission. It comprised William Gautier, chair; Ralph Marsicano, vice-chair; Joseph Jacobs; Sidney Martin; John Crews; Dick Pettigrew; George Hollahan; and Tom Sebring.

Under the 1885 Constitution, Florida counties and cities had few powers unless they were given individual charters by the legislature.[73] Unlike some other states, Florida did not provide uniform legislation regulating and providing for the government of counties and the municipalities within them, and its constitution prohibited special legislation for cities, towns, and counties. Counties and cities had only those powers stated in their charter, whether given by general law to all cities or counties throughout Florida or by special law applying to a single area.[74] Counties and municipalities had to seek a grant of power from the state legislature to undertake some new service, such as firefighting. As a result, these special bills were choking the legislature. In fact, we have just seen that even in the March 1966 special session, the House spent time clearing a backlog of local bills while waiting for the Senate to pass its version of a reapportionment bill; the Senate did likewise. In its 1961 session the legislature had passed 1,266 special acts relating to counties and municipalities.[75] And as a practical matter, bringing a local bill before the whole legislature was a waste of time: local bills were traditionally passed by the legislature if they had the approval of the House and Senate members from that county.[76] Whether to change this scheme had been the subject of controversy for years, and groups such as the Florida League of Municipalities and the League of Women Voters attended committee meetings that spring and weighed in with suggestions.[77]

The problem areas involved with home rule, as the shift from legislative to local control of local matters was called, were already known to CRC members. Dade County had provided an example for the state when it achieved home rule by constitutional amendment in 1957. The friction points between state laws and agencies on the one hand and counties and cities on the other hand, and between county ordinances and municipal ones, had been litigated. Courts had established a body of judicial decisions guiding which laws trumped others.[78]

Home rule, a movement that began in the early 1900s in the United States, allows elected leaders of local entities such as counties and municipalities to authorize new services through local legislation rather than by seeking a grant of power from the state legislature. Home rule is based on the idea that locally elected bodies are better able to respond to local needs than a state legislature is. Advocates of home rule were vocal in the decades leading up to the CRC. In the late 1940s several counties gained the constitutional right to assess and collect taxes within their own territory.[79] In 1965, Hillsborough County joined Dade in attaining a home-rule charter.[80]

Municipalities were wary of home rule being given to counties. Counties were traditionally considered less true localities than administrative subdivisions of the state that implemented state functions such as elections, tax collection, law enforcement, courts, and road building at a local level. In addition to allowing the legislature to control each city and county directly, the 1885 Constitution enumerated each essential office at the county level: a court system to administer justice, a clerk of courts, a sheriff for law enforcement, a property appraiser to assess the value of property for taxes, and a tax collector to collect certain taxes. The form of each board of county commissioners was likewise fixed to a five-person board elected by district.[81]

Municipalities, however, were more specialized. They provided local services to urbanized areas. The delivery of municipal services costs less per person the more highly concentrated the population. For example, one police officer can cover one hundred people located within a one-square-mile urban area at about the same cost as covering ten people in a one-square-mile rural area. The areas surrounding the cities became urbanized, however, as people moved to the suburbs. Traditionally, the county would spend its tax dollars to provide increasing levels of infrastructure and service to the populated fringes, and the municipality would then annex the area into the city. The county lost its investment; the city gained an addition having a high tax base with little additional capital infrastructure costs.

Annexation into a city required voter approval in the area to be an-
nexed. Voters generally approved annexation because they received urban services and a lower tax rate due to the city's lower per-person cost.
Home rule for counties threatened this progression. Counties having
home rule could provide municipal-type services to the urbanized
fringes surrounding cities without having to seek legislative approval
for the new services. Annexation would become less attractive to sub-
urb dwellers. The city's cost per person for services would increase as
people left the city core and moved to the suburbs, and tax rates would
increase in the city as the city's tax base decreased. But if a county were
to have home rule and the ability to levy taxes for its services, those
representing the interests of cities wanted to make sure that county
taxes were not levied on residents inside city limits.

Ralph Marsicano, who had served as counsel for the City of Tampa
since 1931 and as president of the Florida League of Municipalities,
wrote the proposed sections of the constitution having to do with municipalities and ensuring that counties could not tax for services within
city limits.[82] Like many who had tried to govern cities under the 1885
Constitution, he favored home rule so that cities would not have to go
hat in hand to the legislature to have all but the most routine business
approved. Marsicano had had to spend entire legislative sessions in Tallahassee just to serve Tampa's needs. However, he acknowledged that
some opposed home rule because they had doubts about the ability of
local officials to handle increased power.[83]

Human Rights

Ralph Turlington would later remember that the members of the Human Rights Committee "were all attorneys who were re-living their law
school experiences" and that their debates "were always accompanied
by some very long philosophical discussions."[84] Interestingly, however, this committee failed to include two important provisions that
the full CRC added later: juvenile rights in criminal proceedings, and
limitations on sovereign immunity. The Declaration of Rights draft
that emerged from this committee did contain, however, an expanded

Figure 8. Justice B. K. Roberts was influential and wielded power astutely. Many watched his behavior on the Constitution Revision Commission with concern. However, he fought for broader individual rights in the constitution's Declaration of Rights. Photo courtesy of State Archives of Florida, *Florida Memory*, https://floridamemory.com/items/show/30215.

section on collective bargaining, especially by public employees; an explicit exclusionary rule on evidence obtained through illegal searches; and a provision allowing the state to regulate how firearms were kept.

The Human Rights Committee was composed of Justice Roberts, chair; Charlie Harris, vice-chair; Donald Reed; Raymond Alley; and Richard Earle. Roberts was the perfect person to shepherd the committee. Politically active, constantly monitored by Smith's "spies" throughout the revision process, and grounded in earthy practicalities and casual disregard for inconvenient laws, Roberts was fifty-one years old in 1966 and exercised considerable power in state government.[85]

Roberts was a study in contrasts. He was born in Sopchoppy in Wakulla County, not far from Tallahassee, on an unglamorous stretch of the Gulf of Mexico. At age seven he was blinded in one eye in an accident with a BB gun. Undaunted, he excelled in school and received a certificate to teach school when he was thirteen years of age, after attending a six-week-long teachers' course one summer. He attended the University of Florida in Gainesville, but his poverty meant that he sometimes had to live in a tent.

Roberts rapidly became a successful businessman and attorney. An important client and friend of Roberts was Edward Ball, who controlled vast stretches of timber for the du Pont estate and also controlled the Florida National Bank and the Florida East Coast Railway. In 1966 the railway was involved in a union strike that had already lasted three years and would become the longest-running strike in U.S. history.[86] And, coincidentally, an amendment to Florida's right-to-work constitutional provision, which was unfriendly to union organizing, was being considered by the CRC's Human Rights Committee, which brings us back to Justice Roberts, Ball's friend, who chaired that committee. *Sotto voce*, there were persistent murmurings that an *ex parte* link ran between Edward Ball and Justice Roberts on matters before the state supreme court.

Roberts, however, not only possessed an unusually able legal mind but also was a passionate advocate for the powerless. He spearheaded efforts that created the public defender system for indigent defendants following the U.S. Supreme Court's *Gideon v. Wainwright* decision in 1963. Roberts also did not forget the powerless when guiding his committee to craft the Declaration of Human Rights. He paid attention to small dignities not often attended to at the time. For example, he fought to have the constitution drafted in gender-neutral language.[87] Though many were suspicious or even fearful of Roberts's use of power, the basic rights of Floridians were safe in his hands as Human Rights Committee chair.

Education and Welfare

The Education and Welfare Committee had little controversy in creating its draft proposals, and its proposed certified questions wound up being subsumed into those proposed by other committees. In fact, Turlington later said there wasn't much for its members to have long discussions on, and that his role was to "go around and act pleasant and let the events shape themselves."[88] Its draft article was composed of seven short sections, considerably shorter than the then-existing constitution. The committee's members were Ralph Turlington, chair;

Beth Johnson, vice-chair; Tom Sebring; Gordon Vickery; and William O'Neill.

The article on education occupies the area between structuring government and legislating policy at a constitutional level. In theory the legislature could handle both the structure of the education system and appropriations without the need for constitutional restraint. The Model State Constitution, a document published periodically by the National Municipal League, contains only a single paragraph regarding education, stating that a state legislature should "provide for the maintenance and support of a system of free public schools, wherein all the children of this state shall be educated."[89] On the other hand, Florida's 1885 Constitution's article on education contained no less than fifteen sections, for a public school system that was still in its infancy, including section 12: "White and colored children shall not be taught in the same school, but impartial provision shall be made for both."[90]

Two long-term influences required the CRC to deal with education: Florida's history of emphasizing education, and the disproportionate amount of tax revenues devoted to the education system. Since the 1940s, education had been the state's largest expense. Florida had passed the Minimum Foundation Program in 1947, which set a minimum amount of funding per pupil.[91] When the state's population began to explode, so too did the mandatory funds required.

The draft continued the constitutional Florida Board of Education; recommended that, unlike in the 1885 Constitution, the principal of the State School Fund could now be spent; and, of course, erased the segregation language of the old constitution. Turlington, a former University of Florida faculty member, saw to it that the Board of Regents that oversaw the state university system was elevated to constitutional status, although the legislature would later delete this provision. One source of the committee's harmony was its ability to use language from the McRae Committee's proposed constitution a decade earlier—the very language that Maxine Baker had fretted over.[92]

Suffrage and Elections

The 1885 Constitution placed interesting restrictions on voting. While nonwhites were not constitutionally restricted from voting, voters had to have lived in Florida a full year, have all their mental faculties, and be male and twenty-one years of age. In addition, no one convicted of betting on an election, committing perjury, larceny, or bribery, or fighting a duel could vote or hold public office.[93] One change the Suffrage and Elections Committee—George Stallings, chair; Bill Young, vice-chair; Dick Pettigrew; Warren Goodrich; and Richard Earle—proposed was removing the restrictions on dueling and betting. Another proposed question it certified for discussion was whether to create a method by which citizens could initiate revisions to their constitution.

6

Drafting a Constitution, Drafting a Legislature

March and April 1966: Meetings on the Certified Questions

After the committees had submitted their initial recommendations and identified their certified questions, Chesterfield Smith used the unusual procedure of having the certified questions debated before the full commission as a preliminary introduction to these issues. No constitution revision process in Florida had used this procedure before, nor has one repeated it since. The procedure was intended to keep everyone informed and to prevent issues on which there might otherwise have been a consensus from going unquestioned.[1] As the committees met and drew up their questions, Smith assigned different CRC members, not necessarily from the proposing committee, to argue for and against each question with an eye to forcing commissioners to argue against their normal positions and to create tension in the debate. It was also at this time that Smith noticed that commissioner Bill Baggs, the editor of the *Miami News*, had not attended any CRC meetings. Smith publicly criticized him, saying that if anyone was not ready to appear and do the work, Smith did not want him on the CRC.[2] Word must have gotten to Baggs, because his attendance was excellent for the rest of the year.

The commission met in Tallahassee on March 25 and 26 and April 11 to hear, discuss, and vote on the certified questions the committees had proposed in their individual meetings. At the outset, Smith skipped the invocation. Reubin Askew reminded him to do it, remarking, "We're going to need all the help we can get in this convention."[3] The meeting opened with speeches by political scientists from Florida State University and University of Florida. Professor Albert L. Sturm, of FSU's Institute of Governmental Research, addressed the commissioners and produced several constitutional analyses and comparisons for their use.[4]

Much of the opening proceedings took the form of general advice on constitution writing. Jack Mathews urged his fellow commissioners to draft their sections in unambiguous language, to "save the difficulty of the litigation that so plagues our brothers that sit over here across the street in telling us what we meant to say in the constitution," an obvious reference to the state supreme court.[5] Richard Earle articulated a basic philosophy of constitution writing: set broad parameters for the structure of government, and then get out of the way. He advised his fellows that they must have confidence that government officials could and would carry out their duties according to the constitution. He also reminded them that they should worry less about writing a constitution that would meet with the approval of the legislature or voters and worry more about writing "the best constitution of which we are capable." Earle urged the commissioners to "do the best job we know how and let somebody else knock it in the head."[6]

Among the first of the certified questions discussed at the March meeting concerned whether a maximum and minimum number of legislators should be specified. To distant observers of government this may not seem an important question, but a constitutionally prescribed number of legislators in the still-current 1885 Constitution had been part of the problem in creating the gross malapportionment Florida was just now trying to get out of. After debate, the full commission voted to allow the Legislative Committee to set, not a precise number, but a minimum and maximum on the size of each house of the state legislature.

The related issue of legislative apportionment also was argued. The question was whether the Legislative Committee should draft a provision for automatic apportionment if the legislature should fail to reapportion itself. This issue struck at the core of the apportionment troubles of the past several years. The members of a malapportioned legislature could not be expected to find it easy to vote themselves or each other out of their districts. When, for example, thirty of forty senators represent only 20 percent of a state's population, the remaining

80 percent of the population has only the voting power of the remaining ten senators. That was approximately the situation of the legislature in the Pork Chopper years. The thirty senators, to accomplish fair reapportionment, must vote to shrink the representation of their area to fewer than ten senators, and most of them would lose their seats. The CRC realized that the new constitution might need to have a backstop in place, an alternative method to accomplish fair apportionment, in case the legislature could not do the deed itself.

Charley Johns, who was then in the middle of a primary election battle to retain his seat in the Senate, spoke eloquently and emotionally on the subject. Johns had not been assigned to argue this issue, but he, more than any other commissioner, had lived through it. He pointed out that reapportionment battles "have caused more wounds in the Florida Legislature than anything that has ever happened" and that he would "shed tears when I would see some senator's district eliminated." He was keen on the idea of having some means of reapportioning that did not involve the legislature in making the decision: "Whenever you mention legislative reapportionment to me, I shiver all over."[7] The CRC voted for the backstop. The commission also voted to direct the Legislative Committee to propose annual sessions of the legislature, to propose a bicameral legislature, and not to propose longer terms for legislators.

Home rule for counties and municipalities was approved in theory. Two of the certified questions were whether the constitution should provide methods by which counties and municipalities, taken separately, could "provide for home rule or other type of self-government." Although both provisions were approved, home rule for counties passed nearly unanimously, while home rule for municipalities passed with several no votes. Because municipalities are independent small governments, while counties are merely political subdivisions of the state, it might seem more logical to provide home rule for municipalities than for counties. But that is not how the commission voted.

Also in the March meeting on certified questions came the particularly contentious subject of whether the cabinet should be elected or appointed. The cabinet was composed of six members, each independently elected statewide and with no term limit. This resulted, some said, in six fiefdoms in which resided all the real state power, while others believed that it resulted in more stable government and provided an effective check on the governor's power. Smith asked two of his most eloquent and powerful speakers to address the issue: Pettigrew in favor of changing it to a cabinet appointed by the governor, and Taylor in favor of keeping the cabinet elected.

Pettigrew believed passionately that the cabinet should be appointed. He was young, smart, well educated about political science, and idealistic. His conviction that the cabinet should be appointed arose from his belief that the mess of committees composed of various cabinet members amounted to a shell game protecting cabinet members from revealing their protection of special interests. And, unlike more experienced and entrenched politicians, Pettigrew was unafraid to argue against having the cabinet members elected, as he didn't feel that he owed any cabinet member allegiance.

Taylor represented the more conservative view: he was suspicious of any scheme that would place too much power in the hands of the governor. Most of the CRC members held this view. They were so strongly in favor of maintaining the status quo, in fact, that Ralph Turlington later said he did not remember that it "crossed anybody's mind" that the cabinet should be appointed.[8] The elected cabinet—the "seven governors," as some called it, referring to the cabinet and governor—barely had to break a sweat as the CRC upheld it, by a vote of twenty-four to three.

The commissioners also voted, by a narrow margin, to direct the Executive Committee to draft a provision creating a lieutenant governor, "assuming satisfactory allocation of responsibility and power." Although the vote in this meeting favored a lieutenant governor, the members had much debate on the subject. Its detractors mostly argued that the lieutenant governor would have no real duties, while the proponents believed the successor to the governor's seat needed to be elected statewide.

The CRC voted that the Supreme Court of Florida should be given supervision and control over the housekeeping and budget functions of the court system, including collecting statistics and assigning judges to equalize workload. Properly drafted and implemented, this provision could modernize Florida's court system. The commission also advised the Judicial Branch Committee regarding how much control the legislature should have over the courts: the legislature should not be able to create "purely statutory" trial courts, but it should be able to change the jurisdiction of trial courts, so long as it did so uniformly, and to authorize additional judges for trial courts.

The commission also recommended that the governor have some degree of control over making appointments to fill judicial vacancies. However, in an early sign of the group's tendency to quarrel over judicial matters, the CRC nearly deadlocked over whether incumbent judges should have to run for reelection against opponents, rather than face a yes-or-no vote on the ballot for retention in office. The vote was thirteen for and eleven against reelection; rather than considering such a close vote from such a small number of members to be a recommendation, Smith urged the Judicial Committee to work harder on the question and come up with a better recommendation.[9]

As for taxes, the CRC voted to limit the legislature's taxing powers, eliminate millage restrictions for school funding, limit the legislature's power to issue bonds and revenue certificates, and allow the legislature to earmark revenue sources. The group also recommended that the Human Rights Committee draft a section allowing for eminent domain, the government's right to seize private property under certain conditions.

On the final day, the group was unable to reach a decision on a question that would continue to resound for decades: whether to allow Florida's voters to initiate revisions or amendments to their new constitution. Although the vote was seventeen to nine in favor of allowing voter initiatives, Smith did not consider this a clear mandate and asked the Suffrage and Elections Committee to give "original thought" to solving the issue.[10]

After the debates and votes on the certified questions, the committees were instructed to draft their portions of the constitution accordingly and submit them to the Style and Drafting Committee in time for it to blend the separate articles into one document and harmonize the terminology used throughout the constitution. The Style and Drafting Committee had to have a draft ready for public release by the end of

June, before the public meetings that the CRC would conduct around the state in July. The Style and Drafting Committee began its work after the eight substantive committees had submitted their sections, although its members did participate in the March and April meetings.

This procedure solidified the issues the CRC would consider, as well as their likely response, thereby eliminating repetitive argument and allowing early drafts of major parts of the constitution to be worked on simultaneously. While the March and April answers were not binding on the various substantive committees, they would allow each committee to draft its section with confidence as to what the sense of the full commission would be.

In the political world outside the CRC's deliberations—the world of constant confusion about legislative apportionment—yet another thunderbolt hit the House of Representatives between the March and April meetings on the certified questions. The Speaker-designate of the House, George Stone, was killed in an automobile accident in Pensacola. Stone was not on the CRC, but he was popular and respected.[11] His death left an opening for the leadership of the House for the next session, which would begin in 1967. Ralph Turlington decided to run for House Speaker against Bob Mann of Tampa, who otherwise had the job lined up for 1969.[12] In addition to his CRC responsibilities as chair of the Education Committee, Turlington sent letters to the estimated four to five hundred candidates who were running for the legislature in the topsy-turvy primary elections that were just then getting under way, and he succeeded in getting enough votes pledged to become the Speaker-designate.[13] To accomplish this he had to work with the Republican minority leader, Don Reed, who was also a CRC member. Reed pledged the Republican votes to Turlington, believing that because he was from Gainesville in North Florida he might be more conservative than Mann.[14]

In the meantime, the committees drafted their proposed constitution sections and mailed them to the chairman of the Style and Drafting Committee, Hugh Taylor. It was this committee's job to put the whole thing together, to make the various sections, each drafted without exposure to the others, into a cohesive whole. The committees' proposals were in some cases incompatible; it would be nearly impossible to draft a whole that included all of the parts as proposed by the committees. The Style and Drafting Committee's job was thankless, and Smith knew it. He wrote Taylor in late May, probably as a pep talk, giving him discretion to meet with his committee "anywhere in the state at your discretion, and spend such travel and per diem as is necessary. . . . The job which you have is the most difficult and burdensome, and yet the most important single one facing any member of the Commission. It is a great pleasure to me to know that you are the one who is assigned this task."[15]

As the committee drafts arrived in Taylor's mailbox in May, he became concerned. He wrote to his fellow committee members, fretting that his committee would have "a monumental task in getting any reasonably presentable draft" ready by June 30:

> Apparently some committees have merely outlined general views in many areas and left it up to us to work out details. In other instances, ideas have been incorporated which, to me at least, appear unnecessary or improperly placed. In the hope of expediting our work when we get together, I . . . am making notes of changes which I personally feel should be made. Of course, I am not attempting to dictate what our committee should do.[16]

And even though Frank Fee had complained to Taylor in May 1966 about his State Finance Committee's work, Fee did have something to mail in before the end of May. However, in his transmittal letter he explained that his committee had failed to address one of the finance-related sections of the former constitution with which it had been charged. He also noted in his letter that the committee had not made a comprehensive review of its section and that the committee had asked him to number the various sections according to his best judgment.[17]

Taylor's committee did succeed in knitting together a reasonably comprehensible and consistent first draft of the constitution. But it is obvious they were aware of how much substance they had had to change to produce a draft that would make sense. On June 22, about a week before the full draft was due to be released publicly, Taylor sent a memo to all the CRC members in which he admitted that, because of inconsistencies in the different committee reports, "it was completely impossible to present an harmonious whole." Taylor continued:

In order to avoid the criticism that would inevitably follow the presentation for discussion of a Constitution with radically conflicting provisions, the Committee on Drafting and Style, after conferring with Chairman Chesterfield Smith, made those changes which it felt were necessary in order to present to the public for consideration and discussion a document that would not reflect upon the Commission at the outset.

We sincerely hope that all members of the Commission will recognize the problem that confronted the Drafting Committee and will recognize that we have not tried to substitute our views for theirs, but merely to coordinate the various views that have been expressed by the different committees.[18]

Smith took steps to make sure that the public would see the draft constitution as soon as it was finished. Through good public relations and well-placed phone calls, most major newspapers in the state published the full text of the draft constitution in late June. In the meantime, transcripts of the committee meetings and full commission meetings were generated and made publicly available. And planning began for the next step: just three weeks after the first draft of the proposed constitution was made public, public hearings were to begin throughout the state to receive input and suggestions from members of the public.

The May 1966 Primaries: Hog-Slaughtering Day

In the meantime, things were changing all over the United States. President Lyndon Johnson had been changing the idea of what it meant to be a southern Democrat by hustling the Civil Rights Act of 1964 and the Voting Rights Act of 1965 through Congress; socially conservative, segregationist southern white Democrats didn't appreciate that. Johnson was also building his Great Society, including such broad entitlements as Medicare; fiscally conservative Democrats didn't care for that. And he stepped up the Vietnam War; as the bodies of fallen soldiers came

home in growing numbers, the country began roiling with antiwar protests. Race riots were becoming more numerous as blacks insisted on
equal rights that white segregationists were unwilling to grant.

In Florida, things were changing, too. On May 3 the Democratic primary election for governor was held. The incumbent, Haydon Burns,
was eligible to succeed himself, because the term he had just served
was a special two-year one created as a transition as Florida shifted its
gubernatorial elections from presidential election years to off-years.
After the primary, Burns faced a runoff against the liberal Miami mayor
Robert King High. On May 6, Scott Kelly, whom Burns had defeated in
the first primary, endorsed High.[19] Immediately after the press conference announcing Kelly's endorsement, the news hit that Burns was
accusing Kelly of trying to sell his support to Burns for half a million
dollars, using Kelly's campaign manager, Ben Hill Griffin, as the go-
between.[20] That attempt at a blow to Kelly's integrity made him so angry that he decided, instead of endorsing High mildly and leaving on
vacation, he would stay and help High fight to defeat Burns. Although
Burns later retracted his claim, it had already backfired on him. Kelly's
and High's efforts paid off, and the runoff election went to High on May
24. Whether the naturally conservative and rural Kelly was actually able
to switch many votes to High in the final Democrat primary or whether
he simply inspired Burns supporters to stay home, High became the
Democrat nominee in the general election against the political upstart
and insurance executive Claude Roy Kirk Jr. It was assumed that High
would win the general election, as Democrats always had for more than
ninety years: High wrote Chesterfield Smith on July 9 promising his
"complete cooperation" with the CRC in the coming months.[21]

In the same primaries, the old guard of Pork Choppers began its
cannibalism. At least one redrawn district pitted two old colleagues
against each other: Charley Johns of Starke, in Bradford County, and
Emory "Red" Cross, of Alachua County. Johns eliminated Cross in the
first primary, but in the second he met his match. He now had to win
votes in a county that his FLIC had terrorized when it investigated left-
leaning and gay professors and students at the University of Florida.
That county, Alachua, voted for Hal Davis, a relative unknown from
Quincy. The districtwide margin was just 282 votes. After thirty years in

office, Johns was now free to "go fishing when I want to."[22] B. C. Pearce, the longtime Pork Chopper representing Palatka, was also was defeated in that election. Dilworth Clarke, the old dean of the Senate, had been wise to retire the previous year. It was this reapportionment—not the famous one, the following year, imposed by the federal court—that first began to break up the Pork Chop Gang.

After the primary season, some of the surviving candidates decided to school themselves about constitution revision. Bob Graham, who was running for the state legislature for the first time that year, met in June with Manning Dauer in Gainesville to discuss constitution revision over dinner. The Grahams gave Dauer an electric carving knife as a thank-you gift.[23] It is not clear whether either man considered the gift an appropriate one to use as a redistricting tool in the ongoing legislative apportionment battles.

The Public Hearings: "We Are Little Men"

In July, Smith and a majority of other CRC members, which varied according to city, slogged from Miami to Pensacola to conduct five public hearings on the proposed constitution. At the CRC's request, most major Florida newspapers had printed the entire first draft shortly before the hearings. The draft had never been before the full CRC; that would come in the fall meetings. This draft was simply the aggregate, amended by the Style and Drafting Committee for cohesion, of the work of each committee on the specific subject matter to which each had been assigned that spring.

The hearings lasted from one to three days in each city; they were held in Miami, Tampa, Orlando, Jacksonville, and Pensacola. Organizations of people who stood to lose in the proposed constitution, such as county tax assessors and the Justice of the Peace and Constables Association, had representatives appear and speak in every city. The League of Women Voters, although nonpartisan and disinterested, also sent representatives to speak in each city. Individuals also attended, listened, and spoke their concerns. Sometimes they got more response than they may have expected from the commission members. If a commissioner had questions of a speaker, he did not hesitate to ask them, and sometimes sharply. John Crews, who had just lost his legislative seat to reapportionment, could be especially acid. When questioning a county tax assessor who claimed to be in favor of abiding by the voted "will of the people"—except he did not want residents of individual counties to have the right to vote his own office out of existence— Crews lit into him with repeated pointed questions typical of a cross-examining lawyer. Finally, Smith intervened in an attempt to soften the exchange. Crews turned on Smith, noting that he had learned what it meant to abide by the will of the people "when I was a legislator and had to abide by the will of the people as expressed by the law and had to vote to abolish my office."[24]

In Miami, Representative Maxine Baker addressed the CRC. She reminded them that she had served by appointment of Governor Collins in 1958 on the Special Constitution Advisory Committee. Baker had examined two drafts of the proposed new constitution. It turned out that one of the drafts had been issued to legislators by the CRC, three days before the version published in the newspapers. Baker noted places where the Style and Drafting Committee had, in her opinion, changed the substance, not just the wording, of proposed provisions. One example was the methods of amending the constitution that the Suffrage and Elections Committee had proposed. The Suffrage and Elections Committee had proposed amendment by legislature, by commission, or by convention, but the Style and Drafting Committee's edition omitted the convention option. Baker implored the CRC to prevent essential elements of the constitution from becoming "lost in the process of editing and polishing."[25]

Some citizens who spoke before the commissioners were let off easily, either out of sympathy or because the commissioners were wary of them. For example, in Pensacola the committee heard from James Sideris, who proceeded to provide a detailed critique seeded with warnings about government unchecked; about the Council of Foreign Relations, a bête noir of conspiracy spotters; and about encroachments on the "sovereignty" of Florida. Smith interrupted to ask whether Sideris was referring to the draft of the proposed constitution. He said no, he was unaware there was a new proposed constitution. He blithely continued until his time expired.[26]

On the other hand, an eighty-year-old gentleman appeared in Orlando and related an alarming story about county workers who had diverted the water supply of his small water company, and how he now had no income and felt the government had too much authority. He concluded simply, by declaring: "We are little men, but we are the people that made this State of Florida."[27]

The public hearings were memorable in another way to CRC member Richard Earle. After a long day of hearings, Earle had returned to his hotel room at the Dupont Plaza, which overlooked Biscayne Bay in downtown Miami. As Bill O'Neill recalled, Earle settled into bed and lit his last cigarette of the day. Then he began to smell smoke, and not from the cigarette: his mattress was on fire. Earle sprang out of bed to try to put out the fire. Taking no chances, he decided to get help. Earle ran out into the hallway in his nightclothes and heard his hotel room door lock behind him. His key was in the room with the smoldering bed. He was locked out.[28] And his fellow CRC members would kid him about it for decades.

As the public hearings were held around the state that July, one CRC member, Ervin appointee Tom Alexander, a member of the State Finance Committee, died, making necessary the CRC's third substitution. Ervin's successor as Florida Bar president, Fletcher Rush, replaced Alexander with a young state representative and lawyer, Lawton Chiles, from Lakeland. Chiles, though joining the CRC near its halfway point, schooled himself and prepared to contribute to the effort.

Some of the CRC members later said that they believed the public hearings were unhelpful because the suggestions from attendees often seemed to be mostly quick and less-thought-out reactions to the draft constitution, whereas the CRC members had invested weeks of time and expertise working on the draft. Nevertheless, all agreed that putting the constitution before the people was necessary so they could participate in the constitutional revision process, even if nominally.[29] Earle later recalled that the public hearings were just an exercise in lip service, "more for public relations than they were for education."[30] John McCarty of the Legislative Committee claimed the public input resulted in very little change to the proposed text.[31] The public hearings did give CRC members the opportunity to socialize with each other in the evenings. At least one, Richard Earle, has said the members often discussed matters regarding the constitution revision work.[32] These meetings violated no public meetings laws in existence at the time.

After the public hearings were concluded, the CRC members got a brief respite from their constitutional labors, but some members of the press were still thinking about how to communicate constitutional concepts in a way that laypeople would understand and find interesting. Bill Sweisgood of the *Jacksonville Journal* had an idea. He proposed putting the constitutional revisions in comic-strip form:

> "Holy Homestead Exemption, Batman! If they make it limited by local option you're likely to lose stately Wayne Manor," says Robin. "Yes, Boy Wonder, but on the cheerful side remember that if the new constitution goes through, the Penguin will have to get an order from a court of competent jurisdiction before he can tap our telephone," replies the Caped Crusader.[33]

Next Drafts: Constitution and Legislature

The substantive committees met in September to review the public suggestions for the draft constitution and make any changes they considered appropriate based on those suggestions. The Style and Drafting Committee altered the first draft over the next weeks to incorporate the input from the public hearings, and printed a second draft of the full constitution in early November. That was the first time the CRC members would see the full draft of the constitution that they would consider as a group between Thanksgiving and the Christmas holidays. This became the "final draft" used at the three-week final CRC debates to which the CRC members submitted proposed amendments and finalized the substance of the proposed constitution. Not all of the CRC members were satisfied with the November draft. During the debates, the Style and Drafting Committee, and Hugh Taylor in particular, would be criticized for changing the preferred language of the committees, particularly when it involved a member's pet project.

The November 1966 Election

On November 8 a general election was held under the March 1966 apportionment. The newly expanded Dade County delegation took shape:
Talbot "Sandy" D'Alemberte was a freshman Democratic representative in that group, as was Bob Graham. Representative Edmond "Eddie"
Gong, a Miami native and Florida's first member of a racial minority
elected to the legislature since Reconstruction, was now in the state
Senate.

South Florida was represented in large numbers for the first time, as
were Republicans. The election of 1966 reflected Florida's new apportionment as well as the Republican backlash against the liberal streak
of Democrats led by President Johnson.[34] Charley Johns's son and
daughter-in-law later vividly remembered the day that they and their
friends made a party of marching to the courthouse to change their
registration to Republican.[35]

An underlying assumption of reapportionment was that urban areas
in the state would radically shift legislative policies away from rural,
conservative values. This simplistic view, however, ignored the conservative pull of the rapidly growing suburban areas surrounding South
Florida metropolises, the strongly conservative midwestern population filling southwest Florida, and the conservative character of North
Florida's Duval County, home to Jacksonville.[36]

The result of the governor's race accurately reflected the shifting
statewide politics that reapportionment plans were trying to follow.
Republican Claude Kirk was elected governor, becoming the first popularly elected Republican governor of Florida since Reconstruction. Political analysis of the time chalked his victory up to a few things. First,
his opponent, Robert King High, was a "Miami liberal" aligned with
the national Democratic Party. By relentlessly characterizing High as
an "ultraliberal," Kirk succeeded in splitting the formerly monolithic
Democratic Party in Florida into old-style conservatives and newer,
Kennedy-and-Johnson-style, liberals.[37] Kirk ran on a law-and-order
platform, and he knew how to use coded language, such as criticizing
High for supporting open-housing legislation, to appeal to white segregationists.[38] Second, Kirk—although a newcomer to politics—had

charm and persuasiveness on his side. Known to the press as "Kissing Claude," Kirk was a divorcé who wowed the crowds by smiling and promising "white papers" on the issues. Other than a quixotic run for the U.S. Senate in 1964 he had zero experience in government.[39]

Choosing between High and Kirk, the former Burns supporters overwhelmingly voted as "Demo-Kirks." Kirk carried all but eleven counties in what had until that moment seemed a Democratic state.[40] The urban voters, who were the most crucial group for High, voted for Kirk. Kirk carried most of the populous counties. Although High carried his own Dade County, his margin there was far too narrow to make up for his shortfalls statewide.[41] Florida's conservative voters were no longer hesitant to vote Republican when the alternative was a liberal; this was the beginning of a broad Republican expansion in Florida and in the South. Ironically, the growing social liberalism of the national Democratic Party is why Florida Democrats had changed the gubernatorial election year to the "off years" between presidential elections, even at great expense to the party.[42]

The November 15 Legislative Organizational Session

Also a winner on the November 1966 ballot was an amendment to the 1885 Constitution authorizing a legislative organizing session. Now, for the first time, the legislature would be authorized and funded to meet one week after the election to choose leaders of each chamber and assign members to committees. This, it was hoped, would help the many new legislators become oriented to their new jobs.

The legislature convened in its first one-day organizing session on November 15. Both chambers had optimistic sessions. The Senate began by installing longtime reform legislator Verle Pope as its President for the upcoming two years. Pope then addressed the Senate and noted that events were "progressing at lightning speed." He reported that only nineteen of the forty-eight senators present were reelected; the rest were new faces. He acknowledged the past problems of legislative strangulation and predicted that the new apportionment plan would be an absolute solution: "I think for the first time, we will have a state in which fears are abolished and in which we can count on moving

ahead in the solution of all the problems of all the state."[43] In concluding he acknowledged the newly installed legislature's unique situation:
"I think this legislature has been charged with a responsibility unsur-
passed by previous ones. For the first time in the history of Florida, the
legislature is based on one man, one vote."[44] This claim was almost true.

In the other chamber, veteran legislator Ralph Turlington was officially elected Speaker. In his address to the House he politely referred
to the past malapportionment, and promised cooperation with the federal government and greater legislative responsibility and efficiency.
The legislature would be "responsible to all and not just a part of the
state," he said.[45] Then, perhaps to assuage Pork Choppers' fears of exclusion from tax benefits in this new legislature, Turlington called for
a reexamination of the allocation of tax money, claiming that those
funds should be allocated based on needs, not source of revenue. On
the other hand, he acknowledged that it was due to poor apportionment that Florida had lost ground to the federal government in areas
like education and health. He urged his members to be active and informed in order to regain state control.[46]

7

The CRC Debates

November and December 1966

When the CRC met for final debates on amendments in late November 1966, it found itself in a very different political climate than when its formation had been proposed in the legislature just a year and a half earlier. Florida had its first popularly elected Republican governor in ninety years. The urban areas had secured greater representation in the legislature. Republicans had established a notable presence in the legislature, and expectations were that the party would grow both in the legislature and in local elected offices throughout Central and South Florida in subsequent elections.

On Monday, November 28, less than two weeks after the legislative organizing session, the CRC gathered, "with an extraordinarily cheerful sense of duty and calm temper," as one reporter said, for its three weeks of final debates.[1] It met in the Senate chamber of the capitol, on a hilltop in the center of Tallahassee with a view east across the North Florida hills.

Governor-elect Claude Kirk attended most of the daily sessions for the three weeks while his transition team prepared for Kirk to govern the state.[2] The governor-elect later acknowledged that he could have spent the time organizing his new administration, which would begin in January, but believed his presence at the debates would attract media attention for constitutional revision and spur the commissioners to the finish.[3] Smith seated the governor-elect with him on the speaker's dais overlooking the well and the chamber where the commissioners sat at the senatorial desks. Recognizing the potential unpopularity of the first Republican governor since Reconstruction, Kirk quipped that he "came in through the back door of the Senate chambers and up to the podium where the people could not really reach me."[4] Smith, however, recalled: "Often, I did not do too good a job presiding because I was trying to explain to him the simplest things about what this really was and what the proposal would do to the government." According to Smith, "nobody has ever been elected, or ever will be, who knew less about the governmental structure of the state than he did initially."[5]

The governor-elect, meanwhile, did pay attention to the action on the floor. Although he knew many of the more seasoned members, he noticed one unfamiliar young member who impressed him. He asked the chair: the young star's name was Reubin Askew.[6]

Each commissioner had a desk and chair on the floor of the Senate chamber and would stand when speaking or when requesting to be recognized by Smith to speak. Smith sat in a raised dais at the head of the room, with Kirk to his left. Beneath Smith at the center front of the Senate floor sat a recording clerk behind a desk; the clerk would receive written amendments filed by CRC members. Smith, as chair, was in charge of who sat where in the chamber. He must have wanted to shake things up, because he seated Pork Chopper critic Bill Baggs next to conservative Pork Chop stalwart Charley Johns. "They got along famously," wrote one columnist. "I'm rubbing a little pork chop on Bill and it's doing him a lot of good," Johns joked.[7]

Even with the governor-elect and the handpicked lions of the state in attendance, there was little public interest in the convention. One reporter remarked that, except for "a scattering of reporters, no one watches."[8] The reporter continued: "The speakers keep talking of 'giving the people the right to decide' in this or that area. But you wonder if 'the people' want to take the trouble."[9]

The Steering and Rules Committee adopted procedural rules for the debates. The debates would follow a quasi-legislative procedure in which the November 10 draft would be treated as a proposed legislative bill and the commissioners could file amendments to it.[10] The commissioners would then debate the proposed amendments. Most members appeared in Tallahassee without having filed their amendments, so that became the first order of business. Even after all the work the substantive committees had done over the past ten months, the commissioners still proposed more than two hundred amendments.[11]

The rules prevented repetitive arguments on amendments. The vote on an amendment was final unless a CRC member moved for reconsideration of the vote; only one reconsideration vote per amendment was allowed.[12] The person proposing an amendment was given the floor to speak. A member wanting to question the proponent of an amendment would stand and ask if the proponent would yield the floor. Almost invariably the answer would be yes, and the questioner then could ask one question. A few additional questions might slip in, but still a very limited number, with no back-and-forth debate. The amendments were put in writing and distributed to all members. Many of the amendments were written by hand and later typed. Throughout the proceedings, Smith insisted that all members know exactly what they were voting on for each amendment.

The plan was to go through the entire constitution three times during the CRC's three-week session. The rules of the CRC provided that amendments would be relatively easy to propose during the first two rounds through the constitution; in the final round, the only amendments allowed were those offered by a general committee or by the Style and Drafting Committee.[13] This way, commissioners were subtly discouraged from repetitive attempts to propose losing amendments. In fact, Smith had a humorous way to let commissioners know it was time to stop talking: he would appoint them to the "Christmas Party Committee," implying that too much talk would push the CRC's work past the scheduled December 16 end date.[14]

The eight substantive committees were disbanded on the eve of the three-week debate period, and four new committees, titled General Committees A, B, C, and D, were formed; all CRC members except the chair were on one of these committees. Amendments filed after the start of the convention were randomly assigned to one of the four new committees. Smith reserved the authority to assign an amendment to a particular committee if a closely related amendment was already with that committee. Random assignment was to prevent the perception that a committee would control a particular issue. The purpose of the general committees was initially simply to discuss amendments

Figure 9. The Constitution Revision Commission did its plenary work in the Senate chambers in what is now referred to as the Historic Capitol. Photo courtesy of State Archives of Florida, *Florida Memory*, https://floridamemory.com/items/show/34936.

with their introducers; in the final round, however, general committees were the only means to further amend the draft constitution. If a general committee rejected a proposed amendment, a majority vote of that committee was required to resubmit it. If approved, a proposed amendment was sent to the Steering and Rules Committee to schedule for full CRC debate.[15] This procedure was used so that the structure of the November 10 draft would largely be the final form of the new constitution, as none of the proposed amendments substantially altered the structure of the document.

This final three-week push reflected the growing familiarity the commissioners had with one another. There were jokes; there were also snarky comments. The mix of urban and rural commissioners made for some interesting remarks, such when Dick Pettigrew of Miami mentioned, as he began to speak, "I hesitate to rise during deer season to oppose this amendment."[16] And even though all the commissioners

Figure 10. The Constitution Revision Commission on the capitol steps, December 1966. Photo courtesy of State Archives of Florida, *Florida Memory*, https://floridamemory.com/items/show/18745.

agreed Smith was a strong leader, he occasionally had to scold them for failing to pay attention. One day he took several minutes to admonish the group for its lack of decorum: members were wandering around the chamber, whispering loudly and refusing to acknowledge defeat on pet points: "We should learn to accept the issue and realize again that we may not be the sole depository of wisdom in the chamber, that there may be others who also have fine and splendid ideas." He added, "I hate to have to say things like this and I apologize for it, because certainly it is a minor thing . . . I would not want the best group I have ever seen or ever worked with to get down to a lower plane."[17] Immediately, Charley Johns rose to Smith's support: "You don't owe anybody any apologies for your comments this morning. And I have thought within myself why you didn't get harder with us."[18]

Two concerns ran through the debates: whether a particular provision would help or hurt eventual adoption, and whether the matter was something that should appear in the constitution or be left to ordinary legislation. Neither issue was cut and dried. Members repeatedly argued for or against amendments based in part on their probable effect on eventual adoption of the whole constitution. However, Smith criticized the members when the horse trading moved to the hallways outside the chamber and influenced votes on amendments.[19] The horse trading would be reserved for the legislative debates on the CRC proposal, which were outside Smith's control.

Whether a particular matter should be placed in the constitution or be left to statutory law was likewise a matter of much debate. Arguably, the only time something is required in the constitution is to organize government or to grant or restrict power to some part of the government. For example, no details about a state education system appeared in the Florida constitution until 1868.[20] The Model State Constitution drafted by the National Municipal League, available to all CRC members, contained only a one-paragraph, forty-four-word article that guaranteed free public schools.[21] The article on education that eventually became part of Florida's constitution, however, is one of its more detailed portions and is tied to other articles, such as taxation and bonding.

Conversely, the issue of private economy appeared only minimally in the constitution, in the "right to work" guarantee in the Declaration of Rights. Regulation of businesses and the private economy is otherwise left entirely to the legislature, which has passed volumes of laws governing economic relationships within Florida.

The following discussion of some of the areas of debate will illustrate how the members viewed and disposed of the contested issues in each area, and will provide insight into their intent within each article. A schedule outlining the transition from the 1885 Constitution to the proposed new constitution received debate and was included in the final CRC document as Article XII. However, this book will not discuss that transition article, because of its temporary nature.

Article I: Declaration of Rights

Sovereign Immunity

Commissioners later recalled different times in the proceedings when the debate became heated. Most often the transcripts do not corroborate those recollections. The transcript regarding sovereign immunity, however, does demonstrate a heated debate. Interestingly, it was between sitting Florida Supreme Court justice B. K. Roberts, Human Rights Committee chair, and his nominal subordinate, circuit judge Hugh Taylor, chair of the Style and Drafting Committee.

The section on sovereign immunity was one of the most significant sections of the draft constitution. The doctrine of sovereign immunity prevents citizens from suing their own government either for personal injuries caused by a government official or employee or for a breach of contract by the government. This ancient doctrine is based on the premise that the King can do no wrong, even if his actions have caused evil consequences. The Human Rights Committee, headed by Roberts, proposed to abolish the doctrine in a proposed new section of the Declaration of Rights in its draft sent to the Style and Drafting Committee, headed by Taylor. The draft that Style and Drafting sent to all CRC members, however, deleted the proposal. But Roberts was having none of that. He immediately entered an amendment seeking to restore the provision to the constitution. that Chairman Smith himself, however, stood in to defend the deletion as a necessary reconciliation between two committees' drafts.[22]

Justice Roberts, though politically conservative in many ways, urged passionately that the new constitution allow citizens to sue their own government. As he pointed out in the floor debate, "if a truck that the State Road Department owns runs over you and kills you, you are just as dead as if it had been a truck operated by the Florida Power Corporation."[23] Roberts argued for sovereign immunity to be waived to correct this wrong, and had proposed a detailed set of instructions to be included in the constitution's Declaration of Rights. The Style and Drafting Committee had replaced Roberts's provision with terse language directing the legislature to deal with the subject. This language had not even directed the legislature to waive sovereign immunity. Although Taylor attempted to explain its reasoning, Roberts swatted him down, breaking the veneer of collegiality: "Would you let me finish?"[24] Taylor never said another word in that debate, letting his committee vice-chair, Jack Mathews, argue with Roberts. Roberts's detailed provisions never made it back into the draft, but a simple statement did, stating that sovereign immunity would not exist. During the three-week CRC debate period, CRC member and news editor Bill Baggs complimented Taylor, commenting he would make "one hell of a rewrite man."[25]

Basic Rights

Another passage in the constitution that highlighted the strain between Roberts and Taylor concerned the prohibition on aliens ineligible for citizenship to own land in Florida, a provision included in the 1885 Constitution. The Human Rights Committee sought to keep that provision in the new constitution, proposing language in section 2 that provided that "foreigners who are not eligible to become citizens of the United States may be regulated or prohibited" from "the ownership, inheritance, disposition, possession and enjoyment of real estate in the State of Florida." The Style and Drafting Committee shortened the language substantially, substituting, "the real property rights of aliens ineligible for citizenship may be regulated by law." Roberts explicitly wanted the word "prohibited" restored. Taylor mildly replied that his changes were just making the language briefer and broader; he did not address the substitution of the word "prohibited" with "regulated," even though that was clearly what was bothering Roberts. Finally, Roberts said: "If the head of our foreign enemy to the south of us should come into Polk County and start buying up the citrus industry, or the phosphate industry, I think that the Legislature of Florida should have the right to say, 'Mr. Castro, you are an alien, you cannot own any property in Florida.'" Did Roberts mean to imply that Taylor was a communist, or simply naive? One can imagine Roberts then pausing and leaning back, as he said, "I'm not particularly upset about it . . . just whatever the Commission wants to do." The commission agreed with Roberts and put the language back in.[26]

Equal Rights for Women

Bill Baggs proposed an amendment to guarantee women equal protection under the law, an addendum to section 2. Unfortunately, he was ahead of his time. Baggs, age forty-five, was the editor of the afternoon paper the *Miami News*. He was an outspoken opponent of racial segregation, the Vietnam War, and Fidel Castro. He networked with the anti-Castro Cuban exiles while maintaining links to the CIA in Miami. In the fall of 1962, the *Miami News* reported on the presence of Soviet missiles in Cuba eight days before the White House announced them.[27] Baggs was persistently rumored to be associated with Operation Mockingbird, a secret CIA campaign to influence the media to present the CIA's views, although proof of such an association is elusive. His editorials advocated services for South Florida retirees and environmental protection of Key Biscayne. The latter campaign was successful; a state park on Key Biscayne is now named after Baggs.

One of Baggs's primary opponents on the subject of equal rights was George Stallings. Stallings was fifty-eight years old at the time of the meetings. A representative from Jacksonville since 1958, Stallings had twice chaired the House Committee on Reapportionment[28] and was a member of the FLIC when that group published its notorious "Purple Pamphlet" in 1964. Although perhaps representing an extreme, Stallings was not alone as a conservative member of the old guard. He had company in Charley Johns, Hugh Taylor, and others.

Rowell, for example, implied that a federal ERA would have spelled the end of common courtesy:

> One day up in the Legislature . . . [a] bunch of girls got on the elevator. I was standing close to the front door. When we got down, I had to stand aside for them all to get out.
>
> I said, "Well, if the ERA had passed, I wouldn't have had to do this. I could have been gone on down the street."[29]

Baggs's equal rights amendment would change the equal rights guarantee from discrimination "because of race or religion" to "because of race or religion or sex." As he geared up to defend his proposed amendment, other members were chatting and Baggs chided them: "Gentlemen, we are talking about sex, and I'd like your attention." Baggs's proposed amendment generated controversy in the group. Smith had to ask again for order. When he tallied up those who wanted to speak for or against the proposal, there were four against and five in favor, in addition to Baggs. Beth Johnson, the only female commissioner, spoke in favor of it, saying, "If you are going to say that no person shall be deprived of his rights because of race or creed, then you should add 'or sex.' Because there are, I have to remind you, more women than there are people of differing races; there are more women than there are people of differing creeds." Also in favor were Davis, O'Connell, Roberts, and Crews. Opponents were Stallings, Friday, Taylor, and Ervin.

Although Don Reed, one of the few Republicans on the CRC, had not asked to speak as either a proponent or opponent, he proposed an amendment to the amendment: he asked for equal rights regardless of political party. Given the floor, and amid laughter, he immediately withdrew his proposal.[30] Next, Stallings began by declaring that he was not "against women. I am not against wine or song either," but then he stated seriously and risibly: "I wish someone would show me honestly and truly where women have been deprived of their rights just because they are women."[31] Ervin responded by noting that the wage classifications in Florida state government classified female employees separately and at lower rates; Crews observed that because Stallings had said nothing against the prohibition against deprivation of rights because of race, Stallings must be ready to live with mixed-race marriages.[32]

Turlington asked Crews whether men were not also being discriminated against by not being included in the declaration of equal rights. Crews answered that "man is either one sex or the other." Crews next had to field questions from two supreme court justices, Sebring and O'Connell. When Turlington had another question for him, Crews got testy and refused to receive any more questions from him:

MR. CREWS: . . . You probably have some other silly questions. I'm not going to yield to anybody that doesn't know that a man is a male man, and a woman is a female man.
CHAIRMAN SMITH: Just a minute, Gentlemen.[33]

The debate examined the effect of adding the equal rights phrase on other parts of the law, such as curtesy and dower rights of married men and women, and laws allowing pregnant women to be excused from juries. When Goodrich asked what effect the amendment would have on dower and curtesy, Justice O'Connell shot back:

MR. O'CONNELL: I wouldn't attempt to give you even a guess, much less a judicial opinion, as has been attempted here. But I would say this, that if—

CHAIRMAN SMITH: Watch your step.

MR. O'CONNELL: It has been attempted by others than you, sir, so it's not directed only to you. I am not excluding you, however.[34]

Ervin stated that he was "not too far apart from Mr. Baggs" on the issue but noted that the amendment would not help the constitution gain approval by the public. Many times speakers had to say that they were speaking "seriously." Similarly, several times the chair had to ask for order. It is obvious the subject of women's rights was controversial and, in a gentlemen's-club kind of way, was subject to jokes and side comments. Nevertheless, the amendment to prohibit discrimination on the basis of sex in the declaration of rights passed.[35]

The next day, the CRC atypically approved both a motion to reconsider the amendment and a motion to refer the matter to a select committee composed of Baggs, Earle, Faircloth, and Goodrich. The debate on the motion for reconsideration revealed the commission's polarization on the issue. Goodrich, arguing for reconsideration, stated: "We do not speak against women's rights, but for them. We have, in our society, a theory that women do have some right to be protected by nature of their sex, by virtue of it, in some circumstances. . . . You are about to destroy that basic theory."[36] When Mathews challenged the equal rights opponents, hypothetical worst-case scenarios emerged, revealing fear of changes like those brought by the 1954 *Brown v. Board of Education* decision:

MR. MATHEWS: But you don't honestly think that a constitutional guarantee against deprivation of rights in and of itself does not prohibit classification with reference to rest rooms, honestly?

MR. GOODRICH: Well, since you bring that up, I think that is a rather far-out extension of it, but I think this would be possible. But I'll give you a better one than that. The Florida statutes provide that prisoners shall be segregated according to sex. And I don't think that would be upheld if we did this, because the supreme court has held that separate but equal facilities are discriminatory.[37]

Stallings closed the debate:

> Here is one thing that gives me great concern. . . . What is going to happen if sexual deviates, and there are plenty of them in this state and in this country, bring forth the argument that there is a third connotation on sex, and they take the position that they would be discriminated against if the State of Florida attempted to pass any laws against such a deplorable situation as homosexual marriages.
>
> And I finish on this theme. You hear so much about our Judeo-Christian heritage. What are you doing to that when you put this thing in the constitution? Because our Judeo-Christian heritage has protected the woman. . . . I think we are doing something dangerous in the name of a righteous movement, something that we are trying to throw a sop to the women. And I think it is a mistake. . . . I hope you will reconsider this and get this nonsense out of the constitution.[38]

The select committee's report to the full CRC provided a straightforward legal analysis: an equal rights provision in the Florida constitution would allow either spouse to receive alimony and have custody of children; it would allow, but not require, women to be drafted into the military; and it would not abrogate criminal laws against sexual offenses. The committee then recommended that the convention indefinitely table the amendment. The vote in the select committee was three for that recommendation and one, Baggs, against. The select committee's report bears Baggs's handwritten rejection.[39]

The December 16 debate on indefinite postponement of the equal rights amendment reprised the previous arguments. Critically for the amendment's survival, Beth Johnson now reversed her position and argued against it. She noted that the League of Women Voters had traditionally opposed equal rights amendments since 1925 because they would strip women of protective labor legislation. Johnson said that it would be premature of the convention to legislate equal rights through the constitution. She noted this was a commission composed of men: "I am only one woman on this Commission and I haven't been able to find too many [women] around in these halls to discuss this matter with in the last few days."[40] She suggested instead that the legislature handle the issue after allowing women to form a commission and debate the issue more widely.[41] Mathews then urged that the amendment go forward to adoption, noting that this section of the constitution dealt with basic rights and that a person could not be deprived of basic rights just because she is female.[42]

Crews also argued against indefinite postponement:

> Let me tell you, from the time that woman was a mere chattel, bought and sold, then through the common law when her property became the property under the control of her husband, until she was partially emancipated, and then with the 19th Amendment of the United States, . . . this would be the culmination of securing for her all the right of other citizens.[43]

Nevertheless, the full CRC voted seventeen to fifteen to postpone consideration of the amendment indefinitely.

Other Rights

The CRC crafted a "right to work" provision as section 6. The term "right to work" is sometimes scoffed at by people with pro-labor interests, because it declares that persons have the right to work regardless of their membership or non-membership in a union. However, unions generally do have a harder time taking hold in right-to-work states. It is tempting to wonder, however, whether Roberts's good friend Edward Ball, who controlled the Florida East Coast Railway, had any influence over the provision. After all, at the time the CRC met, that railroad was years into one of the nation's longest railway strikes. And Roberts was chair of the Human Rights Committee, which wrote the "right to work" language.

In addition, the CRC decided that the state could regulate the right to bear arms, particularly the manner in which arms are borne, in section 8, and it wrote into the constitution that information obtained through wiretaps without a warrant would be excluded, not trusting the courts to uphold this "exclusionary rule," in section 12.

Article III: Legislature

Sections 2 and 3: Legislative Auditor and Annual Sessions

The CRC discussed many aspects of Article III. Although the CRC's decision to call for annual legislative sessions was almost uncontested, it did face a small bump in the road. Reubin Askew proposed an amendment keeping sessions biennial. His proposal lost overwhelmingly.[44] Although biennial sessions would keep the legislature from having too much time to make unnecessary laws, which was the basic fear Askew and others expressed, the need to set a budget over a two-year window made budgeting a nightmare in a state growing as rapidly as Florida. The move to annual sessions was seen as a move toward a modern and professional government.

Another move seen as key to a modern government was to add a legislative auditor to review legislative expenditures. That proposal passed with little discussion.[45]

Section 16: Apportionment of the House and Senate

The apportionment debates were the most poignant of all. The legislators on the CRC were fresh from the shock of the political realignment that the November elections had just accomplished. When the debate on legislative apportionment came to the floor it took on an awkward, almost strained quality. Every member of the Legislative Committee except Robert Ervin had been either a current or a past member of the legislature. This fact, together with the ongoing pain of the pending federal reapportionment legislation, made any talk of constitutional legislative apportionment seem both politically loaded and futile. Attorney General Faircloth would be leaving the following week to argue for the state's latest apportionment scheme before the U.S. Supreme Court in *Swann v. Adams*. Faircloth was in an uncomfortable position during the reapportionment litigation. He had supported reapportionment as a legislator, but as attorney general he was obliged to argue for the Pork Chop majority's halfhearted reapportionment plans during the reapportionment court wars. At one point during the debate, Faircloth pointed out to the commission that its attempts to propose new apportionment plans made it difficult for him to defend the legislature's present plan to the U.S. Supreme Court.[46] The commission barely acknowledged Faircloth's dilemma; it kept on debating plans.

The transcripts of the floor debate on reapportionment reflect indirect language and a seeming unwillingness to discuss details. For example, at one point in defending a proposed apportionment amendment, Ervin said he brought the proposal at the request of members who "have their own problems in their own areas, which I do not think it proper to discuss here."[47] Whether his reluctance was because the debate was being transcribed or because the commissioners were simply weary of wasting more time chewing the same old rag is unclear.

The debate was not without substance, however. The members considered the latest plan's twenty-four-county Senate district in rural North Florida, which had displaced some of the state's most powerful senators, to be a big problem. And they repeatedly discussed the U.S. Supreme Court's one-man, one-vote benchmark. The members recognized they must meet that goal, but they had questions about exactly what that standard required and allowed. Specifically, they wondered whether the Senate could be apportioned according to geographical features while the House remained apportioned by population.

During these debates, Johns addressed the group. Although his career had benefited from the malapportionment that allowed areas with tiny populations to be overrepresented, he now said that malapportionment was wrong. Johns acknowledged that he had recently lost a narrow reelection attempt that had ended his thirty years in office. He told the group he had voted for the twenty-four-county "monstrosity" of a senatorial district that had led to his defeat, not because he liked it, but because he "didn't want those nine gentlemen in Washington reapportioning the State of Florida. And it was the best we could get out of it."[48]

The commissioners were divided on how they thought the reapportionment drama would play out in the coming months. Some seemed confident that the next legislature would apportion itself fairly, while others were skeptical. Most agreed, however, that the November election had amounted to a referendum by voters that fair apportionment should occur. The commission also discussed four amendments proposed by Ervin. Each attempted to prevent overlapping or identical districts except for the two large one-county districts, Duval and Dade. But the committee opted for keeping the constitutional constraints on apportionment minimal and giving the legislature maximum flexibility; all amendments regarding apportionment were defeated.[49]

Several proposed amendments not directly related to apportionment also commanded debate. The commissioners discussed the advisability of having a large number of at-large candidates. Would having many at-large seats help legislators take a broader perspective, or would it simply hinder the average citizen's ability to know his or her legislator? Would it increase effectiveness, or simply encourage ward-style politics?[50] Not every commissioner came off well in these debates. Jack Mathews occasionally addressed fellow commissioners sarcastically. He also broke protocol and referred to his fellow Jacksonville legislator, George Stallings, by his first name. When the chair reminded him to "refer to Mr. Stallings by his proper title," Mathews replied, "Mr. George."[51]

Legislative Investigations

The final matter the commission took up under the legislative article was that of legislative investigations. Legislative investigations were mentioned in several sections of the legislative article under the 1885 Constitution, authorizing compulsory attendance of witnesses and of legislators, and authorizing punishment. The CRC sought to authorize investigations explicitly in one unified section, section 5, of the proposed constitution and to provide broad parameters for them.

Students of midcentury politics often associate legislative investigations with committees such as Senator Joseph McCarthy's House

Un-American Activities Committee (HUAC), which had blacklisted many Americans for alleged Communist sympathies, and Florida's notorious Florida Legislative Investigation Committee, which had investigated the NAACP and gays on college campuses in the name of rooting out communism. Usually, though, legislative investigations are an essential part of the legislative process, since they allow legislators to directly determine facts that will influence what legislation is passed. The legislative investigative committee must have the power to compel reluctant witnesses appear before it and to punish witnesses who refuse to answer questions.

By the time of the CRC debates began in November, one prominent investigative committee of the Florida Legislature had recently completed its work: the FLIC had completed its ten years of investigations ranging from searching the NAACP for Communist infiltration to rooting out homosexual state university faculty members. During its life, the FLIC had used the threat of contempt to coerce witnesses into providing information. The CRC members continued it in the proposed new constitution. In fact, four of the FLIC's former members were on the CRC: Bill Young, George Stallings, Henry Land, and founder and sometimes chair Charley Johns. The FLIC, while powerful, gradually lost credibility as its investigations embarrassed not only its targets but eventually its members. It had been defunded in 1965.

Ervin recalled that the FLIC experience did not shape the debate over legislative investigations. The FLIC was never explicitly mentioned during the CRC debates, nor were there any obvious references to its proceedings. Perhaps the FLIC was a largely self-healing wound, cauterized by its own "Purple Pamphlet." Instead, the CRC split its debate on investigations into two parts: investigations while the legislature was in session, and those when it was out of session. The CRC decided that incarceration should be available as a constitutional option for persons defying legislative investigations only during session, which was consistent with the 1885 Constitution as amended.[52] But 1885 sanctions were harsh when incarceration was allowed: violators could be imprisoned for up to ninety days without access to a judge. The CRC amended this practice to require a judicial proceeding before an investigative committee could punish a person.[53]

Article IV: Executive

Lieutenant Governor and Succession in Office

John McCarty, brother of Governor Dan McCarty, who had died in office in 1953 at age forty-two, proposed an amendment, creating a new section 2 to the executive article, to add a lieutenant governor to the cabinet.[54] After the death of Governor McCarty, Senate President Charley Johns had become acting governor, and this had thrown into focus the old constitution's problem with succession: the state was run for two years by a man who had gotten into office with the votes of only a few thousand voters in his rural district. The accession of Johns to governor illustrated the need, as some saw it, to have a person elected statewide to succeed the governor. John McCarty must have had his brother in mind when he pleaded, "The strain and press of schedule for a governor is just almost more than an individual can stand."[55] McCarty also pointed out that taking the succession to the governorship out of the legislative branch would have the effect of strengthening the executive branch. But not everyone agreed. Turlington maintained that a lieutenant governor would "stand . . . around the office and that's about the size of it." He added, "The best thing to do is to elect healthy governors."[56]

Turlington also believed that, because Florida already elected seven members of the executive branch statewide, it was unwise to add an eighth for the voters to distinguish from the others: "You can only get so much attention from a mule at one time, even with a two-by-four." Years later, Reubin Askew dryly observed that the only duty of the lieutenant governor was "to wait for the Governor to stop breathing."[57] The amendment was at first adopted, but the next day was reconsidered and failed.[58]

The matter of whether the governor could succeed himself was another warmly contested issue. Section 3 of the executive article in the November 10 draft provided that the governor could do so. Debate started with Ervin recommending an amendment that would take away the governor's ability to serve a second term but leave the cabinet members able to be reelected. In other words, Ervin's amendment would retain the succession scheme of the executive branch that had been in effect since 1885.[59]

Predictably, Ervin met resistance on the issue. He made the mistake of seeming to claim that something about the office of the governor gave the governor a greater "opportunity to build the machinery" to keep himself in office for "a long, long time" and implying that the cabinet members did not have that machinery. Jack Mathews's somewhat sarcastic questioning revealed, of course, that most cabinet members (unlike the governor) indeed did stay in office for a long, long time.[60]

At this point, Bill O'Neill, Warren Goodrich, and Richard Earle asked Smith to read their substitute "seven governors" bill:

The supreme executive power shall be vested in seven governors as follows:

1. The presiding governor, who shall be in charge of booze, bridges and bangtails.
2. The governor in charge of the state bird and seal.
3. The governor in charge of litigating, bookmaking and wire tapping.
4. The governor in charge of literacy, illiteracy and lethargy.
5. The governor in charge of tombstones and shylocks.
6. The governor in charge of farms, feed and fertilizer.
7. The governor in charge of agents and arsons and adjusters . . .

Each governor shall be elected for a term of four years and shall not succeed himself more than 12 times.[61]

After the laughter died down, the mood turned serious again with Mc-Carty's eloquent defense of having a one-term governor. He argued that a governor should "do that job for the term that he is there without any other thought, to re-election or to anything else," and that "if we allow a governor to succeed himself, he is not going to for those first four years be the man in that office that he should be."[62] Under the 1885 Constitution, the legislature met once every two years, and the governor had only a four-year term. The first time the legislature met during a governor's term, the governor was brand new and inexperienced. By the second time the legislature met, the governor was a lame duck with less than half his term left. The timing of the sessions and the short term of the governor left him weak not only as to the cabinet but also as to the legislature. Some members remarked, in apparent levity, that if a term-limited governor wished to succeed himself, he could always run his wife or mother as his successor, so who needed the second term?[63] Askew then reported that legislators at a conference of large-state legislators he had attended had pointed out that a two-term governor did not eliminate his lame-duck period, but simply postponed it. Askew also reported the perhaps surprising news that many of those legislators considered Florida's system of having an elected cabinet and weak governor to be "the model" in allowing executive leadership to continue.[64]

Also speaking in favor of keeping a one-term governor, Turlington, who had been a state representative for sixteen years, argued that in reality Florida's governor was quite strong. If the governor should become eligible to serve two terms, he said, the commission should then look for ways to restrict the governor's authority. Turlington claimed that the appointive authority of the governor in Florida "is one of the very strongest" in the United States, and the veto authority was also among the strongest in the nation.[65] Turlington threw an oblique zinger at his former professor, Manning Dauer, when he added: "We have allowed political scientists to apologize for our system for a long time without calling their hand and pointing out our governor in many respects has authority that exceeds the authority of many other governors in America."[66] Turlington, however, did not provide examples of how Florida's governor was so strong.

Finally, Richard Earle, always a voice of reason, spoke up: constitutionally limiting the governor to one, or any number of, terms amounts to nothing more than denying the people the right to elect whomever they please as governor. The people should have the right to make unwise, as well as wise, choices; the constitution should "return . . . the government to the people."[67] The amendment limiting the governor to one term failed and never went to the legislature.

Elected versus Appointed Cabinet

Of all the proposed amendments, number 100 carried the most political dynamite. Naked politics swirled around the CRC's debate on the committee substitute for amendment 100, which proposed that Florida's cabinet members, proposed to be defined in Article IV, section 4, be appointed by (and removable by) the governor, instead of elected statewide as it had been since 1885. McCarty dubbed it "high octane 100" and predicted that debate on it would "separate the lady and the men from the boys in the commission."[68]

On December 14, the morning the debate on the amendment was to be held, Governor Burns addressed the full CRC. To the surprise and chagrin of the amendment's proponents Chesterfield Smith and Dick Pettigrew, the lame-duck governor urged the CRC to maintain the elected cabinet.[69] This was an unexpected position for a governor to take, since an appointed cabinet would have given much more power to the Florida governor.

But the governor's voice was not the only powerful one speaking about the cabinet system that day. Smith stepped down from the chair to speak in favor of an appointed cabinet. He began by stating he spoke on behalf of Pettigrew, whose passion was government reorganization and whose political pony was the appointed cabinet idea. Pettigrew was absent that day, and for much of the constitutional convention, because of illness. Smith, his expansive personality having been constrained to enforcing parliamentary procedure for so much of the convention, spoke eloquently: "I am a trial lawyer. I have had to sit up on the Chair and preside. I felt that I was entitled to one major argument." He began by noting: "I have tried to be fair in this convention. I did not mean to be so fair, however, when I knew this was coming up, as to permit the Governor of Florida to take an opposite point right beforehand. I regret that he did so. But neither he nor I were aware of the other's plans."[70]

Smith stated that he was advocating for several interests, not just Pettigrew's and not just his own. Among others, he declared, he was arguing on behalf of Manning Dauer, who had educated many of the CRC members while they were in college and who had mailed his own reapportionment plan to the federal court in Miami. Smith also stated he was advocating for the League of Women Voters, whose "yardstick for constitutional revision" favored an appointed cabinet. In the mid-1960s women were still expected to stay at home; their involvement in civic affairs was not always taken seriously. Smith, however, did take the League seriously. He told the commissioners, "Those who sneer at [the League's] efforts are no friends of mine. They have furnished the spark of leadership for constitutional revision for 20 years in this state, when nobody else has been able to."[71]

He then exhorted his fellow commissioners to summon their political courage and "worry about my state for a hundred years," not just the next four. He declared the issue of the cabinet to be the most important in the new constitution. He said that having six cabinet members elected statewide with no supervision by the governor created, in reality, seven governors, and that the tangle of some 150 overlapping state agencies headed by one cabinet member or another created "a hydra-headed monster, without any control or direction."[72] He argued that just one person needed to head the state—to, "at midnight, . . . go look the owl in the face, and . . . make the decision."[73] He challenged his commissioners: "We have to decide, is this a reform commission, convention, or is it a rewrite."[74]

After Smith sat down to applause from the audience, Bill Young stood up and described Smith's words as "one of the finest speeches in behalf of the people and a form of state government that any of us have ever heard."[75] But as compelling as Smith's speech was, he did not change every mind on the CRC. After all, the amendment he advocated represented radical change: that was why it had been dubbed "high octane 100" in the first place.

Tom Sebring led the debate by making the basic opposition argument that the substitute amendment ceded too much power to the governor.[76] Warren Goodrich then spoke in favor of the amendment, noting that "There has been hovering over this entire convention a feeling and a conviction that there is one thing we cannot do, and that is change the cabinet system. It has been said that we cannot do this, for if we do, we will surely arouse political opposition, which would defeat the entire constitution."[77] Goodrich appeared to have been inspired and emboldened by Smith's speech. Noting that it had taken courage for

Smith to advocate against the status quo, Goodrich admitted that "it will not be easy to look [my cabinet member friends] in the eye and say that I rose to support the conscientious position of our Chairman." But Hugh Taylor spoke in opposition and said, "A wiser man than I recently said that all change is not improvement, and all movement is not forward."[78] Taylor doubted whether a cabinet appointed by a governor would ever exercise independent judgment, noting that "most folks that hire folks like the folks they hire to agree with them."[79] Nothing in the record suggests that Taylor did not believe in his stated position, but he had received a handwritten note from former secretary of state R.A. Gray pleading for the CRC to keep the cabinet elected, arguing that this was the only "internal check" in the executive branch.[80]

Ralph Marsicano also spoke in favor of keeping the cabinet elected, stating that it provided continuity in government—an understatement, considering that some cabinet members had been reelected for decades.[81] John Crews argued in favor of the appointed cabinet. Referring to the space program, he characterized Florida as "the Gateway to the Moon" and therefore deserving of a modern, efficient government.[82] The elected cabinet, he argued, was just the opposite. The fact that most of them stayed for many terms led to too much mutual backscratching: the state's budget would never decrease because the cabinet members would always trade votes for other members' increases.[83] Crews contended the governor should be "the Executive of Florida" and "not just the governor in charge of a few departments."[84]

Ralph Turlington later said that changing the cabinet from elected to appointed was so politically unlikely as to be insignificant, akin to changing to a unicameral legislature. He attributed the issue's existence to "outspoken" CRC members and the trumpeting of the League of Women Voters.[85] But at the time, he thought it was significant enough to speak for several minutes about the danger of putting too much authority in the hands of a single executive. Then incoming Speaker of the House, Turlington, deadpanned, "I don't really know of but one person that I would trust with such responsibility, and I [don't] feel . . . that I could offer for both House and Senate." He then switched to an appeal to the intellect, claiming that college professors—"they are fine people, some of them"—would vote against the appointed cabinet with him, because "a no vote is the proper and intellectual answer to this."[86]

More discussion followed, and more substitutes for the "high octane 100." The final vote was to keep the cabinet elected.

Executive Branch Reorganization

The CRC debated proposed language that would have created a new section, proposed to be section 6, that mandated that the number of executive departments be reduced to no more than thirty. Ervin proposed removing the limit, as the number was admitted by all to have been completely arbitrary. However, the commissioners agreed that the present number of committees was not only huge but also almost impossible to determine. Members pointed out that no one seemed to know exactly how many existed: one legislator or another would guess that there were 136, 156, or 158 different departments, agencies, and boards. Those who had tried to find out confessed frustration not only with determining the number but also with figuring out who served on particular boards or how a board operated. The system was "a jungle and a maze," remarked Goodrich.[87]

As the debate continued, it became clear that fundamental differences existed among the commissioners as to whether the executive branch really needed a complete overhaul. Again, Ervin spoke in favor of the cabinet system, with its many overlapping boards, remaining intact. Ervin acknowledged that many of his ideas for the executive department had not prevailed, and that he was "licking a good many wounds." Nonetheless, he questioned the necessity of "repudiating that which has been a highly effective system of government," and, referring to the cabinet members, repudiating "these gentlemen who [are] equally as dedicated as you members of the legislature."[88] Jack Mathews, on the other hand, described what it was like to watch the cabinet members meeting in their various capacities as members of overlapping boards. Said the man who was generally acknowledged to be an expert on Florida's government, "Unless you know a lot more about government than I do, I'm sure that without a program . . . you couldn't tell which were the members of the boards working officially as a member of that particular board during that particular time, because they sit in the same seats, and they go right from one board into the other."[89] But Ervin argued that changing from overlapping boards to a system in which each of the proposed thirty boards would be headed by the governor and cabinet, as one proposed amendment provided, would result in an inefficient and tumultuous transition period. Ultimately, Ervin argued for leaving the decision of organizing the executive departments and boards up to the legislature. That is exactly what his opponents disliked, worrying that without constitutional protection, a governor could be hamstrung by an unfriendly legislature bent on taking him off cabinet boards and therefore reducing his influence. Ultimately, the commission voted against Ervin's position and in favor of the substitute amendment, which guaranteed that the governor and full cabinet would sit on all cabinet boards.[90]

The draft had also included a provision for a three-person budget commission that would inspect budget requests. Referred to by its detractors as a three-headed monster, the budget commission died a quick death on the floor of the convention. The budget commission had been criticized by the press as a three-man fourth branch of the government,[91] because of its independence from those it would audit and because the budget commissioners would be elected statewide. As the *Tallahassee Democrat* put it, popular election is "the worst way to choose a financial expert."[92] In defense of the budget commission idea, Taylor gave a persuasive reason for its proposed existence: the budget commission would be another means of keeping the mutual back-scratching club at bay, by keeping the various cabinet members from just approving each other's budgets without looking too closely at them. But Taylor appeared to be the only strong proponent. Raymond Alley proposed an amendment deleting the three-person budget commission from the proposed constitution completely, and the amendment passed.

Governor's Power to Suspend Officers

The commission voted to give the governor power to remove municipal officials who had been indicted. After some discussion, the group adopted an amendment, carrying section number 7, that made this power optional rather than mandatory. However, many felt that the governor should be mandated to remove indicted municipal officials, so that the governor would feel protected by the law and the municipal official would, indeed, be removed. Jack Mathews of Jacksonville sponsored this amendment, and from the oblique talk among the commissioners it appears the amendment was pointed at rooting out corruption in Jacksonville. However, others acknowledged, just before the vote adopting it, that it would be useful elsewhere in the state as well. And, in fact, the incumbent governor who had just been defeated earlier that year in the Democratic primary, Haydon Burns, had been mayor of Jacksonville and trailed an odor of corruption that may well have nudged him out of reelection. Governor-elect Kirk became known for colorful and rowdy personal behavior and erratic political behavior, but he also ran on the promise of rooting out corruption from localities throughout Florida.

Game and Fresh Water Fish Commission

The language governing the Game and Fresh Water Fish Commission (GFWF), an agency already in the old constitution but proposed to be revised with a new section number, section 9, received a lot of discussion from the CRC members, many of whom hunted and fished in their spare time and likely had done so in the Florida woods, swamps, and waters their whole lives. The principal disagreement concerned whether the GFWF should be answerable to the legislature—a position advocated by Ervin, who mistrusted the carte blanche nature of the power then currently granted to the commission—or be constitutionally given its own rule-making authority, which some considered to be far too much power. The hunters and fishermen in the CRC immediately set to discussing how, if the legislature had the power to grant power to the commission, individual legislators would keep for themselves the ability to "set the bag limit, the days of hunting," and other specific rules, ostensibly for their own convenience and pleasure rather than in the interest of maintaining and managing wildlife populations. "Believe me," said John Crews of rural Baker County, "hunting is a sensitive point to many people in this state," and giving the legislature power over wildlife management would hurt "the hunting public, . . . the sportsmen and . . . the people of this state." When Ray Alley pressed him, Crews admitted that it would help preserve the wildlife and fish as well.[93]

Turlington was another who spoke knowledgeably about letting the GFWF Commission have its own authority. He claimed one of the soundest pieces of advice he ever heard from a legislator before the GFWF Commission existed was, "Son, don't ever get in no trouble with no fish bill." He described having been set upon in his early years in the legislature by "all these worrisome people . . . and they'd want to take up half your time telling you about the habit of dove, and when you should hunt dove." His position was joined by all but those who, like Bob Ervin, didn't like the independence the GFWF Commission had. Eventually the young turkey hunter, Lawton Chiles, pointed out that the legislature would have plenty of power over the GFWF commissioners by controlling the amount they could charge for hunting and fishing licenses and penalties for violations.[94] This point settled the feathers of the CRC members, who voted for the GFWF's independence.

Article V: Judiciary

The commission entered the November debates with a fundamentally revamped proposed judicial system drafted in detail by its Judicial Committee. But of all the amendments proposed to the November 10 draft, the greatest number—55 out of 216—sought to amend the proposed revision of the judicial branch. The members of this committee had to listen to everyone else tell them that, in essence, their baby was ugly. This was to be expected from a CRC dominated by lawyers. The criticism started with Taylor, who sent Smith a letter as the commission began its meetings. Addressed to the "Top Sergeant," the letter presented "for study and comment a suggested revision of the judiciary article which you will notice is four pages instead of the ten contained in the committee draft."[95] The fate of Taylor's truncated version is not found in the CRC records.

The full commission then set about dismantling the Judiciary Committee's proposals in the hopes of producing a constitution that the public would vote to accept. The result of the full CRC's amendments was to make Article V more cumbersome and showed that the commissioners had no clear consensus on the court system.

The most significant change was the elimination of the feature providing for merit selection and retention of all judges and for the substitution of nonpartisan elections of judges. Chiles proposed a simple amendment that provided for nonpartisan elections.[96] Although he said it had no effect on merit selection, his amendment had the effect of eliminating it.

The commissioners were blunt about eliminating merit retention simply to gain voter approval of the whole constitution.[97] They fanned out along predictable philosophical lines. Taylor favored merit selection but noted the need for continued accountability to the public: "As a judge, . . . when I feel like throwing my weight around in a courtroom, where nobody is going to tell me no, it's a salutary thing for me to look out there and say, 'Those folks can take me down off this bench any time they feel like it,' when the election comes around."[98] O'Connell spoke to the unsuitability of popular election when the candidates are restricted in what they can talk about and when the voters therefore cannot make informed decisions because of the restricted topics. He noted that popular elections do not ensure that the best candidate will be elected, but rather that the winning candidate will have the best-financed campaign or be the most telegenic or the most networked one.[99] O'Connell and Crews spoke wistfully in favor of having a merit retention system someday.[100] Moderate commissioners such as Reed and Turlington approved of the Chiles amendment providing for nonpartisan elections.[101] The more conservative commissioners, such as Stallings and Taylor, opined that the public would not forgo direct elections.

Stallings said the Chiles amendment was the most the voters would accept, predicting that merit selection and retention "hasn't got a snowball's chance" when it came up before the voters.[102] He agreed there was a risk that only a small percentage of voters would be sufficiently interested to vote in favor of merit retention, and that small group could swing the results based on "an overnight campaign." He said that the Florida Bar's urging of merit selection and retention was itself a political move and that "this business of saying you are removing the selection of judges from politics is just so much hogwash."[103]

Midway through the deliberations, Crews offered a compromise amendment that would allow trial-level circuit and county judges to be elected in nonpartisan elections but would preserve merit retention for appellate-level judges of the district and supreme courts. Stallings opposed it, claiming that what the amendment "says to the public is we will let you elect the horse's rear end [trial judges], but the Bar Association is going to elect his head [the appellate judges]." Mathews then asked whether they shouldn't "assure Judge Taylor that we don't consider him one particular end or the other."[104] Turlington objected that the dual system would be incomprehensible to the public given the inconsistent explanation why some judges should be selected and other elected.[105] Crews's compromise failed.[106]

The CRC voted to preserve the Judicial Committee's proposal of merit selection by providing for a judicial nominating commission to provide three candidates from which the governor would choose.[107] The constitution would not specify the composition of the judicial nominating commissions. The CRC also preserved the creation of a judicial qualifications commission (JQC) that would discipline errant or unhealthy judges. The JQC had just been created as a constitutional amendment a few weeks before the CRC met, in the November 1966 election. The CRC, however, did add that the JQC disciplinary procedure would be supplemental to the Senate's right to impeach a judge.[108]

The CRC voted to pass this compromise plan to the legislature. But, in a way, the CRC's proposal for the judicial branch represented a regression in court design. It continued a mandatory, not optional, magistrate's court for small claims and misdemeanor offenses.[109] County courts became optional in counties with populations greater than 100,000.[110] Thus, the proposed court system retained qualities that would keep it unnecessarily complicated and non-uniform.

Article VI: Suffrage and Elections

Voting Age

The proposed amendment regarding voting age, like the one concerning equal rights, generated an impassioned debate that demonstrated the impossibility of separating elevated constitutional principles from immediate politics. And, like equal rights, the issue of voting rights pitted Baggs against Stallings.

Baggs's opposition to the Vietnam War led him to be a crusader for the right of eighteen-year-olds to vote, a small change to section 2 in the suffrage article, but an issue that was gaining momentum around the nation.[111] Baggs noted that even in Georgia, which, he drily admitted, "at this season is not the Jeffersonian citadel," eighteen-year-olds had had the vote for many years.[112] He also made the point that eighteen-to-twenty-year-olds, while perhaps immature, were likely at least as informed as older voters because of the influence of television—"quite a confession for a Gutenberg type to make," Baggs admitted.[113] The CRC was split on the issue. Goodrich asked whether all eighteen-year-olds should have the right to vote, as only a small minority were actually serving in the military.[114] Stallings argued against lowering the voting age, pointing out that car insurance companies recognize that eighteen-year-olds lack judgment and hence require them to pay higher premiums.[115] Stallings also said he believed that the impetus for the eighteen-year-old vote came from Dade County and its gambling interests.[116]

Lawton Chiles, only thirty-six at the time, suggested that eighteen-to-twenty-year-olds might have a higher-than-average voter turnout if granted the vote, because of their political enthusiasm. Stallings disagreed, saying he believed youth were the "bread and circuses" crowd, wanting something for nothing.[117] In retrospect, it seems likely that the debate was not simply whether eighteen-to-twenty-year-olds should vote, but whether the eighteen-to-twenty-year-olds of 1966 should vote. They, after all, were the ones burning draft cards, protesting the war, and taking hallucinogenic drugs—at least that was who was making headlines. In the end, the CRC voted to lower the voting age to eighteen.[118]

Article VIII: Local Government

Local Government

Relatively few amendments to the draft were proposed regarding local government and how to fund it. Even though this area of the constitution demanded little time in the final weeks of proposed amendments, it was one of the most far-reaching changes to governance statewide. Most of the November and December discussions on these areas of the proposed constitution dealt with the definition of public purpose in the context of whether bonds could go toward funding private buy-ups of blighted areas in urban-renewal projects.

Home Rule

The home-rule provisions proposed for sections 2 and 3 in the local government article were the most far-reaching provisions; they would also be the provisions that caused organized groups to advocate for rejection of the revised constitution during the public campaign in the summer and fall of 1968. For example, a group called Women for Constitutional Government sent a telegram to Taylor during the convention urging the commission to remove the provision for home rule, which they described as "a socialistic, dictatorial, un-American form of government at [sic] has abolished the checks and balances of America."[119]

As discussed above, under the 1885 Constitution, counties and cities had only those powers given to them by the state. Generally speaking, cities had greater powers to enact laws and taxes within their geographical boundaries, and counties were less powerful subdivisions of the state over rural areas. Home rule would remove restrictions on cities and significantly increase the power of counties. Cities were therefore wary of the potential for county home rule to encroach on their traditional power. The political tug-of-war between counties and cities located within a county were fought out through the Florida Legislature, usually controlled by the elected local delegation of legislators from the affected area. Cities could politically control the less powerful counties in the legislature through local bills restricting a county's power.

In 1966, four localities had various forms of home rule: Dade County; Hillsborough County; Duval County and the City of Jacksonville; and Monroe County and the City of Key West.[120] Home rule was heavily blended with the consolidation of county and city governments into one body that governed the whole county area at that time.

There were two recurring points of conflict with county home rule in the CRC debates: first, the extent to which counties could create ordinances that were effective within a city, and second, how taxes were to be assessed between county areas and cities. Both issues were further complicated by the ability of a county or city to offer both traditional government services, such as policing, road construction, or creation of a hospital, and the ability to deliver so-called proprietary services that otherwise could be performed by a private company, such as running a power or water utility for profit.[121]

Provisions for home rule had always been part of the proposed constitution. The draft presently before the CRC provided an option for constitutional home rule for counties and cities. Counties could choose to become self-governing through a charter, or they could remain subject to the legislature's general direction as a non-charter government. Cities would become full-fledged self-governing bodies restricted only by general laws that applied to all cities. Because the members proposed no amendments during the debates that would substantially change the draft, the home-rule provisions were never in doubt, and were approved by the CRC.

Article XI: Amendments

Robert Ervin considered Article XI, which concerned future amendments to the constitution, as the most important change the CRC proposed for Florida's constitution.[122] Other CRC members and commentators agree. The core purpose of the additions to this article was to take sole control away from the legislature and place the power to amend the constitution in the hands of Florida voters. The debates over

Article XI, however, reflected the legislators' interest in maintaining control over changes to the constitution.

There were two new methods proposed for future constitutional revisions: a recurring Constitution Revision Commission and a provision by which voters could directly amend the constitution by initiative. The first method, the provision for a recurring CRC, was not found in any other state constitution. According to this provision, ten years after the adoption of the new constitution and every twenty years thereafter, a new CRC would convene to review the entire constitution and determine if it needed to be revised. The concept of such a commission was never challenged, though its composition was. The original proposal called for a thirty-seven-member CRC consisting of the attorney general, one Florida Supreme Court justice and five others appointed by the chief justice, eight appointed by the governor, six appointed by the Senate, six appointed by the House, five appointed by the Florida Bar president, and five appointed jointly by the cabinet. Other proposals included one in which the governor was forbidden to appoint lawyers and one in which each branch of the government chose twelve members.[123]

The debate concentrated on whether the Florida Bar president should have the power to appoint future CRC members. The bar was the only nongovernmental entity with appointments to the CRC, and some resented the privileged role it gave lawyers. One proposed amendment attempted to ensure lay representation by restricting the governor's appointments to non-attorneys.[124] Earle called this proposal "ridiculous" and suggested it would put the governor in shackles, although he also recognized that the governor-elect himself was watching the debate from the dais, and smiling.[125]

The legislature's attempts to retain control over the 1966 constitutional revision were laid bare during the debates. House Speaker Turlington proposed in his argument that either a select committee work out the composition or that the future CRC composition be left to the legislature to specify by general law. O'Neill objected to the latter method, suggesting that Turlington was trying to position himself so that he could tell the next legislature that the CRC agreed with letting it decide future CRC composition.[126] The Pork Choppers were gone, but the remaining legislators still knew how to hoard power. No legislature, not even a reformed one, was a guaranteed friend to constitutional reform. Ultimately, the CRC proposed a composition that gave each branch of government twelve appointments plus the attorney general's automatic membership; Turlington's suggested choices never became formal proposals and went nowhere.

The second new method the CRC proposed for future constitutional revision was the citizens' initiative. Ervin knew from his long experience interacting with legislators that the legislature was not always responsive to the people's interests, wants, or needs. He wanted the new constitution to have a method for citizens to amend their constitution without having to depend on the legislature.[127] The initiative provision was uncontroversial during the November–December debates and was approved by the commission.

On December 16, after signing copies of the group picture that Smith nagged them all day to sign, the convention adjourned. All but one of the commissioners went home. Hugh Taylor stayed in his office in the capitol; his next round of work as chief drafter was just beginning.[128]

8

Putting It Together, Part II

One Labor Ends, Another Begins: The House and Senate Debates

January 3, 1967, was a foggy, mild day for Florida's first Republican governor of the twentieth century to be inaugurated in Tallahassee. Claude Roy Kirk Jr. stood hatless in a business suit as his audience, the men in suits and the ladies in hats, raised their umbrellas against the drizzle. After his opening remarks, in which he promised "constructive action" and stated his intent to "mak[e] Florida number one," he startled his audience, stunned the legislators, and infuriated their leaders by calling the legislature into special session on January 9 to consider the proposed new constitution.[1] Never mind that legislators were howling that six days did not give them enough time to pause their day jobs, organize a legislative session, and find lodging in the capital. Never mind that the majority of legislators were novices who had never worked in a regular legislative session together. Never mind that the CRC had not even submitted the proposed constitution. The newly inaugurated governor wanted to demonstrate that he was a different brand of leader. The office of governor may have been weak, but its new occupant need not be weak with it: he was going to move the state's business.[2]

Perhaps oblivious to the chaos he had just caused, or perhaps in an attempt to escape it, Governor Kirk left on vacation immediately after the inaugural ball with Erika Matfeld, the lovely Brazilian who was his date at the ball and whom he soon married.[3]

Although the announcement of the special session seems to have surprised almost everybody, Smith later claimed he had urged Kirk, in a meeting that also included Don Reed, to call an early session.[4] Smith had warned the press about a possible special constitutional session, but it received only a minute mention in the *Tallahassee Democrat*. Smith had told an Associated Press reporter that he believed the legislature could not possibly complete the revision in a sixty-day session; a special session would be needed.[5] Smith also alerted at least one CRC member, Beth Johnson, in a thank-you letter dated December 30, that he had decided to ask the governor to call a special session. He just omitted stating when that session would be announced.

What appears certain is that the announcement did not surprise the chair or the vice-chair of the CRC. Tom Barkdull recalled that in December, after the commission's work was done, Smith had phoned him and told him to come up from his Miami home to West Palm Beach, where governor-elect Kirk lived. After the three men had gathered, Smith gave Barkdull a tough assignment: go to Tallahassee, get hold of the other two members of the Style and Drafting Committee (Taylor and Mathews), and tell them to come to Tallahassee to finish drafting the constitution. But don't tell them why, Smith said. Barkdull did as he was told. The committee found a few secretaries and finished drafting the document between Christmas and New Year's Day in an empty capitol.[6] All that remained was for the entire commission to come to Tallahassee to formally sign off on the draft.

The Final Draft Is Signed

On January 7, two days before the special session began, the commissioners had just one last slog to the capital to put ink to the final document. Only Stallings was not present to vote: he had taken violently ill with a gallbladder attack the previous night, after a dinner with Turlington, and "almost kicked the bucket."[7] The vote for the full proposed constitution was thirty-five to one. Only one member voted nay: Elmer Friday. Friday later remembered the day he cast his vote: "As I drove by myself from Fort Myers back to Tallahassee for the final meeting, at which we were to vote yea or nay, there was a most intriguing, difficult debate all the way—'yea' or 'nay.' I really decided before I got as far as Polk County [less than halfway] to vote 'no.'"[8] He so strongly opposed a provision that would have allowed county commissions to appoint constitutional local officers, such as sheriffs, without the involvement or approval of the electorate that he voted to reject the whole constitution. He recalled: "I will never forget the moment when I said 'no.' The look on Chesterfield's face as he looked over! He could not believe it."[9] Although when Kirk had announced the special session the draft was not even signed by its authors, by the time the session started the legislature's new constitution was waiting.

Viewed objectively, there was reason to believe the legislature could approve the new constitution speedily. The CRC version was high-quality work. This legislature had a big influx of new legislators who closely reflected the more populous urban areas of the state. The draft constitution favored urban areas through its provisions enabling counties and cities to have home rule; this would minimize the need for local bills. The proposed constitution made up for this reduction of legislative power by otherwise favoring the legislature with annual sessions and a legislative auditor.

However, politically savvy observers were not so sure of the success of the proposed constitution. An editorial in the *Gainesville Sun* on January 5 outlined the waiting snares. More than half the legislators were brand new and would be no match for the "vested interests," such as boosters for citrus, phosphate, and race tracks, who were lying in wait like the wolf for Red Riding Hood: "These people are prepared. . . . Their arguments are written, their amendments are drafted, their persuasive talents at the ready. They are flushed with success and infused with vigor and mellow with experience. For them, a green lawmaker is no match." And Kirk, not being an "experienced watchdog of the people's interest," would be in no position to help.[10]

In Kirk's proclamation calling the session, he stated he expected there to be a special election in April 1967 for the public to vote on the new constitution; at the subsequent 1967 regular session the legislature could "enact legislation" under the new constitution. Kirk returned from vacation in time to address the joint session of the legislature.

No one knew it at the time, but the legislature would meet in four sessions spanning eighteen months before it would offer the voters a new constitution. But the legislature's adoption of the constitution, though not speedy, would resist most attempts by special interests to corrupt it.

The January Extraordinary Session: A Lightning Bolt

At 9:30 a.m. on January 9, the legislature convened. Members both old and new had made hasty arrangements to be absent from work in their hometowns, had made the long drive or flight to Tallahassee, and had found a place to sleep in the capital city and a place to park near the capitol. The swarm of freshmen legislators waded through the flower-laden House and Senate chambers. The chambers were decked out as for a lavish funeral or wedding, as was the tradition on opening day for every session. When the legislators had finished finding their desks and locating the restrooms, they settled in.

In the Senate, Reubin Askew offered the opening prayer.[11] In the House, as the lawmakers found their seats, the new Speaker, Ralph Turlington, contemplated the situation. This was not the situation Turlington had hoped for when he had become Speaker. Instead of an experienced legislature stacked with people he knew he could depend on, he led a chamber in which a majority of the members were brand new. Also, his party, the Democratic one, was looking more vulnerable than it had in ninety years. Not only was the new governor a Republican, but so were many of the new representatives. As Turlington later recalled, "it looked like the world was going to wipe out all the Democrats."[12] For Turlington, facing the unexpected new makeup of the House was "a rather traumatic experience."[13] Nevertheless, he had appointed a twenty-five-member Select Committee on Constitution Revision, with himself as chair and James Sweeny and Donald Reed as vice-chairs. The committee had six former CRC members: Turlington, Reed, Frank Fee, Henry Land, Dick Pettigrew, and George Stallings.[14]

The first order of business that day in the House was an address by Chesterfield Smith. Smith began by exhorting the representatives that now, for the first time, they had the "clear legal authority" to rewrite the constitution, indicating that a constitutional amendment had recently allowed the wholesale revision that the CRC was now recommending.

He spared no words when he described the current constitution, describing it as "antiquated," "obsolete," and even "confusing," and the state's "dire" need for a new one. After concluding his address to the House, Smith crossed the length of the capitol building, walked down the long hall bisected by the central stairway to the opposite end of the building, and entered the Senate chamber to deliver a similar speech.

But as Smith addressed the Senate, alarming news came: the U.S. Supreme Court had that morning, for the third time, reversed the Southern District Court's opinion in *Swann v. Adams* and held Florida's reapportionment, and the legislature elected under it, unconstitutional.[15] The Court rejected both the apportionment plan and the failure of the State or the district court to provide reasons for the remaining variations in population of the proposed districts in the latest plan. The Court did not ask Florida's historically recalcitrant legislature to do the reapportioning. Instead, it simply reversed, leaving the question of how to accomplish the next reapportionment in the district court's hands.

However, the legislature did not give up immediately. The Senate proceeded to introduce a bill proposing that the new constitution be adopted in toto.[16] The *House Journal* tersely reported that at 2:45 that afternoon, Speaker Turlington and Senate President Verle Pope were in conference with the governor "regarding the situation produced by today's decision of the U.S. Supreme Court on Florida reapportionment."

The *Swann* opinion was a low-key affair in Washington, but was a perhaps unintentionally far-reaching opinion for state legislatures. As political scientist Robert Dixon Jr. has observed, "There is not the slightest indication in the Supreme Court's subsequent opinion that the Court realized invalidation of Florida's plan would also imply invalidation of post-*Reynolds* judicially approved plans in nearly half of the states."[17] And, in fact, the latest *Swann* decision seemed, surprisingly, to make no particular impact on the legislators who had just been told that they finally, definitively, legally, did not exist. Dick Pettigrew remembered the decision as simply as a good opportunity for the urban areas to gain power.[18] Sandy D'Alemberte did not recall that the news was particularly earth-shattering, but he dreaded the inevitable repeat election.[19] And Turlington returned from his meeting with Kirk and Pope to announce that he "felt the House should continue with its immediate task of constitutional revision."[20] Askew, however, remembered that "even a motion to adjourn wasn't in order—they just said, 'you're null and void. You no longer exist.'"[21]

For the first time, the Court plainly stated that arithmetic would be the touchstone for apportionment. Other factors, such as natural geography, political subdivision boundaries, and economic similarities or disparities, were irrelevant. The Court denied rehearing the same day it released its opinion. This was the death knell of any attempt to stall, any attempt to finesse.

Governor Kirk addressed the joint session that afternoon and made a provocative declaration: his proclamation to convene the special session, he claimed, had "triggered a legal move" to prevent the session, which in turn had caused the Supreme Court to issue the apportionment ruling the previous morning.[22] Kirk offered no specifics about what the "legal move" consisted of, and his extraordinary claim that his own proclamation could influence the U.S. Supreme Court went uncommented on.

By the next day, January 10, Kirk had expanded the scope of the extraordinary session to include apportionment. As a body that no longer legally existed, it was questionable whether the legislature could make decisions even regarding that. All remaining efforts went to reestablishing a state government. Because the Supreme Court opinion had put final reapportionment in the hands of the Florida federal district court, anyone wishing to propose an apportionment scheme had to present it to that court in writing in an amicus curiae brief. But before the free-for-all in which legislators proposed alternative plans, the House, with the Senate concurring, passed a resolution. It resolved first to defend the existing apportionment scheme and, failing that, to argue for yet another chance to devise a new scheme, arguing that under Florida law, a reapportionment by the court presented an "insurmountable legal impediment."[23] In other words, Florida's legislature still hadn't gotten the message: further reapportionment was out of its hands. It gave a practical reason for its stubbornness, in a we-know-ourselves-better-than-you-do resolution:

The natural barriers, the shape of the state, and the varying density of population are such that beginning at any point and carving out districts of exactly equal population would inevitably result in splitting counties, putting in the same district people lacking those affinities desirable in local government, and, many times, separated by great rivers, swamps or lakes and, sometimes, by traditional rivalries.[24]

Desirable affinities; traditional rivalries. The legislature's will to control its apportionment died hard, and so did its refusal to understand what the Supreme Court had told it. Despite the plain requirement of the *Swann* opinion that mathematical balance be achieved, individual legislators expended substantial energies proposing additional apportionment factors. The legislature also involved itself with the ongoing Southern District Court proceedings, rushing to get a new proposal to the court in time for a January 25 hearing in Miami.[25]

Other issues and emergencies intruded into the legislative chambers as well. A rural schoolhouse burned down, and the legislature, though still officially illegitimate, had to appropriate funds for a temporary school.[26] A fire burned three Apollo astronauts to death as they sat in their rocket on the launch pad at Cape Kennedy; the Senate passed a memorial resolution.[27] Journalists tried to take over the Senate chambers to protest being banned from secret "executive sessions."[28] The Senate President made a speech in which he described the journalists' behavior as like that of "schoolchildren," but defended the necessity of executive sessions.

But the main business was apportionment, and the need to find a way to become a legally constituted legislature meant the proposed constitution could not be considered in this special session. Then, less than a month after the *Swann* decision, on February 2, 1967, the Disney Company presented its legislative package to a select audience of politicians. With great fanfare, with Roy Disney, Governor Kirk (who arrived by limousine flying the Florida state flag), and nearly half the legislature in attendance at a large theater in Winter Park, the company presented its plan to change Central Florida forever. First, Disney executives softened up the crowd with a movie describing the project;

the movie was narrated by the iconic Walt Disney, who had died just weeks earlier. The vision of Walt mesmerized the politicians, as it was surely meant to do. When the lights came up, Roy Disney laid out the company's needs: bonding authority, highway interchanges, increased trademark protection, two new municipalities, and no less than an autonomous political district.[29] This was a very large bite for the legislature to chew.

Members of the legislature at that time, even those who had been on the CRC, did not remember there being any controversy about the abrupt change in direction.[30] In January the legislature had been called to Tallahassee to work on the proposed new constitution. That same day, they had been cast into legal and political limbo, told they didn't exist. Before new elections could be held, they were being told by the corporate and tourism equivalent of Cinderella herself that their new priority was passing whatever legislation Walt Disney's shade would request. Out went the new constitution. In came the Disney legislation. The legislature was not in session, but it appeared to have new work cut out for it once it could reconvene as a legitimate body.[31]

Meanwhile, in Miami . . .

On January 11, in Miami, the Southern District Court held a pretrial conference with the litigants, their lawyers, members of the media, and enough other people to pack the courtroom. The U.S. Supreme Court decision had returned the case to the district court to determine if any reason existed to permit population variances among districts in the Senate and House. The Court had made clear, however, that population equality among districts was the paramount consideration.

Several creative suggestions entered the melee. Defendant and Secretary of State Tom Adams jumped on fractional voting, a method that would allow a voter to vote for more than one candidate by dividing his or her vote into fractions; D'Alemberte filed a plan along similar lines.[32] Several members of the legislature filed amicus briefs advocating particular plans. Bob Graham advocated a smaller legislature. Another amicus brief suggested a unicameral legislature, arguing that if both houses were required to follow the one-person, one-vote standard, there was no reason to have two houses. The supervisor of elections for Dade County, Claude Brown, found racial discrimination would necessarily result if the court adopted multi-member, at-large districts. Another amicus brief proposed using 1965 population figures instead of the 1960 census figures in calculating district populations, since this move would have reflected recent growth in Central and South Florida.

In its response, the legislature presented affidavits from legislators explaining how the current apportionment had been reached. Turlington detailed in a sixteen-page affidavit the process he followed and the problems certain apportionment decisions entailed. Askew's six-page affidavit detailed why the legislature's bill was, if not perfect, at least better than any alternatives that "the computer at the Florida State University" had produced.[33] The named plaintiff, Swann, filed a joint response with one of the defendants, the supervisor of elections for Dade County, urging the court to find the present apportionment unconstitutional.

Attorney General Earl Faircloth was in a fix. Any attorney representing a large group of clients simultaneously in a single lawsuit would recognize the dilemma he confronted. He had to represent the legislature—which was now illegally constituted—in yet another attempt to come up with a plan that would satisfy the U.S. Supreme Court. The best procedure in such a situation is to listen to the well-meaning suggestions of all the clients, choose the best suggestions, apply one's own expertise, and then go to court. And, even though he had personally advocated reapportionment throughout his career, Faircloth went to court to defend his clients.

Faircloth had worked as a private attorney in Miami with U.S. senator Claude Pepper, and had organized a citizens' committee for reapportionment in 1959. Faircloth was elected to the Florida House in 1962 and served one two-year term; he was elected attorney general in 1964, defeating the incumbent, Jimmy Kynes, even though his friend Emerson Allsworth later described him as "a great politician but an average lawyer."[34] Now, as state attorney general, Faircloth was forced to advocate against further reapportionment. His response to the court order was tepid: he stated in bland language that the current apportionment scheme was fine, although he conceded that the scheme had failed to achieve arithmetical equality.

On February 8, in a packed courtroom, Judge Warren Leroy Jones, an appellate judge sitting as part of the Southern District Court three-judge panel, announced the court's decision: it adopted Manning Dauer's friend-of-the-court reapportionment plan. Dauer's plan included a detailed breakdown for districts that resulted in population variances that were smaller than those in other plans. He did this by grouping counties into districts, but he did not follow federal congressional districts. The court ordered new elections immediately.

After Judge Jones finished reading the full text of the court's order, he gazed around the courtroom at all those who had argued on all sides of this issue for five years. He asked the crowd: "Is there anything else that needs to be said?" After a brief silence, the courtroom erupted in laughter.[35]

Reactions around the state and nation varied. Governor Kirk proclaimed that the judges had usurped Florida's sovereignty.[36] Former governor Collins told a reporter for the *Palm Beach Post* that this could have been expected to happen because the state had failed to take care of its own business in the mid-1950s.[37] Some legislators disliked the Dauer plan; John McCarty called it a "monstrosity."[38] Malcolm B. Johnson's column in the *Tallahassee Democrat* protested the lack of democracy inherent in the decision:

> Came the mail, it seems, and Judges Dyer, McRae and Jones seized the Dauer plan, thanked him in Latin as a "friend of the court" (an amicus curia) and thereupon promulgated the Dauer, Dyer, McRae and Jones apportionment. . . .
>
> There are a thousand men in Florida who could have drawn as good a plan, if they had been amicus enough to the curia. But the point is that here we have a Legislature made up according to the view of one man, elected by nobody, representing nobody, responsible to nobody except to a few judges elected by nobody and responsible to nobody for their judgment.[39]

But others were sanguine. "The GOP will come back in an even stronger position," said Senate Minority Leader Bill Young of Pinellas Park.

"Reapportionment always helps Republican chances."[40] Faircloth expressed relief that the matter was finally over.[41]

On February 9, Judge Bill McRae, who had chaired Governor Collins's Special Constitution Advisory Committee before becoming a federal judge, wrote a letter on court stationery to "Dear Manning," enclosing Dauer's plan, a copy of the court's order, and a copy of the in-court statement announcing the court's decision. The letter informed Dauer that the judges had examined all the plans submitted, "experimented on our own with variations," and arrived at the unanimous conclusion that Dauer's plan was "the most acceptable and practical plan that could be devised."[42]

The March 1967 Elections

In March 1967, for the first time in thirty years, Charley Johns wasn't running for election. He would have had to try to regain his Senate seat. Because of the new apportionment, his old district had been absorbed into a district that also included the much larger and much more liberal Alachua County.

This election saw even more Republicans come to the legislature, although the changes it brought were not as far-ranging as those brought in the November 1966 election. That election had brought many new faces to Tallahassee: thirty of the winning candidates in the Senate had been freshmen, of a total of forty-eight members. By contrast, the March 1967 election had only eleven more new senators.[43] It did continue the trend of kicking out the old and bringing in the new, however. New legislator Bob Graham, who had been elected to the House in the November 1966 election and attended just one organizing meeting, returned after the March 1967 election and found himself chair of a subcommittee by virtue of being the only remaining Democrat on it.[44]

No one could deny that the elections of the mid-1960s, especially the two most recent ones, had put a new and very different face on Florida's legislature. In contrast to the 1963 legislature, the last in which the Pork Choppers held firm control, the new crop had less than half as many of ranchers and farmers, more attorneys, 50 percent more real estate workers, and nearly 50 percent more insurance and banking professionals. It had barely half as many hunters and fishermen, and more than twice the number of tennis, golf, and handball enthusiasts. The new legislature even included a few surfers. The new legislators still spent time outside, but in ways that did not directly extract resources from Florida's soil.[45] The new legislators, of course, reflected the new urban distribution of Florida's population.

How would this new group of lawmakers behave once they took office? The April 1967 regular session, which began on April 4, offered some hints. For one, the importance of constitution revision had slid to third place in the view of House Speaker Turlington. In his opening address, Turlington told the legislators that more than three thousand separate pieces of legislation had been proposed, and declared the three most pressing problems to be, in order, education, property taxation, and constitution revision.[46] Governor Kirk, however, urged the legislators in his opening speech to "unshackle Florida from the dead past" by taking up the constitution as its first priority.[47] In the other chamber, Senate President Pope mentioned constitution revision, but only as one item in his opening speech. Speaking on behalf of his colleagues who had toiled fifteen years for a new constitution, he said that he would like to see a new one passed by voters by November of the following year. He also mentioned he would like to see a lieutenant governor, an interesting preference from the man who would otherwise be next in line if the governor died.[48] Pope concluded by admitting, unlike his peer Turlington, that his chamber was filled with "inexperienced men" but that their inexperience could be replaced with "great determination."[49]

As a sign of the times, bills proposed at the start of the session included those that would ban LSD, advocate for voluntary school prayer, and fund the construction of fallout shelters. Another declared a "Steve Spurrier Day" honoring the University of Florida's Heisman Award–winning quarterback. Buried among the bill proposals was one revising the state constitution; as all bills were, it was assigned to committees in both the House and Senate.[50] Disney's three goliath bills were introduced in the House on April 18. Eight days later all three were passed unanimously; one week after that, the Senate passed them. Only one senator voted nay, and on only one bill: Democrat Tom Spencer of Miami was the lone no vote on the bill creating the shockingly independent Reedy Creek Improvement District, which allowed Disney to create its own infrastructure with essentially no oversight. Dick Pettigrew recalled, and the record supports, that taking up and passing the Disney legislation was not controversial.[51] The regular session dragged on and on, extended until July 14; the bill proposing the new constitution died in committees in both the House and the Senate, the victim of a budget feud.[52]

The legislature returned ten days later for a one-week extraordinary session, but constitution revision was not among the urgent issues: the session was called for appropriations for junior colleges and to consider a crime bill. Twice, Representative George Stallings and others tried to put constitution revision bills forward, but because revision was outside the subject matter of the extraordinary session, both times they were stopped.[53] No matter: on July 26, Governor Kirk had called a session to begin on July 31 for the legislature to finally consider constitution revision.

The July 31 Special Session

Four days before the special session on constitution revision was to begin, Kirk's legislative aide, Wade Hopping, sent a memorandum to the legislature recommending that it "embrac[e] this constitution in toto."[54] However, the memorandum went on to recommend several changes. One predictable one claimed that although the governor did not take a stand either way, the legislature should consider limiting the number of terms the cabinet members could serve, or reducing the number of elected cabinet members, "or both."[55] Kirk strongly endorsed home rule, explicitly took no position on voting age, and agreed with the provision calling for citizens to have the power to initiate constitutional amendments.[56]

The special session began at noon on July 31. Each chamber created a Constitution Revision Committee to work on the details of the proposed constitution. Turlington named Murray Dubbin, a Democrat from Miami, chair of the sixteen-member House committee; it also included former CRC members Henry Land, Dick Pettigrew, Don Reed, and George Stallings. Pope appointed Jack Mathews as chair of the

Senate committee; that committee was also loaded with former CRC members, including Bill Young, Reubin Askew, Lawton Chiles, Elmer Friday, and George Hollahan.

Two full constitutions were proposed in the Senate. Neither was identical to the proposed constitution the CRC had signed in January; legislative committees had been developing alternative provisions since then. One, SJR 1-XXX(67), contained provisions that represented a greater break from the old constitution than the other, SJR 2-XXX (67), did. SJR 1-XXX (67), for example, prohibited sovereign immunity, provided for annual sessions of the legislature, and allowed eighteen-to-twenty-year-old citizens to vote. It also strengthened the governor, providing for reelection and allowing the governor to reorganize the executive branch. Neither proposal provided for a lieutenant governor, though SJR 1-XXX changed the succession to the Secretary of State instead of the President of the Senate, as the 1885 Constitution and SJR 2-XXX provided. Both bills proposing constitutions were sponsored by the Senate Constitution Revision Committee. While SJR 1-XXX represented greater change, only SJR 2-XXX had a companion bill in the House (HJR 3-XXX [67]).

In the afternoon, four speakers from the CRC addressed the joint houses.[57] First, though, Justice Caldwell spoke. He caustically commented on the "former" rule of law in the U.S. government. Although his ostensible theme was states' rights, a listener alert to the issues of the day would recognize his anger at having been told by the federal courts to integrate schools and the Florida Bar and to put an end to poll taxes: "[States] no longer have the power to say who can . . . practice law in the State courts; . . . to control education within their boundaries . . . nor to control State elections."[58] Caldwell cautioned the legislature not to experiment with the constitution and not to change it merely for change's sake.[59] Sandy D'Alemberte later recalled that the gist of Caldwell's speech was that he hoped the legislature would make, at most, a few tweaks.[60]

Chesterfield Smith was the next to speak. Smith was indignant. After all the long, difficult, and heartfelt work of his team, here was one of the state's highest-ranking judges undermining his mission. Rather than step up to the dais, Smith stood at the recording clerk's desk, where he could address the legislators at eye level.[61] Although Smith reprised much of the speech he had given on January 9 at the aborted special session, he added some fire. He provided examples of "garbage" language in the old constitution and drew attention to parts of the 1885 Constitution that the U.S. Supreme Court had found unconstitutional, such as the prohibitions against segregated schools and interracial marriage.[62] His message was clear: Anyone who didn't believe that Florida needed a new constitution didn't understand much about Florida or about its constitution.

Never afraid to let his position be known, Smith wasn't about to meekly stick to his prepared remarks. The troops needed to be reminded of their duty—plus, so many faces were different from the ones present at the January 9 special session. He explained the peculiarities of the 1885 Constitution, with its weak legislature and weaker executive, as a reaction to the departed post–Civil War carpetbaggers. As he liked to say, the people in Reconstruction government "were not the best people then in our state, nor were they the best people in the States from which they had recently come."[63]

Smith suggested that the most difficult aspect of drafting the constitution would be facing the reality "that someone else besides you has intelligence."[64] But most important, he told the legislators, was keeping the new constitution flexible enough that future voters could mold it: in 1967, a politically and socially tumultuous year all over the United States, one of the top members of Florida's "establishment" had just said the most important thing was to "give to the people forevermore the power" over their own constitution.[65]

Bill Baggs was the next man to address the legislators. "You have just been introduced to the bold, if not brutal, Chesterfield Smith," he began, "and you should now realize why the Constitutional Revision Commission completed its draft of the proposed revised constitution and submitted it to you—we were afraid not to."[66] Baggs asked the legislators to keep the vote for eighteen-year-olds, and saved a few sardonic remarks for "Chesterfield Smith's pet idea that we should appoint the Cabinet."[67]

Richard Earle then spoke. He pointed out that although the chambers had plenty of experienced lawmakers, there is no such thing as

an experienced constitution revisionist: "If you do the job expected of
you . . . this will be your sole experience in this field."[68] The fourth CRC
member to speak was Tom Sebring. He pointed out that the proposed
constitution contained six or seven wholly new provisions.[69] They were
amendment by public citizens' initiative; a voting age of eighteen; elimination of sovereign immunity; selection of judges on a nonpartisan
basis; authority to apply different rates of taxation on different kinds
of property, such as intangibles; and legislative apportionment by the
Florida Supreme Court if the legislature should fail to apportion.[70] Curiously, Sebring neglected to mention home rule, which was entirely
new as a general provision, although it was already in place in Miami
and Dade County.

The second day of the session began similarly. In the House, Speaker
Pro Tempore James Walker urged the legislators to put aside partisan
politics (mentioning the recent four months of partisan "frustration
and failure"); to set aside selfish interest; to participate actively; to try
to know what the electorate wanted in the constitution; and to keep in
mind that the constitution would last beyond their lifetimes.

The next order of business in the House was the Constitution Revision Committee's proposal of HJR 3-XXX(67) for ratification by the
voters. That bill was a proposed constitution, which was the same as
SJR 2-XXX (67), described above. But the House did not act further as a
whole right away; although House Revision Committee members Robert Mann, Ray Osborne, and Stallings organized debates, and Dick Pettigrew managed an end run around the CRC to get a provision for a lieutenant governor inserted into the House proposal,[71] the bill languished
without a vote. The House Style and Drafting Subcommittee's chair,
Louis Wolfson, a Democrat from Miami, did not yet have an agreed-
upon product. Instead, a concurrent resolution asked the governor to
call another special session to continue the work on the constitution
the week after the current special session was to expire. The resolution
passed, although some nay-voters grumbled that the legislators were
fatigued from spending so many months in session.[72]

The Senate, however, remained busy, meeting often as a committee of the whole to discuss and tweak the proposed constitution. It
rehashed many of the same issues the CRC had already talked to death,

such as whether to have a lieutenant governor, whether to have the cabinet appointive rather than elective, and whether to lower the voting age to eighteen. It also found time to commemorate the entertainer Jackie Gleason and to comment on the governor's many appointments and removals of public officials.[73] But like the House, the Senate ended the session without an agreed-upon document.

One reason that the constitution work may have been delayed was the large amount of time that would be required when so many people turned their attention to such a radically changed document. More than 150 lawmakers examined the proposed documents, and many of them found issues to chew on and worry about. An example is a memo from Senator Lee Weissenborn to Senator Elmer Friday fretting about language in the Declaration of Rights that mentioned "corruption of blood" and "forfeiture of estate for treason." This obsolete language would be the subject of several memos to and from senators leading up to the August 21 session.[74]

Many written requests came to legislators recommending changes to the draft constitution. But when any came to Hugh Taylor, who was assisting the Senate in its consideration of the revised constitution, he had an answer ready: he had nothing to do with the content of the constitution, his job was only in drafting it, and it was improper for him to "attempt to influence the Legislature on questions of policy."[75] Murray Dubbin recalled that Taylor would often insist he was a "mere amanuensis."[76]

August 21, 1967: The Stillborn Session

The House began the special session on August 21 by withdrawing the prior proposed joint resolutions on the constitution and putting forward another, HJR 6-XXXX(67).[77] Throughout the session, for the next nine days, the resolution was neither debated nor touched by the House as a whole. Although the revision committee worked on the constitution revision bill, the House convened and adjourned each day with no recorded evidence of discussion about the constitution.

Five days into the session, however, frustration about the lack of progress became apparent. Representatives Granville Crabtree of Sarasota and Thomas Gallen of Bradenton proposed a joint resolution that a full constitutional convention be called, apparently conceding that the legislature was unable to produce a new constitution. Their resolution was referred to committee and died there.[78] In the meantime, three CRC members were hired as attorneys to assist the legislature in considering constitution revision: John Crews to assist the House, Hugh Taylor to assist the Senate at Jack Mathews's request (Taylor would have done this without pay, as circuit judges were and are forbidden to accept pay outside of their judicial salary), and Bill O'Neill to act as liaison between the two houses.[79]

Only a little House activity occurred during the session. On the second day the House passed a resolution commending the West Tampa Little League All-Stars for winning the Southern Regional Little League title.[80] On the seventh day it successfully passed a concurrent resolution commending the Tallahassee recreational department: "WHEREAS, members of the legislature, bone-weary and mind-fagged from months of continuous session, have found solace and relaxation in a recent round of softball games. . . ."[81] On August 30 both houses passed resolutions expressing sympathy for the death of Robert High, also referred to in the resolutions as "The Little Redhead."[82]

In contrast to the House, debate on the constitution was continuous in the Senate. The Senate began by whittling the proposed version down to two drafts, SJR 1-4X(67) and SJR 2-4X(67).[83] On August 21, the first day of the session, the Senate began debate on amendments to SJR 2-4X(67). The first proposed amendment concerned school funding through statewide ad valorem taxes.[84] The 1885 Constitution prohibited statewide ad valorem taxes; they were exclusively reserved for local governments and funded schools. This meant that schools were funded primarily (but not exclusively) by property owners. The Senate's proposed amendment would keep the school-funding burden on property owners but would allow school funding to be more evenly distributed throughout the state. Thus, poorer counties with less-developed, less-valuable land and businesses could receive a cross-subsidization from more-developed counties. Interestingly, the amendment was passed by a group of senators evenly divided between urban and rural districts. The Senate debated replacing the local-only ad valorem tax provision with either a mandatory .5 percent statewide ad valorem tax collection each year for schools on all assessed property, a 1 percent mandatory tax, or no ad valorem taxes for schools.[85] The Senate at first rejected all options; two senators, Lee Weissenborn of Miami Lakes and Robert Elrod of Windermere, submitted explanations saying the proposals seemed to place a greater burden on the state without identifying an additional source of state funding.[86] Then, the Senate reconsidered its vote and adopted an amendment providing for up to .5 percent statewide ad valorem tax on non-exempt property.[87] This proposal would clearly face an uphill climb if it were to be reconciled with the House version, which maintained the 1885 local-only school-funding provision.

The next day the Senate dealt with the sacred cows of Florida's tax structure. It debated and rejected proposed amendments that would permit taxation of estates and inheritance, on the one hand, or of income, on the other.[88] Either form of taxation would have been an earth-shattering change in tax policy; Florida had always promoted itself as a haven from estate taxation for retirees, businesses, and entrepreneurs. It is significant that such changes were proposed and debated by a newly liberal and liberated chamber straining against moldy precedent.

Finally, the time allotted for the extraordinary session was over. In his closing remarks, Speaker Turlington noted that issues remained to be resolved between the House and Senate versions of a proposed constitution. He did not believe that a subsequent session could dispose of the differences within two days, as some had suggested; his estimate was that the legislature would need a week. The session ended with the opinion of Murray Dubbin, who estimated that four weeks would be required to resolve the "fifty or sixty" unresolved positions between the House and Senate.[89]

In the Senate, President Pope began the final day by appointing an Interim Constitutional Revision Steering Committee to keep working on the constitution until it might be taken up again in a legislative session. The committee was composed of Reubin Askew, Lawton Chiles, Emory "Red" Cross, Louis De La Parte, Elmer Friday, George Hollahan,

Mallory Horne, Jack Mathews, Joseph McClain, Bob Shevin, Tom Slade, Tom Spencer, William Stockton, and Bill Young.[90] In midafternoon the final gavel fell: another special constitution revision session had failed.

The legislature met again for a two-week special session in late January and early February 1968, but its purpose was education, a session the public had been demanding in letters to legislators and letters to editors since the previous year.[91] Once again, the many needs of a growing state kept the legislature busy, but not with revising its constitution. That session ran an extra week; much was accomplished on education, but no bill proposing a new constitution was even raised on the floor.

A Rocket into the Future: June–July 1968

By the late spring of 1968, political pressure was building for legislators to act on constitution revision. After all, every House member had to begin preparing for reelection that fall. The public had heard about a constitution in the making, but so far the legislature had offered nothing. Behind the scenes, in early June, Governor Kirk had called several legislative leaders to Palm Beach to persuade them to pass the new constitution. As Murray Dubbin told the story, the group had drinks and dinner at Kirk's Palm Beach home, "Duck's Nest," and the nearby yacht of a Kirk friend.[92] At one point during the evening, Dubbin and Kirk met in a narrow hallway, the men filling the small space. According to Dubbin, Kirk asked him, "Do you know what they're saying in Europe? 'What does Dubbin have against Claude Kirk?'" For a moment, Dubbin said, he feared the two would "tangle," but then two Florida Highway Patrol officers quietly appeared at Kirk's elbows and led him away. Dubbin recalled the encounter as collegial. Kirk used the evening to persuade the group to redouble its efforts to lead the legislature to agree on a new constitution.[93]

Substantively, an Interim Constitution Revision Steering Committee led by Jack Mathews in the Senate and Murray Dubbin in the House worked during June to coordinate the versions each house had put forth and try to come up with one version that reconciled the differences. The men agreed that the nineteen-year-old vote, local government home rule, and reorganizing the judicial branch were likely to be sticking points.[94]

Governor Kirk had planned to announce a special session in early June, but the assassination of Robert F. Kennedy on June 6 caused him to delay the announcement.[95] Finally, by proclamation dated June 11, Kirk called a special session to begin on June 24, giving the legislators time to prepare to leave their lives for Tallahassee.[96]

On the first day of the session, four joint resolutions were offered in the House. The first was a bill proposing the basic constitution minus the articles on the judiciary, elections, and local government. Each of the other three joint resolutions dealt with one of the omitted articles. Removing the three contentious articles from the main body of the constitution for voting was Dick Pettigrew's idea, and it worked.[97] The House Constitution Revision Committee recommended approval of all four joint resolutions the same day.

The Senate passed a slightly different package that contained five joint resolutions. Four mirrored the four House resolutions; the fifth was the complete, unredacted constitution, just in case the voting public might have the appetite to approve an integrated document drafted to be a complete whole. It is easy to deduce that this fifth resolution was encouraged by Senate consultant Hugh Taylor, who knew better than anyone else how the constitution was drafted to fit together as a functioning whole. However, the next day the Senate Committee on Rules and Calendar recommended only the redacted basic constitution and the sections on elections and local government.[98] It did not recommend the judicial article, and the joint resolution for a complete constitution was abandoned altogether.

For the next several days, legislators from both chambers attempted spurious amendments for political posturing, pettifogging amendments to change minor grammatical or style issues, and substantive amendments that moved the two chambers farther apart than they had been before the session. For example, the Senate wanted to change the voting age to eighteen while the House refused to change it from twenty-one; both sides abandoned the nineteen-year-old voting age compromise they had agreed on the previous year.[99] House members wanted to extend the terms of representatives from two to four years, a move the Senate vigorously opposed.[100] The acrimony surrounding some of the contested issues was so unsettling that it rattled loose even former CRC members. For example, George Stallings, who had served on the CRC, now opposed the proposed revised constitution. Stallings protested the taxation aspects of the proposed constitution, stating that they "reek[ed] with ulterior motives to protect the special interests and penalize the majority."[101]

The House celebrated its approval of a version of the constitution on June 28, when Dubbin led the House through a section-by-section approval of the entire proposed constitution. When his chamber had voted aye to the whole set of documents, they gave him a standing ovation.[102] At the close of the sixth day of the session, July 1, the two chambers again attempted to resolve the remaining differences. On July 3, both chambers, exhausted, collapsed into agreement over the chambers' jointly appointed conference committee's recommendations with the saving rationale that it would be selfish to withhold a proposal from the voters. The article on the judiciary was abandoned, even though almost everyone who had been involved in Florida's court system acknowledged the system was a confusing mess.

The redacted basic document passed both chambers (albeit not nearly unanimously) on the closing day, as did the articles on elections and local government. That afternoon, Senator Askew again proposed a joint Senate resolution for the judiciary article, and it passed by the necessary three-fifths margin. However, Askew's proposal seems to have echoed in an empty hall: there is no recorded evidence that it was ever transmitted to the House before the special session adjourned at 4:00 p.m. on July 3. Dubbin, whom the *Miami Herald* called a "father of this Constitution," may have had the most apt description of the new constitution when he told a reporter, "I think we've launched a rocket into the future."[103]

In the final hour of the special session, Chesterfield Smith returned to the House and spoke briefly.[104] His words were not recorded, but one can imagine the relief he must have felt on seeing his new constitution, though altered, spring closer to being. And the agreement on the new constitution was reached in time for the newspapers to carry the news on July 4.[105] All that was left was to persuade the voters of Florida to approve the new constitution come November.

9

A New Constitution

Public Ratification

The legislators had divided the proposed constitution into three parts for the voters out of fear that controversial provisions, such as home rule and lowered voting age, might sink the whole constitutional ship at the polls. By dividing it, the legislators forced the voters to pay attention to the several separate parts and, by voting on each, signify that they were voting on a part of the constitution that they had actually read and understood. Only Article V, which dealt with the judicial branch of the government, was not submitted to the public.

The public would have four months to learn about the proposed new constitution and vote on whether to accept it. Chesterfield Smith asked all the CRC members to meet in Tallahassee (at their own expense) for one day. At that meeting, which was held at the Governor's Mansion, the group passed a resolution forming a citizens group to acquaint the public with the proposed constitution; the group would be called the ABC Committee (as in "A Better Constitution"), and John McCarty would chair it, although Smith appears to have retained at least some control over it.[1] The League of Women Voters also mobilized in support of the new constitution, as did other citizen groups.[2] Although Governor Kirk supported the new constitution, he kept his polarizing profile low. Later, he quipped that the best thing he did for the constitution was to point out that Edward Ball, who was widely disliked, opposed it.[3]

In the days and weeks leading up to the November vote, newspapers and magazines around the state carried analyses and opinion pieces. The business magazine *Florida Trend*, for example, featured a story in

A NEW

Constitution

RESPONSIVE TO THE NEEDS
OF THE PEOPLE

VOTE IN
the voice of the people

a more efficient government to meet the needs
of a space age society

VOTE OUT
outdated concepts of government

Vote Yes on November 5

Figure 11. The Florida League of Women Voters consistently supported constitution revision. This 1968 pamphlet urges Floridians to vote yes on the proposed revision. Photo courtesy of Beth Johnson Papers, 1957–70, Florida State Archives.

its November issue analyzing how the proposed constitution would affect business. It concluded that the constitution would change business interests very little, except for the fact that it was shorter and more readable and would make for more efficiency in both state and local government, "something that should be welcomed by businessmen and consumers alike."[4] The article also noted that, as both liberals and conservatives were complaining about the proposed constitution, that must mean the legislature had "done a good job" crafting it.[5]

The article did note that the millage ceiling of 10 mills each for counties, cities, and school districts would create a gap for financing local projects, which might force the state to find a way to fill that gap. Under the proposed scheme, the only other option for financing was the state sales tax. The article also pointed out that the homestead exemption (then $5,000) for homeowners would shift some ad valorem tax burden to businesses and that the failure of Florida's revenue bonds to pledge the state's full faith and credit would cost added interest payments because of higher interest rates.

Opposition came from unexpected quarters. Three University of Florida political science professors—Manning Dauer, W. Clement Donovan, and Gladys Kammerer—published a pamphlet titled *Should Florida Adopt the Proposed 1968 Constitution?* through the university's Public Administration Clearing House. They recommended rejecting the proposed constitution.[6] The pamphlet was surprising, partly because Dauer and Donovan had been paid consultants to the CRC but also because some of the group's major criticisms were wrong. Dauer wrote, in a letter to Chesterfield Smith about the pamphlet and the ABC Committee's proposed response to it, that although no one could have expected a perfect document, "there are some gosh awful major items in this one."[7]

Kammerer wrote separately from the other two authors, and she strongly urged rejection of the proposed constitution.[8] She asserted, incorrectly, that home rule was omitted from the constitution and that local legislative bills were still permitted unchecked; she comprehensively criticized the taxing and bonding provisions. She was not alone in her criticism of the taxing and bonding; as noted above, *Florida Trend* also pointed out the shortcomings of those portions of the proposed constitution.[9] Dauer managed an awkward disassociation from the pamphlet, tepidly defending some conclusions while conceding that its assertions regarding home rule were overstated. Dauer was caught between avoiding public criticism of Kammerer and attempting to maintain his recently enhanced national reputation. His straddle accomplished neither goal. The ABC Committee eventually released a public announcement that pointedly but diplomatically challenged the professors' conclusions.

Another unexpected leader in the opposition was George Stallings, who organized a statewide group to oppose ratification of the constitution and wrote a memo to all "Local Public Officials" in which he urged them to join the opposition and promised to keep names of interested people confidential, if desired.[10] In a statement to the press during the months leading up to the popular vote, Stallings called the proposed new constitution little more than a "half-baked revision" of the 1885 Constitution.[11] Another pamphlet in opposition was circulated by a group calling itself the Committee for Integrity. The pamphlet carried a Jacksonville address, mentioned no names of its backers, and urged conservative voters to reject the constitution, pointing out—accurately—that it had been drafted by "the most 'liberal' Legislature in the history of Florida."[12]

The November 1968 Election Results

In the election, 55 percent of voters approved the new constitution. That 55 percent, however, clustered within just sixteen of the sixty-seven counties. The other fifty-one counties voted against the revision. Interestingly, every county voted consistently for each of the three amendments; that is, every county approving the basic revision document also approved the home-rule and suffrage revisions. The percentage voting pro or con for each revision was also steady within each county. None of the three amendments was particularly favored or disfavored. The legislature's concern that the home-rule revision or the suffrage revision could be poisonous to overall adoption was either a prescient strategy or a needless worry: it was prescient if untying the amendments forced voters who were predisposed to constitution revision to also vote for the two trailing amendments to create a unified constitutional structure. It was needless worry if voters had made up their minds that they either supported or opposed a new constitution and would not scrutinize the details of the separate parts of it.

Although most of the counties that voted to reject the new constitution were rural, three populous counties—Orange, Escambia, and Sarasota—also voted to reject the amendments. Orange County, led perhaps by an editorial in the *Orlando Sentinel* urging rejection, voted overwhelmingly against all parts of the new constitution. This is somewhat puzzling, as the home-rule provisions presumably would have aided the Disney Company landholdings, which were mostly in Orange County. Escambia County, still a bastion of old Florida, rejected the amendments despite the labors of its senator, Reubin Askew. It is unclear why Sarasota County voted to reject the new constitution, but it too has historically been a conservative area.

The sixteen counties voting in favor ran up the east coast from Monroe, in the Keys, through Dade and Broward straight north to Volusia, home of Daytona Beach, then skipped one rural coastal county, Flagler, and proceeded with approval through St. Johns and Duval in the northeast and Clay and Alachua just inland. No county west of Alachua voted in favor of revision, including Leon, home of Tallahassee and several of the CRC members. No county that was not on the peninsula voted for constitution reform. Tellingly, only four counties north of the traditional Pork Chop Gang line voted approval: St. Johns, Duval, Clay, and Alachua. The fault line was very clear, as was the implication for the legislature: under the new constitution, legislators from small counties lost their power to vote on local bills controlling the populous counties. Populous counties would now move to home rule.

Supporters of the new constitution said its passage was the birth of a new Florida. But as Chesterfield Smith pointed out, each preceding Florida constitution was the birth of the new Florida of its time, and "a modern Florida is what is happening now."[13]

The 1968 election results revealed an unsettled, if not divided, populace. The voters brought in the new constitution, but cleft along east-west and north-south lines. And though the November 1968 election reestablished Democratic Party control of both chambers of the legislature, it brought in the first Republican senator from Florida since Reconstruction, Edward Gurney, to fill the seat that George Smathers had finally vacated in the U.S. Senate. Gurney defeated former governor LeRoy Collins, revered by many for his attempts to push for reapportionment, racial moderation, and a new constitution during his six years in office. The Florida that had benefited from his reforms—that is, the Florida that voted in 1968—now defeated him. Many have surmised that Florida's steep growth curve resulted in a voting population that did not live in Florida during the Collins years, and therefore did not remember his leadership during the difficult years of racial unrest. Whatever the reason, Florida rejected one of its most distinguished servants for the U.S. Senate in 1968.

Epilogue

Why was Florida able to adopt a new constitution now, when decades of earlier efforts had failed? Looking back on the CRC's work, Bob Ervin, a ninety-year Florida resident, may have nailed it: "Florida was changing, the nation had changed, attitudes had changed, old customs and mores were gone or were changing. Everything from attitudes about racial separation, about education, about the economy, of what goals were and what we would achieve . . . was changing. And so . . . the work of the . . . commission was a result of the accumulation of these many, many changes that we had seen and a desire to look forward."[1]

Causes and Impacts of the 1968 Constitution

Reapportionment's Child

Earl Warren has said that he considered *Baker v. Carr* (1962) his most important case.[2] From Florida's point of view, he was right: without *Baker* and the subsequent reapportionment, Florida was unlikely to have adopted a new constitution. Even after *Baker*, reapportionment occurred only incrementally in the state as the Pork Choppers strategically retreated. Without *Baker*, it is unlikely that the legislature would have passed the bill creating the CRC. The CRC was a temporizing measure on the part of a weakened Pork Chop legislature to move toward reapportionment without ceding too much control.

Without reapportionment, the proposed constitution was unlikely to have been approved by the legislature for voter consideration. After all, the Pork Chop legislature had approved forming constitutional committees and commissions before and then blithely rejected their proposals. Perhaps many of the 1965 legislators who created the CRC had expected to still be in office when the new constitution came up for legislative approval. The Pork Chop legislature was unlikely to have allowed home rule, because doing so would have meant a loss of patronage opportunities. The Pork Choppers were fiscally conservative and accustomed to having South Florida fund North Florida, so it is unlikely that changes to the tax structure or bonding would have occurred. Again, the desire for patronage opportunities would have discouraged changes to the court structure where local judgeships could be distributed. There would be no alternative process to amend the constitution; the citizens' initiative procedure would not exist, and the legislature would have remained the sole channel for amendments. On the other hand, it is possible that annual legislative sessions and a house auditor may have appealed to the Pork Choppers, although having a professional legislature would not. Neither cabinet realignment nor reorganization of the executive branch would likely have occurred, because they would have created a stronger governor in a better position to compete with the legislature in influencing the state.

Fair apportionment meant that Florida would have a meaningful two-party system in state government as the Republicans who lived in newly populated areas began winning elections;[3] it was also necessary for the progressive legislation enacted in the late 1960s and early 1970s, when Florida was a national leader in enacting environmental-protection laws.

Why a New Constitution Mattered

One way to gauge the importance of the 1968 Constitution is to imagine what would have happened if it had not been adopted. The biennial legislative sessions would have continued to be dominated by local bills. With reapportionment greatly increasing urban representation, the preoccupation with local bills would have increased proportionately. Expanding municipalities, urbanizing counties, and special districts created to deliver specific services would battle each other for taxes and favor, and their agendas would likely dominate every regular session to the possible exclusion of other needed legislation. Expensive special sessions to plug isolated, emerging problems would have become even more frequent. Urgent local issues would have demanded that legislators be captured and corralled to ensure passage of each piece of local legislation, leaving them with little time or opportunity to think about statewide issues.

CRC member Henry Land, who had also been a FLIC chair and Sturgis Committee member, remarked later that he thought the home-rule provision adopted in 1968 may have caused some members of the old rural legislative power bloc to drop out of the legislature. Between reapportionment expanding the geographic size of rural legislators' districts and home rule limiting their power over their populace, Land remarked, the cost of campaigning and serving was greater and the rewards fewer than before, when "they had been little czars."[4]

Second, two constitutions would have developed: the written and the actual. Applying the constitution would require knowing which portions had been superseded and were no longer meaningful although present in the document. For example, the 1885 Constitution forbade integrated schools and provided that United States senators would be elected by the legislature, even though both provisions were unconstitutional by 1968. Faith in Florida's written constitution would have eroded even further.

Third, Florida would not have thrived to the extent it subsequently did. Budgeting would, at least officially, have been restricted to two-year projections, making it increasingly difficult to keep pace with growth, especially when the sheer numbers of residents, revenue, and costs became very large. Significant amounts of private investment, taxes, and effort would have been consumed to make the antiquated structure work. The office of governor, remaining at one term with no lieutenant governor, would have had no continuity; the courts would have remained balkanized, unpredictable, and subject to corruption due to political influence and the motivation to use them as fee-generating centers; and the legislature's preoccupation with local matters would have made it unable to set broad agendas. The state's ability to attract business and deliver services would have been significantly impaired.

Because of Smith's planning from the CRC's beginning, the constitution was reformatted along logical organizational themes. It was freed from the need to parrot the 1885 Constitution's arrangement of articles. It was intentionally written sparsely. With few exceptions, notably in areas of bonding and taxation, it included only basic structural features of government and fundamental rights; it fulfilled the CRC's purpose of eliminating provisions more suitable for statutory lawmaking.

The 1968 Constitution had, however, one innovation that militated against constitutional simplicity and sparseness: the new provision that citizens could initiate constitutional amendments on their own, without having to lobby the legislature. The purpose of the provision was noble: to give citizens a say in deciding what was important enough for their constitution. The execution has had some perhaps unanticipated results, though: several amendments are now part of Florida's constitution that look more like statutes. For example, it protects the humane housing of pregnant pigs, limits the number of students that may occupy a classroom, and for several years mandated the development of a high-speed rail system (that constitutional amendment was first voted in, then voted out). The ease with which the constitution could be amended eventually inspired another amendment: to require a 60 percent yes vote rather than 50 percent to pass new amendments. That amendment passed with a 55 percent vote.

Constitutional Interpretation and Original Intent

The complicated manner in which the 1968 Constitution was created raises interesting questions about how it is to be interpreted. What is the "framers' intent" when the constitution had 37 original framers in the CRC and 159 revising framers in the legislature? Hugh Taylor, whom CRC members uniformly identified as a constitutional expert and the "father" of the 1968 Constitution, opined that the history of constitutional development was unimportant in interpreting the constitution:

I think that when the constitution was adopted, the people adopted what was written and not what the people talked about before the vote. I think it is difficult to interpret the constitution in light of all the debates, where one minute you might say one thing and the next minute you might say another. How are you going to determine what the constitution is if everybody has to go back and read all those records and files and so forth to see what was discussed? I think they ought to go by what they say, if you have made a mistake, correct it.[5]

In other words, apply the constitution using the text, and if the text is unclear or does not cover the issue, amend the constitution. Taylor's rule of interpretation accords with the principle that a constitution is interpreted according to the plain meaning of the words, and background material is used only in cases of uncertainty. Even with apparently clear language, however, it is difficult to resist mining the voluminous transcripts of the early meetings, committee meetings, public hearings, detailed reports, drafts exchanged with accompanying correspondence, and recorded hearings for clues as to intent.

Planning for Future Revision

The new constitution also contained the seeds of its own adaptability for the future. It provided that ten years after its adoption and every twenty years after that, a new Constitution Revision Commission would convene. The new CRCs would again contain thirty-seven members. The members would be chosen by a slightly different group of decision makers than the 1966–68 CRC had. Under the 1968 Constitution, no members would be chosen by the Florida Bar. The governor would choose fifteen, including the chair; the Senate President and House Speaker would each choose nine; the chief justice would have only three choices, and would be obligated to do so with the "advice of the justices"; and the attorney general would, as before, automatically be a member.[6]

Post-1968 Developments

Government Reorganization

The first day that the new constitution took effect, Claude Kirk appointed a lieutenant governor, Ray Osborne. Osborne took office on January 7, 1969, becoming Florida's first lieutenant governor since the position had been abolished with the 1885 Constitution.

The legislature had more power because it would now meet annually. Under the old constitution, the cabinet, elected statewide without term limits, was the only institution that both stayed in Tallahassee full-time and could remain in office for a long time. Under the new constitution, the legislature was in town twice as often. More importantly, for the first time it had permanent staff members who could keep the legislators in touch with state business between sessions.

But the governor, in turn, had more power over the legislature than he used to have. When a governor could not be reelected, he typically oversaw only two state budgets of the biannual legislature. The first was passed in the spring after the governor's January inauguration, while the governor was still figuring out his job; the second budget was passed when the governor had less than two years left in office and was already a lame duck in the eyes of the legislature.[7] Now even a one-term governor would oversee four budgets, and a two-term governor would oversee eight. And, importantly, under the new constitution, the governor was the chief budgeter.

The new constitution provided that the wild tangle of at least 150 interlocking state agencies overseen by cabinet members had to be reduced to 28. This meant a complete reorganization of the executive branch. The task of reducing the number of agencies and reorganizing the entire branch fell to the 1969 legislature, and Dick Pettigrew tied a napkin around his neck and put a utensil in each hand in preparation for the carnage. Pettigrew "enjoyed government reorganization the way some people enjoy sex," *St. Petersburg Times* journalist Martin Dyckman remarked later.[8] Pettigrew had been trained at the prestigious Eagleton Institute, which held seminars around the country in 1967 to modernize state legislatures, so his enthusiasm was matched by his preparation for the task.

Reorganization work began in the House just two weeks after the 1968 election, at the post-election organizational session. The House Committee on State Governmental Organization and Efficiency, a group of twenty-one representatives chaired by Pettigrew and dominated by Republicans and urban Democrats, led the House effort to pass legislation reorganizing the executive branch. The Senate Committee on Governmental Reorganization was chaired by George Hollahan, who had served on the CRC. But the Senate committee's bill did not propose change as sweeping as that of the House committee. The conference committee that acted as liaison between the two was dominated by a group of conservative Democrats resistant to the broad change the new constitution called for. For the two chambers to depend on the conference committee would be for them to accept the Senate's tepid bill. Pettigrew's vision of a reorganized executive branch was beginning to look as though it would be suffocated. "This will be a train wreck," Pettigrew told Senate President Jack Mathews. "I'm not abandoning [reorganization], so the failure will be on the Senate's hands."[9] In response, Mathews appointed an informal committee that included Lawton Chiles and Mallory Horne. Pettigrew was able to negotiate with those senators, and both houses passed effective reorganization laws.

Pettigrew paid a price for his activism, though. Although he was Speaker-designate, a group who opposed the reorganization, led by former Speaker E. C. Rowell, tried to put up a coup to dethrone him; it failed. Pettigrew would go on to lead the House through the 1971 and 1972 sessions, the first after Reubin Askew's election as governor. Pettigrew and his chief of staff, Gene Stearns, worked closely with Askew's office to pass Askew's campaign agenda; they worked with Republican Don Reed to sell it to both parties.[10]

Speaking nearly four decades later, Horne reflected on the legislatures of the late 1960s: "You could say, 'They rewrote the Florida Constitution,' and they did; 'reorganized the executive branch of the government,' and they did; 'developed an inventory of the House, created a combined administrative function of the legislature. And, they went from the worst to the best reapportioned state in the nation in ten years.' That's a lot of blood. A lot of blood."[11] Horne was right. Longtime, dedicated civil servants worked and sometimes fell in the service of reform, both on the conservative and on the liberal sides.

Environmental Reform

In his 1974 book *The Florida Experience: Land and Water Policy in a Growth State*, science and geography writer Luther Carter identified legislative reapportionment as the beginning of environmental reform in Florida, noting only tangentially that a new Florida constitution assisted reform of the legislative and executive branches of state government.[12] Other writers have echoed this characterization.[13] Indeed, reports reviewing the 1960s and 1970s cast a bad legislature captured by industry groups against a later, ethically reformed legislature that tried to pass significant environmental protection laws. This account is too simple, however. The push for environmental protection in Florida had earlier beginnings and a few isolated successes. Fighting among industry groups that had formerly been allies against environmental controls broke down some of the unified resistance of the legislature and courts. The factors Carter and others have identified as merely contributing to environmental reform were actually prerequisites: without reapportionment, the new legislature would not have proposed a new constitution; if not for the new constitution, legislative and executive reorganization and local government home rule would not have been possible; and without the reorganization of state government, the wide-ranging environmental legislation would not been passed.

The governmental reform also ushered in one of Florida's strongest voices for the environment, Nathaniel P. Reed. Reed, of Hobe Sound, was Kirk's top environmental adviser and went on to become an assistant secretary of the U.S. Interior Department. Reed has advised several Florida governors and remains an outspoken defender of Florida's natural environment.

A New Article V—Finally

The 1968 Constitution, we have noted, did not include a new judicial article. Strong and organized opposition from those whose ox would be gored stymied judicial reform in both 1968 and 1970. It was not until March 14, 1972, that voters approved a revised Article V.

Why could judicial reform not pass in 1968? And what changed in 1972? It is necessary first to look at what the court system looked like under the 1885 Constitution. Florida had a jumble of different courts—at least eleven different kinds. Among them, in addition to the Supreme Court of Florida, were district courts of appeal, a recent addition as of 1956; circuit courts; municipal courts; justices of the peace; county courts; county courts of record—the list goes on. To complicate things further, the mix of courts and jurisdictions varied from county to county. How could a layperson, or even a lawyer from a different part of the state, understand which court to file suit in? Additionally, all the judges of these courts, even members of the supreme court, were elected by the people; these elections were partisan and therefore political. Many courts were "cash-register courts" in which judges' salaries were funded in part by the fees and fines they generated, creating a conflict of interest. One former judge told of becoming a municipal judge in Jacksonville. On taking office he was told that his predecessor on the bench had brought in a particular amount of money in fines and fees and that he would be expected to bring in even more than that.[14]

In 1970 a proposed Article V set forth a system that eliminated most of these courts but replaced them with a hybrid system that provided for two tiers of trial court in less-populated counties and three tiers in more-populated ones. Many types of judges, including municipal judges and justices of the peace, would be eliminated. Jurisdiction of sensitive cases, such as juvenile delinquency and dependency, was not uniformly provided for. Therefore, it was not only the municipal judges threatened with elimination who opposed the article, but also many lawyers and citizens who believed that the proposed article, as drafted, contained inherent problems.

Reubin Askew's election as governor in November 1970 gave judicial reform a morale boost. Askew had been a proponent of reform since his CRC days. He created a Citizens Committee for Judicial Reform and appointed Chesterfield Smith as chair. In the spring of 1972, a revised proposed Article V passed. It benefited from a strong campaign organized by both the League of Women Voters and Askew's Citizens Committee. The latter group appears to have been organized quite late, little more than a month before the election;[15] at least part of its purpose was to defeat organized opposition feared to arise again from the state organization of municipal judges. Before the end of February, twenty-five thousand "orange and blue bumper strips" reading "I'm for Judicial Reform" and fifty thousand flyers had been printed and were being distributed, and several advertising companies had donated billboard space for the purpose of urging voters to support the proposed article. Members of Askew's group, spurred by Smith, spoke to groups all around the state with the purpose of gaining favorable media coverage. Even Chief Justice B. K. Roberts agreed to be interviewed by any television station in the state.[16]

It wasn't just the media blitz that made the difference this time. The proposed article itself was different, too: the new Article V provided for a uniform court system throughout the state: county courts and circuit courts at the trial level; intermediate appellate courts; and the supreme court. All justice and judge positions remained elected; merit selection and merit retention for appellate judges and justices was still a few years off. The proposed article was the product of the work of House Judiciary Committee chair Sandy D'Alemberte; his aide, Janet Reno; and Senate Judiciary Committee chair Dempsey Barron. Barron was powerful and conservative, and according to D'Alemberte, an avowed liberal, held little respect for judges. D'Alemberte insists that the article would not have made it out of the legislature and onto the ballot without Reno's hard work softening up Barron. The two shared a passion for Wild West novels, and Reno would always have a few to pass along to Barron at their meetings. Reno began to act as a go-between for Barron and D'Alemberte. The respect that grew between Barron and Reno, according to D'Alemberte, helped Barron's willingness to work with the House to pass a proposed Article V.[17]

Later CRCs

The work of the 1977–78 and 1997–98 CRCs and the stories describing the intervening constitutional amendments are sufficient to fill another book, and the varying ways in which each commission addressed the problems of its day and the ongoing challenges in Florida government will provide engaging reading for students of the Florida constitution. This book will briefly address the work of each of these later CRCs.

The 1977–78 CRC convened under the leadership of Representative Sandy D'Alemberte, who had shepherded the revised judicial article into being four years after the rest of the constitution had been passed. The membership of the 1977–78 CRC more closely reflected Florida's populace, with more women and minorities than the 1966 group. The 1977–78 group also included Don Reed, Jack Mathews, Tom Barkdull, and B. K. Roberts from the 1966 CRC. D'Alemberte's CRC attempted broad change, including an appointed cabinet and an explicit right to privacy. However, voters defeated all of the proposed amendments. The proposed amendments had the misfortune of sharing the ballot with a casino-gambling initiative that Askew strenuously opposed; voting no may have been uppermost in voters' minds on that election day. It is also possible that this CRC, heavily Democratic, attempted changes that were too far from the mainstream to be accepted by the voters at that time. However, the commissioners of 1977–78 could take some comfort in the fact that in ensuing years most of its proposed reforms were eventually passed, albeit on a piecemeal basis.

Twenty years after that, the 1997–98 CRC, chaired by Dexter Douglass, who had served on the 1977–78 CRC, had greater success. This group had learned from watching D'Alemberte's CRC, and it attempted more modest change.[18] Its membership was nearly evenly divided between the two major political parties, a factor many believe contributed to its success at the polls: partly because of the evenly balanced membership and partly because the rules of this group required a supermajority vote to place a proposal on the ballot, the group approved only measures that had gained broad support within the CRC. Only Barkdull and Douglass served on both the 1977–78 and the 1997–98 CRCs.

Barkdull was the only person to serve on all three; he died in 2010, so his wisdom will not be available for the 2017–18 CRC.

The next CRC will convene in February 2017 and will be required to have its recommendations for revision, if any, finalized by May 2018, 180 days before the next general election. Like the 1977–78 CRC, this one is likely to be dominated by one political party, but this time it will be the Republican Party. The CRC likely will grapple with issues such as legislative apportionment, privacy, and gun laws; it will do well to learn the lessons from 1977–78 and 1997–98 that balance and broad support will help the success of its proposed revisions.

How CRC Members Turned Out

Two members of the 1966 CRC would later become governor: Reubin Askew and Lawton Chiles. Two other reform legislators of the period also became governor: Bob Graham and Kenneth H. "Buddy" MacKay. Graham, who was elected in 1966 to the state House, became a state senator, then governor, then U.S. senator. MacKay was elected on the same ballot as the 1968 Constitution. He began as a state representative and became a state senator and congressman before becoming Chiles's lieutenant governor and, briefly, governor.

Chiles conducted an unconventional campaign for the U.S. Senate in 1970; then a little-known state senator from Lakeland, he walked the length of the state—putting more than a thousand miles on his feet—and became known as "Walkin' Lawton." He won his campaign for the U.S. Senate and two more after that. Bill Young ran for the Congress the same year that Chiles walked; he became the longest-serving Republican member of the Congress, serving from 1971 until 2013.

Askew defeated incumbent Claude Kirk in 1970; thus, the first governor eligible to succeed himself under the new constitution was unable to pull it off. Indeed, Askew was the first governor to serve two full terms under the new constitution. Graham succeeded Askew and also was reelected. After a four-year term by former Tampa mayor Bob Martinez, Chiles, who had been serving as U.S. senator for eighteen years, was elected governor. His sudden death in December 1998 cut his second term short by three weeks; his lieutenant governor, Buddy MacKay, succeeded him for the interim. Thus the spirit of reform sparked and nurtured by the original CRC and the post–Pork Chop legislature drove Florida through the final third of the twentieth century.

Among the remaining CRC members, Stephen O'Connell was named chief justice of the Florida Supreme Court in 1967, but he left that same year to become the president of the University of Florida. Elmer Friday and John Crews went on to become circuit judges. Tom Barkdull stayed on the bench at the Third District Court of Appeal until retirement. In the early 1970s, Richard Earle courageously investigated sitting Florida Supreme Court justices who were accused of improprieties. Ralph Turlington became Florida's commissioner of education in 1974 and served until 1987.

Jack Mathews never became governor despite two attempts, the final one in 1970 when he lost the Democratic primary to Reubin Askew. Beth Johnson lost her Senate seat in 1966 and never returned to politics. However, Askew said later that he had wanted her to be his running mate for his second term as governor, but "she died on me."[19] Johnson died in 1973 of cancer; she was only in her mid-sixties.

Bill Baggs, too, died young. In January 1967, he and another newspaper editor, Harry Ashmore, led an initially undisclosed effort to Hanoi to explore possible ways to start peace talks between the United States and North Vietnam. They spent time in Washington, D.C., being briefed by State Department officials immediately before and after Baggs was in Tallahassee with the CRC convention in November and December 1966.[20] Their trip was revealed by the *New York Times* after they left for Hanoi and just days before they met with North Vietnamese President Ho Chi Minh.[21] Baggs died in January 1969 at age forty-eight, just months before Ho Chi Minh did.

Charley Johns spent his retirement among his constituents in Bradford County. He never ran for public office again. He took care of his family, his insurance company's clients, and his former constituents, even though he no longer had political power. He gradually transferred his businesses to his son Jerome.[22] His time as acting governor could be seen as the beginning of the end of the 1885 Constitution, for it illuminated brightly one of its failings, that of succession to the governor's office. Johns died in 1990, when two decades of progressive Democrat rule in Florida had wrought economic, environmental, and social change, and just as true bipartisan rule of Florida was about to take hold. His brand of Democrat was gone in Florida by the end of the century. Those whom he might recognize as political kin now—the socially and fiscally conservative—carried the name of Republican.

The chairmanship of the 1966 CRC and the adoption of the 1968 Constitution were still early accomplishments of Chesterfield Smith. Viewed from the perspective of his career, he was just gaining pace. In 1973 he became president of the American Bar Association, and he became a household name that fall for his denunciation of President Richard Nixon's "Saturday Night Massacre" during the Watergate scandal. Many consider his comment about Nixon, "No man is above the law," the turning point in public sentiment against the Watergate cover-up. He returned to Bartow to grow his law firm, renamed Holland and Knight, into a worldwide firm; he kept it ahead of the times in its hiring of women and minorities. He was a legendary mentor. As one of those mentees, Martha Barnett, who served on the 1997–98 CRC, said, "I've never understood how he did it, but I could probably give you 100 names and every one of them would say, yes, Chesterfield Smith is the best friend I ever had, the best mentor I ever had, changed my life, thought about me all the time."[23] As leader of Holland and Knight, Smith became known for his twin mantras, "Do good. Be somebody." He was profiled in Tom Brokaw's book *The Greatest Generation* and honored as a "Great Floridian" by Governor Lawton Chiles in 1997.[24] Chesterfield Smith died in 2003, just before his eighty-sixth birthday.

Adieu, Mr. Chairman

Chesterfield Smith served on neither the 1977–78 nor the 1997–98 CRC, remarking to friends that it was time for others to take the lead. On June 16, 1997, in Tallahassee, Chesterfield Smith addressed his third Constitution Revision Commission. Smith, nearly eighty years of age, reminded the commissioners of the importance of human rights in a new world:

It is pleasing to be here on this historic day before this august group, assembled for a singularly important purpose. I have had the privilege of addressing previous Constitutional Revision Commissions, and the honor today is particularly significant. The convening of this particular Florida Constitutional Commission will undoubtedly be my last.

The eminent Chair of this Commission, Dexter Douglass, has advised me that I have an absolute maximum of 15 minutes in which to address this group. This allotment of time reflects a decision, probably a long-considered decision buttressed over the years by personal experience, that he should make me shut up quicker and sit down sooner.

Back in 1966, when I was Chair of Florida's Constitutional Revision Commission, then I had unlimited time to say whatever I wanted to say, and I said it. Mr. Chairman, it's good to be King, but in your dealings with me, please remember that you, too, will someday be an ex-King. . . . I also will make a bold prediction, some may say I am prone to do that; I promise, I commit, that I will not address the next Constitutional Revision Commission which will convene in the year 2017, the year in which I will celebrate my 100th birthday. . . .

I consider the crowning achievement of our Constitution to be its Declaration of Rights, although, of course, that is not the exclusive source of human rights in Florida. Human rights also arise from the common law principles on which this country was founded. . . . I charge you to be ever mindful of these individual rights, perhaps to expand them and even specifically to include some of them in the Declaration of Rights, to reflect modern life and developing trends, such as: the Internet, the globalization of Florida's economy, and the new and improved communications and computerized knowledge systems. . . .

In 1977, I took the liberty of giving the Commission my personal views on a number of matters that I thought would come before the Commission. I do not do that today, not because I lack opinions, which can never be true, but because, as I said in my opening, one person's opinions are much less important than the integrity of the process and the care taken to protect and preserve a well-spring of individual rights. I thus urge you, foremost and first, to make the great State of Florida a leader, a pioneer, among states, of expanding and protecting human rights. Government structure is important, but in finality, not near so important as human rights. . . .

Take with you, then, the heart of a servant, the wisdom of a god, the savvy of a politician, the nurturing care of a parent; for beginning today you are the potential mothers and fathers of Florida's Constitution, foster parents perhaps, and only for a time, because it does end.[25]

Notes

Abbreviations

Baker Papers   Maxine E. Baker Papers, GSL
Dauer Papers   Manning Julian Dauer Papers, GSL
FSA   Florida State Archives, Tallahassee
FSUL   Special Collections Department, Florida State University Libraries, Tallahassee
GSL   George A. Smathers Libraries, Special and Area Studies Collection, University of Florida, Gainesville
O'Neill Papers   William G. O'Neill Papers, Lawton Chiles Legal Information Center, University of Florida, Gainesville
Sessums Collection   T. Terrell Sessums Collection, Special Collections Department, Tampa Library, University of South Florida
Taylor Papers   Circuit Judge Hugh M. Taylor Papers, FSUL

Introduction

1. Tarr, *Understanding State Constitutions*, 7–9.
2. See Garrow, "Bad Behavior Makes Big Law."

Chapter 1. The Old Constitutions

1. Williamson, "The Constitutional Convention of 1885"; Williamson, *Florida Politics in the Gilded Age*, 139–40; Shofner, "Reconstruction and Renewal," 263–64.
2. Fla. Const. art. IV, §§ 2, 5 (1885).
3. Fla. Const. art. IV, § 19 (1885).
4. Fla. Const. art. XII, § 12 (1885).
5. Fla. Const. art. XVI, § 24 (1885).
6. Fla. Const. art. VI, § 8 (1885).
7. Fla. Const. art. VIII (1885).
8. Fla. Const. art. III, § 23 (1885).
9. Fla. Const. art. III, § 4; art. IV, § 29 (1885).
10. Fla. Const. art. VII, § 3 (1885).

11. Fla. Const. art. VII, § 2 (1885).

12. Fla. Const. art. VII, § 3 (1885).

13. http://fcit.usf.edu/florida/docs/c/census/1890.htm; http://fcit.usf.edu/florida/docs/c/census/1880.htm.

14. Fla. Const. art. XVII, § 1 (1885).

15. R. G. Dixon, *Democratic Representation*, 85–86.

16. Tebeau, *A History of Florida*, 378.

17. Wynne and Moorhead, *Florida in World War II*, 120.

18. Ibid., 14; Revels, *Sunshine Paradise*, 2.

19. Mormino, *Land of Sunshine*, 236–37.

20. Dauer, "Florida: The Different State," 86.

21. 1960 *Census of Population*, table 39, *State of Birth of the Native Population, by Color, for the State, Urban and Rural, 1960, and for the State, 1900 to 1950* (Washington, D.C.: United States Bureau of the Census, 1960); Black and Black, *Politics and Society*, 16–17.

22. Chesterfield Smith address, *House Journal*, January 10, 1967, 20.

23. Powers, *E.C.*, 104.

24. Sturm, *Thirty Years of State Constitution-Making*. See also Terrell Sessums's speech referring to Florida's 1885 Constitution as being "like an old tire, . . . more patch than tire." Box 90, Sessums Collection.

25. Ansolabehere and Snyder, *The End of Inequality*, 73 n. 6.

26. Ibid., 73; Florida House of Representatives, "Reapportionment in Florida," 441.

27. Morris, *Reconsideration*.

28. C. L. Smith, *Strengthening the Florida Legislature*, 2.

29. Sherrill, "Florida's Legislature," 88.

30. Fla. Const. art. IX, § 15, Fla. Const. (1885).

31. Pope interview, 36.

32. Ibid.

33. C. Johns interview, 5. But see Dyckman, *Floridian of His Century* (Johns manipulated the suspension process to plant cronies in state jobs).

34. Fla. Const. art. IX, § 12 (1885 (amended 1930).

35. Air Pollution Control Commission Authority 1961.

36. Ibid.

37. Florida State Bar Association, Constitutional Committee, *A Proposed Constitution for Florida*, 1 [hereafter cited as 1947 Proposal].

38. 1947 Proposal, 6, 63.

39. Ibid., 11.

40. Ibid., 41.

41. E.g., 1960 Florida Bar Proposal.

42. 1947 Proposal, 18, 19.

43. Ibid., 19.

44. Ibid., 18.

45. Ibid., 37.

46. Ibid., 57–58.

47. Ibid., 5.

48. Ibid.

49. Ibid., 7.

50. Ibid.

51. Ibid., 5.

52. Ibid., 6.

53. Ibid., 16.

54. Ibid., 68.

55. Ibid., 11.

56. Ibid., 12.

57. Ibid., 13.

58. Ibid., 7.

59. Ibid., 8.

60. Ibid.

61. 1947 HJR 118 (Fla. Const. art. XVII, § 1 (1885)).

62. Askew interview, May 9, 2001.

63. Sessums interview, May 20, 1974, 3.

64. Havard and Beth, "Representative Government and Reapportionment," 41.

65. SJR 152, 42, April 12, 1955.

66. Senate Bill 179, *Senate Journal*, 45, April 12, 1955.

67. SJ 159, April 2, 1955.

68. Colburn and Scher, *Florida's Gubernatorial Politics*, 110.

69. Florida House of Representatives, "Reapportionment in Florida," 439.

70. Colburn and Scher, *Florida's Gubernatorial Politics*, 110; Wagy, *Governor LeRoy Collins of Florida*, 104.

71. Dyckman, *Floridian of His Century*, 100.

72. Wagy, *Governor LeRoy Collins of Florida*, 104.

73. Senate Concurrent Resolution 1406, *Senate Journal*, June 6, 1957, 1578; adopted by House on June 8, 1957, *House Journal*, June 8, 1957, 1666.

74. Ibid.

75. 105 So. 2d (Fla. 1958) (Thornal, J., concurring).

76. Wagy, *Governor LeRoy Collins of Florida*, 106.

77. Dauer, *The Proposed New Florida Constitution*, 17.

78. Rivera-Cruz v. Gray, 104 So. 2d 501 (Fla. 1958).

79. Hugh Taylor to Jim Hardee, Capitol Correspondent, April 19, 1958, *Orlando Sentinel*, box 173, Taylor Papers.

80. See Florida House of Representatives, "Reapportionment in Florida" (Florida House of Representatives, Committee on Reapportionment, 1991), 439 (characterizing the committee's recommendation as "moderate and respectful of legislative tradition, a tacit acknowledgement that incremental progress towards fair representation had the best chance to succeed"); Havard and Beth, "Representative Government and Reapportionment," 39.

81. Baker to Van Gill and Frances Kilroe, October 5, November 21, 1958, Baker Papers.

82. Baker to Van Gill and Frances Kilroe, October 5, 1958.

83. Ibid.

84. Baker to Van Gill and Frances Kilroe, November 21, 1958.

85. Baker to Van Gill and Frances Kilroe, January 30, 1959, Baker Papers.

86. Fla. Const. art. XII, § 12 (1885).

87. Baker to Van Gill and Frances Kilroe, January 30, 1959.

88. Baker to Van Gill and Frances Kilroe, January 12, 1959, Baker Papers.

89. Baker to Van Gill and Frances Kilroe, January 30, 1959, Baker Papers.

90. Memorandum, Baker to State Board, LWV of Florida, April 13, 1959, Baker Papers.

91. McRae to Dauer, January 27, 1959 (misdated as 1958), box 4, Dauer Papers.

92. CRC hearing transcript, March 25, 1966, FSA, RG 1006, series 720, box 1, folder 7, p. 70.

93. League of Women Voters, "Yardstick for Constitutional Revision," Miami, Florida (undated document, circa 1952).

94. Florida Bar, *Proposed Constitution for Florida*.

95. "Proceedings Annual Conventions: Conference of Bar Delegates, Thursday, April 27, 1950," *Florida Law Journal* 24, no. 6 (June 1950): 190–98. See also Goldstein, "The Bar in Black and White" (discussing racial integration of the bar).

96. Florida Bar, *Proposed Constitution for Florida*, 37.

97. Dyckman, *Floridian of His Century*, 166: "Collins explained [to his six-year-old daughter, Darby] that a lieutenant governor fills in when a governor is away. 'Gosh, I sure wish I had a lieutenant daddy,' Darby said."

98. Florida Bar, *Proposed Constitution for Florida*, 40–41.

99. Ibid., 38–39.

100. Ibid., 43.

101. Dyckman, *Floridian of His Century*, 130; Wagy, *Governor LeRoy Collins of Florida*, 75.

102. Florida Bar, *Proposed Constitution for Florida*, 45.

103. Ibid., 47.

104. Ibid., 56.

105. Ibid., 83.

106. Ibid., 69.

107. Sobel v. Adams, 208 F. Supp. 316, 324 (S.D. Fla. 1962).

Chapter 2. The U.S. Supreme Court Reapportionment Cases

1. Dauer, "Florida: The Different State."

2. Cross interview, 4.

3. E.g., Colburn, "Florida's Governors Confront the *Brown* Decision"; Wagy, *Governor LeRoy Collins of Florida*; Dyckman, *Floridian of His Century*.

4. Morris, *Florida Handbook*, 1963–64.

5. Ibid.; Morris, *Florida Handbook*, 1967–68.

6. Morris, *Florida Handbook, 1963–64*; Morris, *Florida Handbook, 1967–68*.

7. Morris, *Florida Handbook, 1963–64*.

8. Ibid.; Morris, *Florida Handbook, 1967–68*.

9. Gere and Jerome Johns interview.

10. Gong interview ("tyrannical"); Sobel v. Adams, 208 F. Supp. 316, 324 ("stranglehold").

11. Miller, "How Florida Threw Out the Pork Chop Gang."

12. Ansolabehere and Snyder, *The End of Inequality*, 33, 50–51, citing Manning J. Dauer and Robert G. Kelsay, "Unrepresentative States," *National Municipal Review* 46 (December 1955): 571–75.

13. Dauer, "Florida: The Different State."

14. Shiver v. Gray, 276 F.2d 568, 569 (5th Cir. 1960).

15. Ibid., 568, 570.

16. Ibid.

17. CRC hearing transcript, March 25, 1966, FSA, RG 1006, series 720, box 1, folder 7, p. 151.

18. Dauer, "Florida: The Different State," 99.

19. Ibid.

20. Askew interview, May 9, 2001. Askew recalls that he replied: "Well, they're *my* britches."

21. Ibid.

22. Conner and Horne interview.

23. Jewell, "State Legislatures in Southern Politics," 177.

24. Ibid.

25. Ibid.

26. But see Gormley, *Archibald Cox,* 172 n. 58 (disputing contention that Robert Kennedy orchestrated pressure on Cox).

27. Schwartz, *Super Chief*, 423.

28. Kyvig, *Explicit and Authentic Acts*, 371–79. For example, the Virginia Commission on Constitutional Government responded to *Baker v. Carr* with hostility.

29. Neal, "*Baker v. Carr,*" 252–53. See also Garrow, "Bad Behavior Makes Big Law."

30. Dyckman, *Floridian of His Century*, 176; Graham interview, May 15, 2014.

31. U.S. Const. art. I, § 5.

32. See, e.g., Douglas, *Court Years*, 134–35.

33. Newton, *Justice for All*, 388.

34. Ibid.

35. Warren, *Memoirs*, 306–10.

36. Foner, *Reconstruction*, 180–81.

37. Gormley, *Archibald Cox*, 169.

38. Colegrove v. Green, 328 U.S. 549 (1946).

39. Schwartz, *Super Chief*, 413.

40. Gormley, *Archibald Cox,* 170. Accounts differ on this. Schwartz reports that Frankfurter was found slumped in chambers and that he protested loudly when being carried by stretcher out of the building that his shoes had been left behind.

41. Ibid.

42. Baker v. Carr, 369 U.S. 186, 267 (1962) (Frankfurter, J., dissenting).

43. Ibid., 267–69.

44. Ibid., 270.

45. Schwartz, *Super Chief*, 507–8.

46. Ibid., 417.

47. R. G. Dixon, *Democratic Representation*, 139–40.

48. John E. Mathews Sr. to John E. Mathews Jr., March 14, 1947, folder 7, box 1, series 101, John E. Mathews Jr. Collection, Thomas G. Carpenter Library, University of North Florida, Jacksonville.

49. Paulson and Hawkes, "Desegregating the University of Florida"; Sweatt v. Painter, 339 U.S. 629 (1950).

50. Paulson and Hawkes, "Desegregating the University of Florida"; Kluger, *Simple Justice*, 274–84. Paulson and Hawkes state that the Florida Supreme Court had the *Painter* decision available to it during the 1950 *Hawkins* deliberations based on Florida's intervention in *Painter*. Instead, the attorneys for Hawkins explicitly brought it to the court's attention in a separate filing. Virgil Hawkins court file, FSA. Florida was only one of eleven southern states joining in a joint amicus brief in the *Painter* appeal. Kluger, *Simple Justice*, 274.

51. Hill interview.

52. Hawkins v. Board of Control of Fla., 47 So. 2d 608, 609 (Fla. 1950).

53. Sebring was an unusual choice for writing this opinion, as he had recently returned from serving as a judge at the Nuremberg medical trials of Nazi officials. One of the prosecution's arguments was crimes against humanity. Many would argue that southern race laws and the treatment of African Americans in the Jim Crow South amounted to crimes against humanity as well. Harold L. Sebring Collection, Stetson University Law Library.

54. Even historians sympathetic to the Florida court have conceded, though gently, that it was a racist court. Manley and Brown, *The Supreme Court of Florida*, 275.

55. State ex rel. Hawkins v. Board of Control, 347 U.S. 971 (1954).

56. State ex rel. Hawkins v. Board of Control, 71 U.S. 166 (1951); State ex rel. Hawkins v. Board of Control, 347 U.S. 971 (1954).

57. State ex rel. Hawkins v. Board of Control, 83 So. 2d 20, 27–28 (Fla. 1955) (Terrell, J., concurring).

58. Board of Public Instruction of Manatee County v. State, 75 So. 2d 832 (Fla. 1954), quoted in State ex. Rel. Hawkins v. Board of Control, 83 So. 2d 20, 24 (Fla. 1955); emphasis added.

59. State ex rel. Hawkins v. Board of Control, 83 So. 2d 20, 26.

60. Ibid., 27–28.

61. Ibid., 28.

62. See pamphlets on segregation in box 11 of the Justice Glenn Terrell Papers, Claude Pepper Libraries, Florida State University Libraries, Tallahassee.

63. State ex rel. Hawkins v. Board of Control, 350 U.S. 413 (1956).

64. "State of Florida Board of Control for State Institutions of Higher Learning Study on Desegregation," May 1956.

65. State ex rel. Hawkins v. Board of Control, 93 So. 2d 354 (Fla. 1957).

66. Ibid., 367.

67. Jacob, "Remembering a Great Dean."

68. Hawkins v. Board of Control, 162 F. Supp. 851, 853 (N.D. Fla. 1958).

69. Appellee's brief, Supreme Court of Florida Docket No. 29, 491, Gibson v. Florida Legislative Investigation Committee, FSA.

70. Gibson v. Florida Legislative Investigation Committee, 126 So. 2d 129 (Fla. 1960).

71. Lawson, "The Florida Legislative Investigation Committee," 313; Gibson v. Florida Legislative Investigation Committee, 126 So. 2d 129 (Fla. 1960).

72. Gibson v. Florida Legislative Investigation Committee, 372 U.S. 539, 557 (1963).

73. Gibson v. Florida Legislative Investigation Committee, 153 So. 2d 301, 301 (Fla. 1963).

74. McLaughlin v. State, 153 So. 2d 1, 2 (Fla. 1963).

75. McLaughlin v. State, 379 U.S. 184 (1964).

76. McLaughlin v. State, 172 So. 2d 460 (Fla. 1965).

77. Lund v. Mathas, 145 So. 2d 871 (Fla. 1962).

78. Sobel v. Adams, 208 F. Supp. 316 (S.D. Fla. 1962).

79. Ibid., 318.

80. Sims v. Fink, 208 F. Supp. 201 (M.D. Ala. 1962).

81. Moss v. Burkhart, 207 F. Supp. 885 (W.D. Okla. 1962).

82. Sobel v. Adams, 208 F. Supp. 318.

83. Ibid.

84. Bryant interview.

85. Sobel v. Adams, 208 F. Supp. 316, 319 (supplemental opinion).

86. Ibid., 321.

87. Ibid.

88. Jewell, "State Legislatures in Southern Politics," 180.

89. Ibid.

90. Ibid.

91. "U.S. Begins Major Buildup of Air Defense in Florida," *Miami Herald*, October 19, 1962; "Air Buildup at Keys Base," *Palm Beach Post*, October 19, 1962; "No Cuban Assault Set Tonight, Official Says: Defense Aide Denies Exercise Covers Attack," *Palm Beach Post*, October 22, 1962.

92. In re: Advisory Opinion to the Governor, 150 So. 2d 721 (Fla. 1963).

93. Sobel v. Adams, 214 F. Supp. 811, 812 (S.D. Fla. 1963). One of the plaintiff's attorneys was Carl Hiaasen, the father of author Carl Hiaasen Jr.

94. Ibid., 812.

95. Ibid.

96. Foglesong, *Married to the Mouse*. Oddly, Foglesong attributes the episode to an interview with Admiral Joe Fowler, vice president of Walt Disney Productions, from July 1962, seventeen months before the flyover (15 n. 1).

97. Powe, *The Warren Court*, 244.

98. Ibid.

99. Reynolds v. Sims, 377 U.S. 533 (1964).

100. Branch, *Pillar of Fire*, 74.

101. Schwartz, *Super Chief*, 503.

102. Ibid.

103. Critics have argued that Florida's legislative districts are drawn to this effect at the time of this writing, early 2016: statewide party voting records show Florida to be nearly evenly divided between the two major political parties, Republican and Democrat; however, both houses of the Florida Legislature have been dominated by Republicans since the 1990s. A trial judge declared the apportionment illegal in late 2015 and approved a Senate plan that would favor the Democratic Party slightly; no appeal had been filed as of early January 2016.

104. See generally R. G. Dixon, *Democratic Representation*, 191–92.

105. Ibid., 267–69.

106. Ibid., 269.

107. Ibid.

108. Swann v. Adams, 378 U.S. 553, 553 (1964).

109. Described in Swann v. Adams, 383 U.S. 210 (1966).

110. Rep. Richard A. Pettigrew to Rep. T. Terrell Sessums, February 9, 1965. Pettigrew also asked whether Sessums was interested in a unicameral legislature. Box 81, Sessums Collection.

111. Haydon Burns, "Address to the 1965 Legislature," April 6, 1965 (pamphlet), p. 26, box 36, O'Neill Papers.

112. Fla. Const. art. XVII, § 4 (1885).

Chapter 3. The 1966 Constitution Revision Commission

1. See, generally, Chesterfield Smith's opening remarks at each CRC public hearing in Miami, Tampa, Orlando, Jacksonville, and Pensacola, July 1966. E.g., July 11, 1966, FSA, RG 1006, series 721, box 1, folder 4.

2. Ervin interview, November 10, 2010.

3. Webster and Bell, "First Principles for Constitutional Revision," 391, 394 (quoting D'Alemberte); see also D'Alemberte, *The Florida State Constitution*, 11 (quoting Chesterfield Smith TV speech); "Speeches by Chesterfield 1966–1968," box 129, Chesterfield Smith Papers, GSL.

4. Ervin interview, December 16, 1986, 18.

5. C. Smith interview, March 9, 2000, 51.

6. *Senate Journal*, May 13, 1965, 441.

7. Senate Bill 65-977.

8. Ibid.

9. Askew interview, May 9, 2001.

10. Ibid.; Reubin Askew, conversation with the author, August 22, 2012.

11. Dauer, *Florida Reapportionment*.

12. Folder "July 1, 1965 Petition to File," box 19, Dauer Papers.

13. Folder "Brief calculations," box 19, Dauer Papers; David Colburn, conversation with the author, December 1, 2011.

14. Dauer interview, October 3, 1980, 1.

15. Ibid.

16. Ibid., 117–18.

17. Ibid., 118.

18. Ibid., 114–15.

19. Dauer to Faircloth, May 4, 1960, December 2, 1963, folder "Earl Faircloth," box 4, Dauer Papers.

20. Dauer interview, October 3, 1980, 6–8.

21. McRae to Dauer, March 19, 1966, folder "McRae, William A. 1949–1967," box 4, Dauer Papers.

22. McRae to Dauer, October 20, 1969, folder "McRae, William A. 1968–1974," box 4, Dauer Papers.

Chapter 4. Building a Constitution's Foundation

1. Pearce, *Cool Hand Luke*, 226–31.

2. Sherrill, "Florida's Legislature."

3. Emerson, *Project Future*, 82.

4. Ibid., 84.

5. Mitchell, *Gone with the Wind*, 145.

6. Emerson, *Project Future*, 95–114; Emerson, "Merging Public and Private Governance."

7. Gary Printy, conversation with the author, April 10, 2015 ("strut sitting down"); William Reece Smith Jr., conversation with the author, June 21, 2012 ("five blocks away").

8. C. Smith interview, January 14, 2000, 2, 4.

9. Ibid., 13.

10. MacKay, *How Florida Happened*, 16.

11. C. Smith interview, January 14, 2000, 22.

12. C. Smith Jr. interview.

13. C. Smith interview, March 9, 2000, 51–52.

14. Burns to Smith, December 13, 1965, FSA, RG 1006, series 719, box 1, folder 1.

15. Smith to Taylor, December 23, 1965, box 174, Taylor Papers.

16. Barkdull to Smith, December 2, 1965, box 22, O'Neill Papers.

17. Transcript, July 29, 1966, FSA, RG 1006, series 721, box 2, folder 14.

18. Jacobs and Taylor interview, 4.

19. *Chesterfield Smith: A Great Floridian* (Great Floridians Film Series, 1997, available at http://www.worldcat.org/title/chesterfield-smith-a-great-floridian/oclc/61264755) (accessed January 11, 2016).

20. Ibid.

21. Ibid.

22. Ervin interview, December 16, 1986, 2.

23. FSA, RG 900000, Beth Johnson Collected Papers, series M75-74, box 3, folder 16.

24. FSA, RG 900000, Beth Johnson Collected Papers, series M75-74, box 1, folder 17.

25. *Orlando Evening Star,* August 15, 1957, in FSA, RG 900000, Beth Johnson Collected Papers, series M75-74, box 2, folder 7.

26. Ruth Smith, "For and about Women," *Orlando Sentinel,* April 12, 1959.

27. *Orlando Sentinel,* January 30, 1962, in FSA, RG 900000, Beth Johnson Collected Papers, series M75-74, box 2, folder 7.

28. Morris, *Florida Handbook, 1961–1962.*

29. Ann Waldron, "Lady Senator Finds No Room for Tears," *St. Petersburg Times,* November 27, 1962.

30. Ibid.

31. Allsworth interview, August 23, 2013.

32. Ervin interview, January 12, 2011.

33. The friend was Dexter Douglass. Douglass and Ervin interview.

34. Ibid.

35. Dyckman, *A Most Disorderly Court,* 51–60.

36. Ibid., 52.

37. Organizational meeting, January 10, 1966, FSA, RG 1006, series 719, box 1, folder 1.

38. Pettigrew interview, December 16, 1986, 1.

39. Marsicano interview, 1.

40. O'Neill interview, 16.

41. Ibid., 15.

42. Caldwell to Smith, January 17, 1966, FSA, RG 1006, series 719, box 1, folder 2.

43. Memorandum, January 12, 1966, FSA, RG 1006, series 719, box 1, folder 2.

44. Committee listing, FSA, RG 1006, series 720, box 1, folder 21.

45. Earle interview, 9.

46. O'Neill interview, 2.

47. Swann v. Adams, 258 F. Supp. 819 (S.D. Fla. 1966). This published opinion is a combination of a 1965 order and a 1966 opinion on the March 1966 reapportionment.

48. Ibid., 821–22.

49. Ibid., 822.

50. Ibid.

Chapter 5. Putting It Together, Part I

1. Barkdull interview, December 16, 1986, 2–3.

2. Barkdull to Smith, December 2, 1965, box 22, O'Neill Papers.

3. Transcript, January 11, 1966, FSA, RG 1006, series 720, box 1, folder 9.

4. C. Smith interview, March 9, 2000, 53.

5. Stallings interview, December 16, 1986, 5.

6. Transcript, July 11, 1966, FSA, RG 1006, series 721, box 1, folder 4.

7. Askew interview, December 16, 1986, 3–4.

8. Ibid., 3.

9. Hugh Taylor General Statement (undated), p. 5, FSA, RG 1006, series 720, box 1, folder 9.

10. Transcript, March 25, 1966, FSA, RG 1006, series 720, box 1, folder 6, p. 57.

11. Hugh Taylor General Statement (undated), p. 6.

12. C. Smith interview, March 9, 2000, 53.

13. See http://www.unf.edu/library/specialcollections/manuscripts/john-mathews/John_Mathews_Biography.aspx.

14. See, e.g., C. Smith interview, March 9, 2000, 53; Moyle interview.

15. C. Smith interview, March 9, 2000, 54.

16. Dyckman, *Floridian of His Century*, 48.

17. Smith to O'Neill, December 30, 1965, box 22, O'Neill Papers.

18. Transcript, January 11–12, 1966, FSA, RG 1006, series 720, box 1, folder 2.

19. Turlington interview, May 18, 1974, 18.

20. Transcript, January 11–12, 1966, FSA, RG 1006, series 720, box 1, folder 2.

21. Swann v. Adams, 258 F. Supp. at 822.

22. *House Journal*, March 2, 1966, 1.

23. Ibid.

24. Ibid., 5.

25. Ibid.

26. Ibid.

27. Ibid., 3.

28. Ibid., 2.

29. Ibid.

30. Ibid., March 7, 1966, 15.

31. Ibid., March 5, 1966, 13.

32. Swann v. Adams, 258 F. Supp. at 819.

33. MacKay interview.

34. Daisy Parker and Albert Sturm, "The Executive Branch in the Florida Constitution" (Institute of Governmental Research, Florida State University, May 2, 1966), 12.

35. Constitution Revision Commission, 1965–67, Executive Department Committee, minutes, February 16, 1966, *State Constitutional Conventions, Commissions, and Amendments, 1959–78: Annotated Bibliography*, vol. 1 (Washington, D.C.: Congressional Information Service, Inc., 1981) [hereafter cited as *State Constitutional Conventions*].

36. Constitution Revision Commission, 1965–67, Legislative Committee, minutes, February 10, 11, 1966, *State Constitutional Conventions*.

37. Fla. Const. art. III, § 28, and art. VII, § 3 (1885).

38. Ervin interview, December 16, 1986.

39. Douglass, at Florida Supreme Court Historical Society annual meeting, June 20, 2012.

40. Barron interview.

41. Ibid.; Askew interview, May 9, 2001.

42. C. Smith interview, March 9, 2000, 53.

43. Fla. Const. art. V, § 3 (1885).

44. Fla. Const. art. V, §§ 1, 16, 18, 21 (1885).

45. O'Connell interview, 2.

46. "Present Court System in Florida 1966," prepared by Statutory Revision Department, Attorney General's Office, Tallahassee, box 33, O'Neill Papers.

47. Askew interview, December 16, 1986, 11.

48. Ibid., 5, 8.

49. Barkdull interview, December 16, 1986, 11–12.

50. Ibid., 3.

51. Judicial Department Committee, minutes, n.d., *State Constitutional Conventions.*

52. Art. V, § 8, *A Draft of a Proposed Revised Constitution of Florida* (November 10, 1966), FSA, RG 1006, series 720, box 2, folder 8.

53. Art. V, § 13(a), ibid.

54. Campaign correspondence folder (n.d.), Justice Glenn Terrell Papers, Claude Pepper Libraries, Florida State University Libraries, Tallahassee.

55. Art. V, § 14(b).

56. Art. V, § 12(a).

57. Art. V, § 12(c).

58. Art. V, § 14(c).

59. Friday interview, 7.

60. See http://www.mulberryphosphatemuseum.org/whatisphosphate.html (accessed November 27, 2012).

61. Stallings interview, December 16, 1986, 8.

62. Fla. Const. art. IX, § 5 (1885).

63. Fla. Const. art. IX, § 1 (1885).

64. Fla. Const. art. XII, § 1 (1885).

65. Fla. Const. art. IX, § 1 (1885).

66. Dauer interview, November 23, 1976.

67. Ibid.

68. Miami Public Hearing transcript, July 15, 1966, FSA, RG 1006, series 721, box 1, folder 17.

69. Bryant interview.

70. See also Little, "Historical Development of Constitutional Restraints."

71. Fee to Taylor, May 12, 1966, box 174, Taylor Papers.

72. Fla. Const. art. IX, § 6 (1885).

73. Fla. Const. art. VIII, §§ 3, 8 (1885).

74. See, e.g., Fla. Const. art. VIII, §§ 9, 10, 11, 24 (1885).

75. Sobel v. Adams, 208 F. Supp. 316, 322 (S.D. Fla. 1962).

76. Dauer interview, December 16, 1986, 1–2.

77. Constitution Revision Commission, 1965–67, Local Government Committee, minutes, February 18, 1966, May 13–14, 1966, *State Constitutional Conventions.*

78. See, generally, Alford and Wolf, "Constitutional Revision."

79. E.g., Fla. Const. art. VIII, §§ 12–21 (1885).

80. Fla. Const. art. VIII, §§ 11, 24 (1885).

81. Fla. Const. art. VIII, §§ 7 (1885).

82. Marsicano interview, 1.

83. Ibid.

84. Turlington interview, December 17, 1986, 5.

85. C. Smith interview, March 9, 2000, 81.

86. Branch, *Pillar of Fire*; *B. K. Roberts* (Great Floridians Film Series, Florida Division of Historical Resources, Florida Department of State, n.d.)

87. *Tallahassee Democrat*, September 19, 1993.

88. Turlington interview, December 17, 1986, 7.

89. Model State Constitution, Art. X, Section 1000, Model State Constitution with Explanatory Articles, 5th ed. (National Municipal League, 1948).

90. Fla. Const. art. XII, § 12 (1885).

91. Laws of Florida (1947), chapter 23725.

92. Education and Welfare Committee Minutes, April 26, 1966, FSA, RG 1006, series 720, box 3, folder 15.

93. Fla. Const. art. VI, § 5 (1885).

Chapter 6. Drafting a Constitution, Drafting a Legislature

1. Jacobs and Taylor interview, 17.

2. Transcript, March 25, 1966, FSA, RG 1006, series 720, box 1, folder 6, pp. 57–58.

3. Transcript, January 11, 1966, FSA, RG 1006, series 720, box 1, folder 6, pp. 3–4.

4. See, e.g., box 22, O'Neill Papers.

5. Transcript, January 11, 1966, FSA, RG 1006, series 720, box 1, folder 6, p. 16.

6. Transcript, March 25, 1966, FSA, RG 1006, series 720, box 1, folder 7, p. 31.

7. Ibid., 170–72.

8. Turlington interview, December 17, 1986, 4.

9. Constitution Revision Commission, 1965–67, minutes, March 25–26, 1966, April 11, 1966, *State Constitutional Conventions, Commissions, and Amendments, 1959–78: Annotated Bibliography*, vol. 1 (Washington, D.C.: Congressional Information Service, Inc., 1981).

10. Ibid.

11. "Speaker-Designate George Stone Dies in Pensacola Crash," *St. Petersburg Times*, April 2, 1966.

12. Robert T. Mann to T. Terrell Sessums, April 6, 1966, box 82, Sessums Collection.

13. Turlington interview, May 18, 1974, 13.

14. Peter Dunbar, conversation with author, December 11, 2015.

15. Smith to Taylor, May 27, 1966, box 174, Taylor Papers.

16. Taylor to Barkdull and Mathews, May 30, 1966, box 174, Taylor Papers.

17. Fee to Smith, May 27, 1966, Florida CRC, Committee minutes and proposals, January 1966–June 1966, FSA, RG 1006, series 720, box 1, folder 23.

18. Taylor to CRC members, June 22, 1966, box 182, Taylor Papers.

19. Smiljanich, *Then Sings My Soul*, 145; Barnebey, *Integrity Is the Issue*, 132–33.

20. Smiljanich, *Then Sings My Soul*, 145–46; Barnebey, *Integrity Is the Issue*, 133–34.

21. High to Smith, July 9, 1966, box 175, Taylor Papers.

22. "Davis Edges Johns by 282 Votes," *Bradford County Telegraph*, May 26, 1966; "Senator Johns Takes Defeat in Stride," *Bradford County Telegraph*, May 26, 1966.

23. Graham to Dauer, May 25, 1966, folder "Graham, D. Robert (Bob), 1959–1984," box 3, Dauer Papers.

24. Transcript, July 27, 1966, FSA, RG 1006, series 721, box 2, folder 8.

25. Transcript, July 11, 1966, FSA, RG 1006, series 721, box 1, folder 4; draft constitution, box 2, Maxine Baker Papers.

26. Transcript, July 27, 1966, FSA, RG 1006, series 721, box 2, folder 14.

27. Transcript, July 14, 1966, FSA, RG 1006, series 721, box 1, folder 11.

28. O'Neill interview, 9.

29. Ibid.

30. Earle interview, 7.

31. McCarty interview, 5.

32. Earle interview, 4.

33. Bill Sweisgood, "The Comic Look," *Jacksonville Journal*, August 20, 1966.

34. Perlstein, *Nixonland*, chapter 3.

35. Gere and Jerome Johns interview.

36. Ansolabehere and Snyder, *The End of Inequality*, chapter 10.

37. Martin A. Dyckman, discussion with author, August 12, 2012.

38. Kallina, *Claude Kirk*, 70.

39. Ralph Turlington later remarked waggishly that Kirk was so colorful and likable that "for a while, people believed that he really consistently understood what he was doing." Turlington interview, May 18, 1974, 19.

40. Kallina, *Claude Kirk*, 43.

41. Barneby, *Integrity Is the Issue*, 202.

42. Pat Thomas, Chair, Democratic Executive Committee of Florida, to Democratic candidates in the March 1967 special election, February 23, 1967, box 83, Sessums Collection.

43. *Senate Journal*, November 15, 1966, 2.

44. Ibid., 3.

45. *House Journal*, November 15, 1966, 5.

46. Ibid.

Chapter 7. The CRC Debates: November and December 1966

1. Hank Drane, *Florida Times-Union*, December 18, 1966.

2. Douglass and Ervin interview.

3. Kirk interview, December 16, 1986, 4; C. Smith interview, March 9, 2000, 59.

4. Kirk interview, December 16, 1986, 2.

5. C. Smith interview, March 9, 2000, 59.

6. Kirk interview, August 10, 2011, 12.

7. Hank Drane, *Florida Times-Union*, December 18, 1966.

8. *Tallahassee Democrat*, December 5, 1966.

9. Ibid.

10. Barkdull interview, 4.

11. List of amendments, FSA, RG 1006, series 723, box 1, folder 1.

12. Rule 7.7, Florida Constitution Revision Commission, FSA, RG 16, series 720, box 3, folder 6.

13. Barkdull interview, 5; Chesterfield Smith to Steering and Rules Committee members, September 28, 1966, FSA, RG 1006, series 720, box 2, folder 13.

14. Don Meiklejohn, *Gainesville Sun*, December 11, 1966.

15. Barkdull interview, 4.

16. Transcript, November 28, 1966, FSA, RG 1006, series 722, box 1, folder 1, p. 71.

17. Transcript, November 28, 1966, FSA, RG 1006, series 722, box 1, folder 1, pp. 7–12.

18. Ibid., 12–13.

19. Ibid., 9.

20. Fla. Const. (1861); Fla. Const. art. VIII (1868).

21. Model State Constitution (National Municipal League, 1963), 18.

22. Transcript, December 8, 1966, FSA, RG 1006, series 722, box 3, folder 14, vol. 32, pp. 27–52.

23. Transcript, December 2, 1966, FSA, RG 1006, series 722, box 2, folder 11, vol. 11, p. 1003.

24. Ibid., 1004.

25. Don Meiklejohn, *Gainesville Sun*, December 11, 1966.

26. Transcript, December 2, 1966, FSA, RG 1006, series 722, box 2, folder 2, vol. 2, pp. 899–904.

27. Hal Hendrix, "Soviets Build 6 New Missile Bases," *Miami News*, October 6, 1962.

28. Morris, *Florida Handbook*, 1967–68, 514.

29. Powers, *E.C.*, 111.

30. Transcript, December 13, 1966, FSA, RG 1006, series 722, box 2, folder 2, vol. 2, pp. 269, 272.

31. Ibid., 271.

32. Ibid., 273.

33. Ibid., 274.

34. Ibid., 280.

35. Ibid., 293.

36. Transcript, December 14, 1966, FSA, RG 1006, series 722, box 2, folder 2, vol. 2, p. 31.

37. Ibid., 35.

38. Ibid., 41–42.

39. Report of the Select Committee on Amendments No. 127 and 191, FSA, RG 1006, series 723, box 2, folder 7 (with attached *Memorandum Concerning the Probable*

Effect on Existing Laws and Policies of a Constitutional Provision Requiring Equality of the Sexes).

40. Transcript, December 16, 1966, FSA, RG 1006, series 722, box 2, folder 2, vol. 2, p. 113.

41. Ibid., 111–14.

42. Ibid., 116.

43. Ibid., 122.

44. Transcript, December 15, 1966, FSA, RG 1006, series 722, box 2, folder 13, vol. 13, pp. 78–111.

45. Transcript, December 9, 1966, FSA, RG 1006, series 722, box 2, folder 13, vol. 13, pp. 16–27.

46. Transcript, December 9, 1966, FSA, RG 1006, series 722, box 3, folder 4, vol. 22, p. 389.

47. Transcript, December 16, 1966, FSA, RG 1006, series 722, box 3, folder 4, vol. 22, p. 220.

48. Ibid., 492–96.

49. Transcripts, December 9 and December 16, 1966, FSA, RG 1006, series 722, box 3, folders 2–4, vols. 20–22, passim.

50. Ibid.

51. Ibid.

52. Fla. Const. art. III, § 9 (1967).

53. Transcript, December 5, 1966, FSA, RG 1006, series 722, box 2, folder 15, vol. 15, pp. 90–91 (referencing committee legislative subcommittee minutes), 143–44.

54. Transcript, December 6, 1966, FSA, RG 1006, series 722, box 3, folder 8, vol. 26, p. 37.

55. Ibid.

56. Ibid., 42, 43.

57. Askew interview, May 9, 2001.

58. Transcript, December 7, 1966, FSA, RG 1006, series 722, box 3, folder 8, vol. 26, p. 99.

59. Transcript, December 1, 1966, FSA, RG 1006, series 722, box 3, folder 13, vol. 31, p. 675.

60. Ibid., 676–77.

61. Ibid., 679–81.

62. Ibid., 686.

63. Ibid., 689–90.

64. Ibid., 694.

65. Ibid., 713.

66. Ibid., 715.

67. Ibid., 724–25.

68. Transcript, December 14, 1966, FSA, RG 1006, series 722, box 3, folder 7, vol. 25, p. 59.

69. Ibid.

70. Ibid.

71. Ibid., 61.

72. Ibid., 66.

73. Ibid., 99.

74. Ibid., 73.

75. Ibid., 77.

76. Ibid., 79.

77. Ibid., 82.

78. Ibid., 85.

79. Ibid., 90.

80. R. A. Gray to Taylor, n.d., box 182, Taylor Papers.

81. Transcript, December 14, 1966, FSA, RG 1006, series 722, box 3, folder 7, vol. 25, pp. 91–92.

82. Ibid., 93.

83. Ibid., 94.

84. Ibid., 97.

85. Turlington interview, December 17, 1986, 4.

86. Transcript, December 14, 1966, FSA, RG 1006, series 722, box 3, folder 7, vol. 25, pp. 123, 126.

87. Transcript, November 30, 1966, FSA, RG 1006, series 722, box 3, folder 10, vol. 28, p. 578.

88. Transcript, December 6, 1966, FSA, RG 1006, series 722, box 3, folder 10, vol. 28, pp. 224, 226.

89. Ibid., 217.

90. Ibid., 235.

91. *St. Petersburg Times*, November 5, 1966.

92. *Tallahassee Democrat*, November 20, 1966.

93. Transcript, December 8, 1966, FSA, RG 1006, series 722, box 3, folder 14, vol. 32, pp. 198–210.

94. Ibid., 216–18.

95. Taylor to Smith, November 18, 1966, box 181, Taylor Papers.

96. Transcript, December 12, 1966, FSA, RG 1006, series 722, box 4, folder 10, vol. 45, pp. 220–21.

97. See, e.g., ibid., 233, 244.

98. Ibid., 229.

99. Ibid., 230–31.

100. See, e.g., ibid., 236, 252.

101. Ibid., 242, 244.

102. Ibid., 233, 235–36.

103. Ibid., 235.

104. Ibid., 246.

105. Ibid., 244–45.

106. Ibid., 237–57.

107. See ibid., 202–5.

108. Transcript, December 13, 1966, FSA, RG 1006, series 722, box 4, folder 11, vol. 46, pp. 12–15.

109. Ibid., 128–31.

110. Transcript, December 12, 1966, FSA, RG 1006, series 722, box 4, folder 10, vol. 41, pp. 119–26.

111. Pettigrew interview, December 16, 1986, 12.

112. Transcript, December 1, 1966, FSA, RG 1006, series 722, box 4, folder 14, vol. 49, p. 821.

113. Ibid., 818.

114. Ibid., 823.

115. Ibid., 841–42. .

116. Ibid., 845–47.

117. Ibid., 851–52.

118. Ibid., 878.

119. Telegram, Women for Constitutional Government to Taylor, date not available, box 179, Taylor Papers.

120. Fla. Const. art. VIII, §§ 9, 10, 11, 24 (1885).

121. Transcript, multiple dates, FSA, RG 1006, series 722, box 6, folder 11, vol. 81 (entire).

122. Ervin interview, November 10, 2010.

123. Transcript, December 14, 1966, FSA, RG 1006, series 722, box 6, folder 1, vol. 71, p. 346; transcript, December 15 1966, FSA, RG 1006, series 722, box 6, folder 1, vol. 71, p. 174.

124. Transcript, December 14, 1966, FSA, RG 1006, series 722, box 6, folder 1, vol. 71, pp. 337–45.

125. Ibid., 341–42.

126. Ibid., 353–54.

127. Ervin interview, November 10, 2010.

128. Hank Drane, *Florida Times-Union*, December 18, 1966.

Chapter 8. Putting It Together, Part II

1. Governor Claude Kirk Inauguration (1967), at http://www.youtube.com/watch?v=7GSip8DSVlY (accessed January 14, 2016); Turlington, interview, June 13, 2014.

2. Kirk interview, August 10, 2011.

3. Hank Drane, "In Hank's Corner," *Florida Times-Union*, January 11, 1967.

4. C. Smith interview, March 9, 2000, 59.

5. *Tallahassee Democrat*, October 18, 1966.

6. Barkdull interview, December 16, 1986, 8.

7. Final Adoption Composite Draft, FSA, RG 1006, series 723, box 2, folder 17; Stallings interview, December 16, 1986, 10.

8. Friday interview, 4.

9. Ibid.

10. Editorial, "Sampling the Porridge," *Gainesville Sun*, January 5, 1967.

11. *Senate Journal*, January 9, 1967, 2.

12. Turlington interview, May 18, 1974, 19.

13. Ibid.

14. *House Journal*, January 9, 1967, 2.

15. Swann v. Adams, 385 U.S. 440 (1967).

16. *Senate Journal*, January 9, 1967, 5.

17. R. G. Dixon, *Democratic Representation*, 445.

18. Pettigrew interview, October 23, 2012.

19. Talbot "Sandy" D'Alemberte, conversation with the author, June 21, 2012; Barnett and D'Alemberte interview, 13.

20. *House Journal*, January 9, 1967, 18.

21. Askew interview, May 9, 2001.

22. *House Journal*, January 10, 1967, 23.

23. Ibid., January 16, 1967, 32.

24. Ibid., January 19, 1967, 57.

25. *Senate Journal*, January 20, 1967, 59.

26. Ibid., January 19, 1967, 57–58.

27. Ibid., January 28, 1967, 78.

28. Ibid., January 26, 1967, 74–75.

29. Foglesong, *Married to the Mouse*.

30. Pettigrew interview, October 23, 2012.

31. Ibid.

32. Barnett and D'Alemberte interview, 13.

33. Folder "Case 186-62-M-Civil-DD Defendant 1/27/67 Legislative Brief; 1967 Apportionment Statistics Pope, Turlington, Adams," box 18, Dauer Papers.

34. Allsworth interview, August 23, 2013.

35. "Judges Reapportion Florida; New Elections Are Ordered," *Palm Beach Post*, February 9, 1967, in box 26, Dauer Papers.

36. "Gov. Kirk Is Shocked by Ruling." *Palm Beach Post*, February 9, 1967, in box 26, Dauer Papers.

37. "Judges Reapportion Florida; New Elections Are Ordered."

38. McCarty interview, 7.

39. Malcolm B. Johnson, *Tallahassee Democrat*, February 9, 1967.

40. *Orlando Evening Star*, February 10, 1967, in box 26, Dauer Papers.

41. "Judges Reapportion Florida; New Elections Are Ordered."

42. McRae to Dauer, February 9, 1967, folder "McRae, William A., 1949–1967," box 4, Dauer Papers.

43. "Members of the Senate," *Senate Journal*, March 2, 1966, January 9, 1967, April 4, 1967.

44. Graham interview, February 14, 2005.

45. Morris, *Florida Handbook, 1967–68*.

46. *House Journal*, April 4, 1967, 5.

47. Ibid., 21.

48. *Senate Journal*, April 4, 1967, 5.

49. Ibid.

50. Ibid., 17–19.

51. Pettigrew interview, October 23, 2012.

52. 1966–67 *House Journal*, Index, 2150; *Senate Journal*, April 14, 1967, 844.

53. *House Journal*, July 25, 1967, 14, and July 28, 1967, 50.

54. Hopping memorandum, July 27, 1967, FSA, RG 1006, series 923, box 23, folder 1.

55. Ibid.

56. Ibid.

57. Transcription at *Senate Journal*, August 8, 1967, 49–54.

58. Ibid., 50.

59. Ibid.

60. Barnett and D'Alemberte interview, 10; *House Journal*, January 9, 1967, 10.

61. Barnett and D'Alemberte interview, 10.

62. *Senate Journal*, August 8, 1967, 51–52.

63. Transcript, FSA, RG 1006, series 722, box 3, folder 7, vol. 25, p. 427 (no date given).

64. *Senate Journal*, August 8, 1967, 52.

65. Ibid.

66. Ibid.

67. Ibid.

68. Ibid., 53.

69. Ibid., 54.

70. Ibid.; *House Journal*, July 31, 1967, 2.

71. Pettigrew interview, December 16, 1986, 3.

72. *House Journal*, August 16, 1967, 40; Dubbin interview.

73. See generally *Senate Journal*, August 1–15, 1967.

74. Correspondence regarding CRC, folders 761–68, box 93, series 306, John E. Mathews Jr. Collection, Thomas G. Carpenter Library, University of North Florida, Jacksonville.

75. Correspondence regarding CRC, folder 4, box 178, Taylor Papers.

76. Dubbin interview.

77. *House Journal*, August 21, 1967, 2.

78. Ibid., 9, 35.

79. O'Neill interview, 3.

80. *House Journal*, August 22, 1967, 4.

81. Ibid., August 28, 1967, 11.

82. Ibid., August 30, 1967, 16.

83. *Senate Journal*, August 21, 1967, 4–5.

84. Ibid., 5.

85. Ibid.

86. Ibid., 5–6.

87. Ibid., 6.

88. Ibid., August 22, 1967, 9.

89. *House Journal*, August 31, 1967, 19, and September 1, 1967, 25.

90. *Senate Journal*, September 1, 1967, 53.

91. See generally letters to Sessums from citizens in September 1967, box 84, Sessums Collection.

92. Dubbin interview.

93. Ibid.

94. "Revision Panel Ties Up Loose Ends; College Unrest Shakes 19-Year Vote," *Ft. Lauderdale News*, June 17, 1968; "Constitution Revision: Says Legislators Will Avoid Most Emotional Issues," *Daytona Beach Evening News*, June 17, 1968.

95. "Session Decision Due Tuesday," *Palm Beach Post*, June 10, 1968.

96. *House Journal*, June 24, 1968, 1.

97. "Constitution Panel Finds Agreement," *St. Petersburg Times*, June 18, 1968.

98. *Senate Journal*, June 25, 1968, 47.

99. *House Journal*, July 1, 1968, 66; "Gov. Kirk Expands Scope of Session: Senate, House Split on Key Issues," *Palm Beach Post*, July 2, 1968.

100. "Gov. Kirk Expands Scope of Session."

101. *House Journal*, July 3, 1968, 100.

102. Jim Minter, "Dade Delegates' Impact Growing," *Miami Herald*, June 9, 1968.

103. Associated Press, "State's Legislators See People's Okay on the Constitution," *Tallahassee Democrat*, July 4, 1968; "A Constitution to Consider," *Miami Herald*, July 4, 1968.

104. *House Journal*, July 3, 1968, 105.

105. See, e.g., Hank Drane and Everette Williard, "New Constitution Approved," *Florida Times-Union*, July 4, 1968.

Chapter 9. A New Constitution

1. Correspondence, box 182, Taylor Papers; correspondence, box 36, O'Neill Papers.

2. Resolution, October 15, 1968, box 89, Sessums Collection.

3. Kallina, *Claude Kirk*, 123–24.

4. Bill Mansfield, "How Will Constitution Affect Business?" *Florida Trend*, November 1968, 28.

5. Ibid.

6. Dauer, Donovan, and Kammerer, *Should Florida Adopt the Proposed 1968 Constitution?*

7. Dauer to Smith, September 23, 1968, box 36, O'Neill Papers.

8. Dauer, Donovan, and Kammerer, *Should Florida Adopt the Proposed 1968 Constitution?* iv.

9. Ibid.

10. Stallings memo, August 29, 1968, box 36, O'Neill Papers.

11. *Ocala Star-Banner*, September 8, 1968.

12. "Integrity IS the Issue," undated pamphlet, box 36, O'Neill Papers.

13. C. Smith interview, March 9, 2000, 88.

Epilogue

1. Ervin interview, November 10, 2010.

2. Schwartz, *Super Chief*, 507–8.

3. Colburn, *From Yellow Dog Democrats*, 27.

4. Land interview, 3.

5. Jacobs and Taylor interview, 11.

6. Fla. Const. art. XI § 2 (1968).

7. Turlington interview, May 18, 1974, 24.

8. Dyckman interview.

9. Pettigrew interview, October 16, 2012.

10. Stearns interview.

11. Conner and Horne interview.

12. Carter, *Florida Experience*, 48.

13. Colburn and Scher, *Florida's Gubernatorial Politics,* 216; Colburn and deHaven-Smith, *Government in the Sunshine State*, 66–68.

14. Stock speech on ethics, box 127, Chesterfield Smith Papers, GSL.

15. Folder containing information on Citizens Committee for Judicial Reform, box 127, Smith Papers.

16. Ibid.

17. Talbot "Sandy" D'Alemberte, conversation with the author, June 21, 2012.

18. Barnett and D'Alemberte interview, 41.

19. Reubin Askew, conversation with the author, August 22, 2012.

20. Ashmore and Baggs, *Mission to Hanoi*, 13, 21.

21. Associated Press, "U.S. Unit Sends Mission to Hanoi in Behalf of Colloquy on Peace," *New York Times*, January 8, 1967.

22. Gere and Jerome Johns interview.

23. Barnett interview.

24. See https://www.youtube.com/watch?v=IpQfHDZG_8k; https://www.youtube.com/watch?v=8KzPPuQOWUw.

25. Journal of the 1997–98 Constitutional Revision Commission, June 16, 1997, 8–9, http://archive.law.fsu.edu/crc/minutes/crcminutes61697.html (accessed 1/15/2016).

Bibliography

Primary Sources

MANUSCRIPT COLLECTIONS

Claude Pepper Libraries, Florida State University Libraries, Tallahassee
  Terrell, Justice Glenn. Papers.
Florida State Archives, Tallahassee
Florida State University Libraries, Special Collections Department, Tallahassee
  Morris, Allen. Collected Papers.
  Taylor, Circuit Judge Hugh M. Papers.
George A. Smathers Libraries, Special and Area Studies Collection, University of
  Florida, Gainesville
  Baker, Maxine E. Papers.
  Caldwell, Millard Filmore. Papers.
  Dauer, Manning Julian. Papers.
  Graves, William Carlton. Papers.
  Pope, Verle Allyn. Papers.
  Records of the Public Administration Clearing Service.
  Reitz, J. Wayne. Papers.
  Smith, Chesterfield. Papers.
  Stephen C. O'Connell Florida Supreme Court Papers.
  Thornal, B. Campbell. Papers.
Lawton Chiles Legal Information Center, University of Florida, Gainesville
  O'Neill, William G. Papers.
Richter Library, Special Collections, University of Miami Libraries, Coral Gables
  Baggs, William C. Papers.
Stetson University Archives, Stetson College of Law, Gulfport, Florida
  Sebring, Harold L. Collection.
Tampa Library, Special Collections Department, University of South Florida
  Sessums, T. Terrell. Collection.

Thomas G. Carpenter Library, University of North Florida, Jacksonville
Mathews, John E., Jr. Collection.

INTERVIEWS

Allsworth, Emerson. Interview by Mary Adkins. August 23, 2013.
———. Interview by Sid Johnston. December 17, 1986. Samuel Proctor Oral History
Program, University of Florida, Gainesville (hereafter "SPOHP").
Askew, Reubin. Interview by Walter DeVries. July 8, 1974. SPOHP.
———. Interview by Sid Johnston. December 16, 1986. SPOHP.
———. Interview by Mike Vasilinda. May 9, 2001. Tallahassee: Legislative Research
Center & Museum.
Barkdull, Thomas Henry, Jr. Interview by Sid Johnston. December 16, 1986. SPOHP.
———. Interview by Mike Vasilinda. September 6, 2003. Tallahassee: Legislative Re-
search Center & Museum.
Barnett, Martha. Interview. November 18, 2009. SPOHP.
Barnett, Martha, and Talbot "Sandy" D'Alemberte. Interview by Mary Adkins. April
29, 2014.
Barron, Dempsey. Interview by Mike Vasilinda. June 8, 2000. Tallahassee: Legislative
Research Center & Museum.
Barrow, William D. Interview by Mike Vasilinda. August 6, 2002. Tallahassee: Legisla-
tive Research Center & Museum.
Boylston, Gray. Interview by Jack Bass and Walter DeVries. May 22, 1974. Chapel Hill:
Southern Oral History Program, Southern Historical Collection, Wilson Library,
University of North Carolina.
Bryant, Farris. Interview by Mike Vasilinda. February 17, 2001. Tallahassee: Legisla-
tive Research Center & Museum.
Caldwell, Millard. Interview by Ray Washington. N.d. SPOHP.
Chiles, Lawton. Interview by Sid Johnston. December 16, 1986. SPOHP.
Collins, LeRoy. Interview by Jack Bass and Walter DeVries. May 19, 1974. Chapel Hill:
Southern Oral History Program, Southern Historical Collection, Wilson Library,
University of North Carolina.
———. Interview by Ray Washington. March 1979. SPOHP.
Conner, Doyle, and Mallory Horne. Interview by Mike Vasilinda. July 5, 2006. Tal-
lahassee: Legislative Research Center & Museum.
Cross, J. Emory. Interview by R. T. Cross. November 3, 1978. SPOHP.
D'Alemberte, Talbot "Sandy." Interview by Mike Vasilinda. N.d. Tallahassee: Legisla-
tive Research Center & Museum.
Dauer, Manning. Interview by Alfred Diamant. October 3, 1980. SPOHP.
———. Interview by Jorge Guira. March 28, 1982. SPOHP.
———. Interview by Joyce Miller. November 23, 1976. SPOHP.
———. Interview by unidentified interviewer. December 16, 1986. SPOHP.
David, Bill. Interview by Jack Bass and Walter DeVries. May 20, 1974. Chapel Hill:
Southern Oral History Program, Southern Historical Collection, Wilson Library,
University of North Carolina.

Douglass, Dexter, and Robert Ervin. Interview by Mary Adkins. March 8, 2011.

Dubbin, Murray. Interview by Mary Adkins. August 1, 2014.

Dyckman, Martin. Interview by Mary Adkins. June 21, 2012.

Earle, Richard T. Interview by Denise Stobbie. December 16, 1986. SPOHP.

Ervin, Robert. Interviews by Mary Adkins. November 10, 2010, and January 12, 2011.

———. Interview by Denise Stobbie. December 16, 1986. SPOHP.

Friday, Elmer. Interview by Denise Stobbie. December 16, 1986. SPOHP.

Gong, Eddie. Interview by Mike Vasilinda. November 14, 2003. Tallahassee: Legislative Research Center & Museum.

Graham, Bob. Interview by Mary Adkins. May 15, 2014.

———. Interview by Mike Vasilinda. February 14, 2005. Tallahassee: Legislative Research Center & Museum.

Grimes, Stephen H. Interview by Mary Adkins. July 18, 2011.

Harris, Charlie. Interview by Sid Johnston. December 17, 1986. SPOHP.

Henderson, Edward. Interview by Arthur White. December 11, 1972. SPOHP.

Hill, Horace, Sr. Interview by Bill Schumann. N.d. Daytona Beach: Volusia County Bar Association.

Horne, Mallory. Interview by Jack Bass and Walter DeVries. May 21, 1974. Chapel Hill: Southern Oral History Program, Southern Historical Collection, Wilson Library, University of North Carolina.

Jacobs, Joseph C., and Hugh Taylor. Interview by Sid Johnston. December 16, 1986. SPOHP.

Johns, Charley. Interview by Ray Washington. N.d. [spring 1979]. SPOHP.

Johns, Gere, and Jerome Johns. Interview by Mary Adkins. July 11, 2011.

Johnson, Beth. Interview by Mike Vasilinda. October 14, 2003. Tallahassee: Legislative Research Center & Museum.

Karl, Fred. Interview by Mike Vasilinda. June 24, 2002. Tallahassee: Legislative Research Center & Museum.

Kirk, Claude. Interview by Mary Adkins. August 10, 2011.

———. Interview by Sid Johnston. December 16, 1986. SPOHP.

Land, Henry W. Interview by Denise Stobbie. December 16, 1986. SPOHP.

MacKay, Buddy. Interview by Mike Vasilinda. December 14, 2004. Tallahassee: Legislative Research Center & Museum.

Marsicano, Ralph. Interview by Denise Stobbie. December 16, 1986. SPOHP.

McCarty, John. Interview by Denise Stobbie. December 16, 1986. SPOHP.

Morris, Allen. Interview by Jack Bass and Walter DeVries. May 16, 1974. Tallahassee: Museum of Florida History.

Moyle, Jon, Sr. Interview by Mary Adkins. June 22, 2014.

O'Connell, Stephen C. Interview by Sid Johnston. December 16, 1986. SPOHP.

O'Neill, William G. Interview by Denise Stobbie. December 8, 1986. SPOHP.

Pettigrew, Richard A. Interview by Mary Adkins. October 16, October 23, 2012.

———. Interview by Denise Stobbie. December 16, 1986. SPOHP.

——. Interview by Mike Vasilinda. November 16, 2001. Tallahassee: Legislative Research Center & Museum.

Pope, Verle. Interview by Sam Proctor. N.d. SPOHP.

Pride, Don. Interview by Jack Bass and Walter DeVries. May 15, 1974. Chapel Hill: Southern Oral History Program, Southern Historical Collection, University of North Carolina.

Reed, Don. Interview by Jack Bass and Walter DeVries. May 23, 1974. Chapel Hill: Southern Oral History Program, Southern Historical Collection, Wilson Library, University of North Carolina.

Roberts, B. K. Interview by Patricia R. Wickman. July 15, 1986. Tallahassee: Museum of Florida History.

Schultz, Fred. Interview by Mike Vasilinda. September 9, 2001. Tallahasse: Legislative Research Center & Museum.

Sessums, Terrell. Interview by Mary Adkins. July 16, 2014.

——. Interview by Jack Bass and Walter DeVries. May 20, 1974. Chapel Hill: Southern Oral History Program, Southern Historical Collection, Wilson Library, University of North Carolina.

Smith, Chesterfield. Interview by Julian Pleasants. January 14, March 9, 2000. SPOHP.

——. Interview by Denise Stobbie. December 14, 1985. SPOHP.

Smith, Chesterfield, Jr. Interview by Mary Adkins. July 29, 2011.

Stallings, George. Interview by Sid Johnston. December 16, 1986. SPOHP.

——. Interview by Mike Vasilinda. February 9, 2005. Tallahassee: Legislative Research Center & Museum.

Stearns, Eugene. Interview by Mary Adkins. November 21, 2012.

Turlington, Ralph. Interview by Mary Adkins. June 13, 2014.

——. Interview by Jack Bass and Walter DeVries. May 18, 1974. Chapel Hill: Southern Oral History Program, Southern Historical Collection, Wilson Library, University of North Carolina.

——. Interview by Sid Johnston. December 17, 1986. SPOHP.

——. Interview by Mike Vasilinda. March 30, 2001. Tallahassee: Legislative Research Center & Museum.

Verlander, Ashley T. Interview by Peter Klingman. March 4, 1974. SPOHP.

Published Sources

Adams, Alto. *The Fourth Quarter*. N.p.: Privately published, 1976.

Ansolabehere, Stephen, and James M. Snyder Jr. *The End of Inequality: One Person, One Vote and the Transformation of American Politics*. New York: Norton, 2008.

Ashmore, Harry S., and William C. Baggs. *Mission to Hanoi: A Chronicle of Double-Dealing in High Places*. New York: Putnam, 1968.

Barlow, Margaret. *Our Florida Legacy: Land, Legend, and Leadership*. Tallahassee: Legislative Research Center & Museum, 2004.

Barnebey, Faith High. *Integrity Is the Issue: Campaign Life with Robert King High.* Miami: E.A. Seemann, 1971.

Bartley, Numan V. *The Rise of Massive Resistance: Race and Politics in the South during the 1950s.* Baton Rouge: Louisana State University Press, 1969.

Bass, Jack, and Walter DeVries. *The Transformation of Southern Politics: Social Change and Political Consequence since 1945.* New York: Basic Books, 1976.

Becker, Theodore L., and Malcolm M. Feeley, eds. *The Impact of Supreme Court Decisions: Empirical Studies.* 2nd ed. New York: Oxford University Press, 1973.

Belin, J. C., and Braden Lee Ball. *The Edward Ball We Knew: An Untold Story of the Man Who Really Discovered Florida.* Pensacola: University of West Florida Foundation, 1998.

Benson, Charles D., and William Barnaby Faherty. *Moonport: A History of Apollo Launch Facilities and Operations.* Washington, D.C.: National Aeronautics and Space Administration Scientific and Technical Information Office, 1978.

Black, Earl, and Merle Black. *Politics and Society in the South.* Cambridge: Harvard University Press, 1987.

Branch, Taylor. *Pillar of Fire: America in the King Years, 1963–65.* New York: Simon and Schuster, 1998.

Braukman, Stacy Lorraine. "Anticommunism and the Politics of Sex and Race in Florida, 1954–1965." PhD diss., University of North Carolina at Chapel Hill, 1999.

———. *Communists and Perverts under the Palms: The Johns Committee in Florida, 1956–1965.* Gainesville: University Press of Florida, 2012.

Brokaw, Tom. *The Greatest Generation.* New York: Random House, 1998.

Brown, Canter, Jr. *None Can Have Richer Memories: Polk County, Florida, 1940–2000.* Tampa: University of Tampa Press, 2005.

Bullock, Charles S., III, and Mark J. Rozell, ed. *The New Politics of the Old South: An Introduction to Southern Politics.* Lanham, Md.: Rowman & Littlefield, 2003.

Carter, Luther J. *The Florida Experience: Land and Water Policy in a Growth State.* Washington, D.C.: Resources for the Future, 1974.

Cobb, James C. *The Brown Decision, Jim Crow, and Southern Identity.* Athens: University of Georgia Press, 2005.

———. *Red Pepper and Gorgeous George: Claude Pepper's Epic Defeat in the 1950 Democratic Primary.* Gainesville: University Press of Florida, 2011.

Colburn, David R. "Florida's Governors Confront the *Brown* Decision: A Case Study of the Constitutional Politics of School Desegregation, 1954–1970." In Hall and Ely, *An Uncertain Tradition,* 326–55.

———. *From Yellow Dog Democrats to Red State Republicans: Florida and Its Politics since 1940.* Gainesville: University Press of Florida, 2007.

———. *Racial Change and Community Crisis: St. Augustine, Florida, 1877–1980.* Gainesville: University Press of Florida, 1991.

Colburn, David R., and Lance deHaven-Smith. *Government in the Sunshine State: Florida since Statehood.* Gainesville: University Press of Florida, 1999.

Colburn, David R., and Richard K. Scher. *Florida's Gubernatorial Politics in the Twentieth Century.* Tallahassee: University Presses of Florida, 1980.

Crooks, James B. *Jacksonville: The Consolidation Story, from Civil Rights to the Jaguars.* Gainesville: University Press of Florida, 2004.

D'Alemberte, Talbot. *The Florida State Constitution: A Reference Guide.* Westport, Conn.: Greenwood Press, 1991.

Danese, Tracy E. *Claude Pepper and Ed Ball: Politics, Purpose, and Power.* Gainesville: University Press of Florida, 2000.

Dauer, Manning J. *Florida Reapportionment.* N.p., n.d. [1968].

———. "Florida: The Different State." In MacManus, *Reapportionment and Representation in Florida,* 77–138.

———. *The Proposed New Florida Constitution: An Analysis.* Gainesville: Public Administration Clearing Service, n.d.

Dauer, Manning J., Clement H. Donovan, and Gladys M. Kammerer. *Should Florida Adopt the Proposed 1968 Constitution?* Gainesville: Public Administration Clearing House, 1968.

Dauer, Manning J., Michael A. Maggioto, and Steven G. Koven. 1991. "Florida." In MacManus, *Reapportionment and Representation in Florida,* 171–84.

Davis, Jack E., and Raymond Arsenault, eds. *Paradise Lost? The Environmental History of Florida.* Gainesville: University Press of Florida, 2005.

Delzell, John Malcom. *The Moving Finger Writes . . .* East Palatka, Fla.: JoDell Publishing Co., 2011.

Dewey, Scott H. "The Fickle Finger of Phosphate: Central Florida Air Pollution and the Failure of Environmental Policy, 1957–1970." *Journal of Southern History* 65 (August 1999): 565–603.

Dinan, John J. *The American State Constitutional Tradition.* Lawrence: University Press of Kansas, 2006.

Dixon, Karl H. "Reapportionment and Reform: The Florida Example." In MacManus, *Reapportionment and Representation in Florida,* 163–70.

Dixon, Robert G., Jr. *Democratic Representation: Reapportionment in Law and Politics.* New York: Oxford University Press, 1972.

Douglas, William O. *The Court Years: 1939–1975.* New York: Random House, 1980.

Dyckman, Martin A. *Floridian of His Century: The Courage of Governor LeRoy Collins.* Gainesville: University Press of Florida, 2006.

———. *A Most Disorderly Court: Scandal and Reform in the Florida Judiciary.* Gainesville: University Press of Florida, 2008.

———. *Reubin O'D. Askew and the Golden Age of Florida Politics.* Gainesville: University Press of Florida, 2011.

Ellis, C. Arthur, and Leslie E. Ellis, eds. 2007. *State of Florida vs. Ruby McCollum, Defendant.* N.p.: LuLu Press, 2007.

Emerson, Chad. "Merging Public and Private Governance: How Disney's Reedy Creek Improvement District 'Re-Imagined' the Traditional Division of Local Regulatory Powers." *Florida State University Law Review* 36 (2009): 177–214.

———. *Project Future: The Inside Story behind the Creation of Disney World.* Pike Road, Ala.: Ayefour Publishing, 2010.

Evans, Tammy. *The Silencing of Ruby McCollum: Race, Class, and Gender in the South.* Gainesville: University Press of Florida, 2006.

Faherty, William Barnaby. *Florida's Space Coast: The Impact of NASA on the Sunshine State.* Gainesville: University Press of Florida, 2002.

Feldman, Noah. *Scorpions: The Battles and Triumphs of FDR's Great Supreme Court Justices.* New York: Twelve, 2010.

Florida Bar. *Proposed Constitution for Florida.* St. Paul: West Publishing Company, 1960.

Florida House of Representatives, Committee on Reapportionment. "Reapportionment in Florida: Out of the 19th Century into the 21st." In MacManus, *Reapportionment and Representation in Florida,* 437–55.

Florida State Bar Association, Constitution Committee. *A Proposed Constitution for Florida.* Deland, Fla.: Stetson University Press, 1947.

Foglesong, Richard E. *Married to the Mouse: Walt Disney World and Orlando.* New Haven: Yale University Press, 2001.

Foner, Eric. *Reconstruction: America's Unfinished Revolution, 1863–1877.* New York: Harper & Row, 1988.

Freyer, Tony A. *Little Rock on Trial: Cooper v. Aaron and School Desegregation.* Lawrence: University Press of Kansas, 2007.

Gannon, Michael, ed. *The New History of Florida.* Gainesville: University Press of Florida, 1996.

Gardner, James A. *Interpreting State Constitutions: A Jurisprudence of Function in a Federal System.* Chicago: University of Chicago Press, 2005.

Garrow, David J. "Bad Behavior Makes Big Law: Southern Malfeasance and the Expansion of Federal Judicial Power, 1954–1968." *St. Johns Law Review* 82 (Winter 2008): 1–36.

Giardina, Carol. *Freedom for Women: Forging the Women's Liberation Movement, 1953–1970.* Gainesville: University Press of Florida, 2010.

Ginzl, David J. *Barnett: The Story of "Florida's Bank."* Tampa: University of Tampa Press, 2001.

Gormley, Ken. *Archibald Cox: Conscience of a Nation.* Reading, Mass.: Addison-Wesley, 1997.

Hall, Kermit L., and James W. Ely Jr., eds. *An Uncertain Tradition: Constitutionalism and the History of the South.* Athens: University of Georgia Press, 1989.

Hall, M. Lewis. *The Judicial Sayings of Justice Glenn Terrell.* Atlanta: The Harrison Company, 1964.

Hamilton, Howard D., ed. *Legislative Apportionment: Key to Power.* New York: Harper & Row, 1964.

Havard, William C., and Loren P. Beth. "Representative Government and Reapportionment: A Case Study of Florida." In MacManus, *Reapportionment and Representation in Florida,* 21–76.

Heale, M. J. *McCarthy's Americans: Red Scare Politics in State and Nation, 1935–1965*. Athens: University of Georgia Press, 1998.

Hewlett, Richard Greening. *Jessie Ball duPont*. Gainesville: University Press of Florida, 1992.

Hurst, Rodney L., Sr. *It Was Never about a Hot Dog and a Coke! A Personal Account of the 1960 Sit-In Demonstrations in Jacksonville, Florida, and Ax Handle Saturday*. Livermore, Calif.: WingSpan Press, 2008.

Jacob, Bruce R. "Remembering a Great Dean: Harold L. 'Tom' Sebring." *Stetson Law Review* 30 (2000): 71–173.

Jewell, Malcom E. "State Legislatures in Southern Politics." In *The American South in the 1960s*, edited by Avery Lieserson, 177–96. New York: Frederick A. Praeger, 1964.

Kallina, Edmund F., Jr. *Claude Kirk and the Politics of Confrontation*. Gainesville: University Press of Florida, 1993.

Karl, Frederick B. *The 57 Club: My Four Decades in Florida Politics*. Gainesville: University Press of Florida, 2010.

Kilpatrick, James Jackson. *The Southern Case for School Segregation*. New York: The Crowell-Collier Press, 1962.

———. *The Sovereign States: Notes of a Citizen of Virginia*. Chicago: Henry Regnery Company, 1957.

Kline, Kevin N. "Guarding the Baggage: Florida's Porkchop Gang and Its Defense of the Old South." PhD diss., Florida State University, 1995.

Kluger, Richard. *Simple Justice: The History of* Brown v. Board of Education *and Black America's Struggle for Equality*. New York: Vintage Books, 1975.

Kyvig, David E. *Explicit and Authentic Acts: Amending the U.S. Constitution, 1776–1995*. Lawrence: University Press of Kansas, 1996.

Lamis, Alexander P. *The Two-Party South*. New York: Oxford University Press, 1984.

Lawson, Steven F. "The Florida Legislative Investigation Committee and the Constitutional Readjustment of Race Relations, 1956–1963." In Hall and Ely, *An Uncertain Tradition*, 296–325.

Lewis, George. *Massive Resistance: The White Response to the Civil Rights Movement*. London: Hodder Arnold, 2006.

———. *The White South and the Red Menace: Segregationists, Anticommunism, and Massive Resistance, 1945–1965*. Gainesville: University Press of Florida, 2004.

———. "White South, Red Nation: Massive Resistance and the Cold War." In *Massive Resistance: Southern Opposition to the Second Reconstruction*, edited by Clive Webb, 117–35. New York: Oxford University Press, 2005.

MacKay, Buddy, with Rick Edmonds. *How Florida Happened: The Political Education of Buddy MacKay*. Gainesville: University Press of Florida, 2010.

MacManus, Susan A., ed. *Reapportionment and Representation in Florida: A Historical Collection*. Tampa: University of South Florida, 1991.

Manley, Walter W., II, and Canter Brown Jr. *The Supreme Court of Florida, 1917–1972*. Gainesville: University Press of Florida, 2006.

McKnight, Robert W. 2007. *The Golden Years: The Florida Legislature, '70s and '80s.* Tallahassee: Sentry Press, 2007.

Miller, James Nathan. "How Florida Threw Out the Pork Chop Gang." *National Civic Review* 60, no. 7 (July 1971): 366–80.

Mitchell, Margaret. *Gone with the Wind.* New York: MacMillan, 1936.

Mormino, Gary R. *Land of Sunshine, State of Dreams: A Social History of Modern Florida.* Gainesville: University Press of Florida, 2008.

Morris, Allen. *The Florida Handbook, 1961–1962.* Tallahassee: The Peninsular Publishing Co., 1961.

———. *The Florida Handbook, 1963–1964.* Tallahassee: The Peninsular Publishing Co., 1963.

———. *The Florida Handbook, 1965–1966.* Tallahassee: The Peninsular Publishing Co., 1965.

———. *The Florida Handbook, 1967–1968.* Tallahassee: The Peninsular Publishing Co., 1967.

———. *Reconsideration: Second Glances at Florida Legislative Events.* Tallahassee: Office of the Clerk, Florida House of Representatives, 1982.

———. *Women in the Florida Legislature.* Tallahassee: Florida House of Representatives, 1995.

Murphy, Walter F. *Congress and the Court: A Case Study in the American Political Process.* Chicago: University of Chicago Press, 1962

———. "Lower Court Checks on Supreme Court Power." In Becker and Feeley, *The Impact of Supreme Court Decisions*, 66–76.

Myrdal, Gunnar. *An American Dilemma.* New York: Harper & Row, 1944.

Neal, Phil C. "*Baker v. Carr*: Politics in Search of Law." In *The Supreme Court Review, 1962*, edited by Philip B. Kurland, 252–327. Chicago: University of Chicago Press, 1962.

Newton, Jim. *Justice for All: Earl Warren and the Nation He Made.* New York: Riverhead Books, 2006.

Nolan, David. *Fifty Feet in Paradise: The Booming of Florida.* New York: Harcourt Brace Jovanovich, 1984.

Paulson, Darryl, and Paul Hawkes. "Desegregating the University of Florida Law School: *Virgil Hawkins v. The Florida Board of Control.*" *Florida State University Law Review* 12 (Spring 1984): 59–71.

Pearce, Don. *Cool Hand Luke.* New York: Scribner, 1965.

Perlstein, Rick. *Nixonland: The Rise of a President and the Fracturing of America.* New York: Scribner, 2009.

Powe, Lucas A., Jr. *The Warren Court and American Politics.* Cambridge: Belknap Press of Harvard University Press, 2000.

Powers, Ormund. *E.C., Mr. Speaker, E.C. Rowell.* Webster, Fla.: Board of Governors of the E.C. Rowell Public Library, 1977.

Price, Harrison "Buzz." *Walt's Revolution! By the Numbers.* Orlando: Ripley Entertainment, Inc., 2004.

Pritchett, C. Herman. *Congress versus the Supreme Court, 1957–1960*. Minneapolis: University of Minnesota Press, 1961.

Read, Frank T., and Lucy S. McGough. *Let Them Be Judged: The Judicial Integration of the Deep South*. Metuchen, N.J.: Scarecrow Press, 1978.

Revels, Tracy J. *Sunshine Paradise: A History of Florida Tourism*. Gainesville: University Press of Florida, 2011.

Roberts, Diane. *Dream State: Eight Generations of Swamp Lawyers, Conquistadors, Confederate Daughters, Banana Republicans, and Other Florida Wildlife*. New York: Free Press, 2007.

Rose, Arnold. *The Negro in America*. New York: Harper & Brothers, 1944.

Ross, William G. "Attacks on the Warren Court by State Officials: A Case Study of Why Court-Curbing Movements Fail." *Buffalo Law Review* 50 (2002): 483–612.

Schwartz, Bernard. *Super Chief: Earl Warren and His Supreme Court—A Judicial Biography*. New York: New York University Press, 1983.

"Sebring, H. L. 'Tom' and E. Harris Drew Oral History." St. Petersburg: Florida Supreme Court Historical Society, November 2, 1990.

Sherrill, Robert. "Florida's Legislature: The Pork Chop State of Mind." *Harper's*, November 1965, 82–97.

———. *Gothic Politics in the Deep South: Stars of the New Confederacy*. New York: Ballantine Books, 1968.

Shofner, Jerrell H. "Reconstruction and Renewal, 1865–1877." In Gannon, *The New History of Florida*, 249–65.

Sklar, Marty. *Dream It! Do It!* New York: Disney Editions, 2013.

Smiljanich, Dorothy Weik. *Then Sings My Soul*. Cocoa: Florida Historical Society Press, 2007.

Smith, Charles U. *The Civil Rights Movement in Florida and the United States*. Tallahassee: Father and Son Publishing, 1989.

Smith, C. Lynwood, Jr. *Strengthening the Florida Legislature*. New Brunswick, N.J.: Rutgers University Press, 1970.

Stark, Bonnie. "McCarthyism in Florida: Charley Johns and the Florida Legislative Investigative Committee, July 1956 to July 1965." Master's thesis, University of South Florida, 1985.

Sturm, Albert. *Thirty Years of State Constitution-Making: 1938–1968*. New York: National Municipal League 1970.

Talmadge, Herman E. *You and Segregation*. Birmingham, Ala.: Vulcan Press, 1955.

Tarr, G. Alan. *Understanding State Constitutions*. Princeton, N.J.: Princeton University Press, 1998.

Tarr, G. Alan, and Robert F. Williams, eds. *State Constitutions for the Twenty-first Century*. Vols. 1–3. Albany: State University of New York, 2006.

Tebeau, Charlton W. *A History of Florida*. Coral Gables: University of Miami Press, 1971.

Virginia Commission on Constitutional Government. *One Man, One Vote*. 1965.

Wagy, Tom R. *Governor LeRoy Collins of Florida: Spokesman of the New South*. University: University of Alabama Press, 1985.

Warren, Earl. *The Memoirs of Earl Warren.* Garden City, N.Y.: Doubleday, 1977.

Webster, Daniel, and Donald Bell. "First Principles for Constitutional Revision." *Nova Law Review* 22 (Fall 1997): 391–436.

Weitz, Seth A. "Bourbon, Pork Chops, and Red Peppers: Political Immorality in Florida, 1945–1968." PhD diss., Florida State University, 2007.

Williamson, Edward C. "The Constitutional Convention of 1885." *Florida Historical Quarterly* 41 (October 1962): 116–26.

———. *Florida Politics in the Gilded Age, 1877–1893.* Gainesville: University Presses of Florida, 1976.

Woods, Jeff. *Black Struggle, Red Scare: Segregation and Anti-Communism in the South, 1948–1968.* Baton Rouge: Louisiana State University Press, 2004.

Wynne, Nick, and Richard Moorhead. *Florida in World War II: Floating Fortress.* Charleston, S.C.: The History Press, 2010.

Ziewitz, Kathryn, and June Wiaz. *Green Empire: The St. Joe Company and the Remaking of Florida's Panhandle.* Gainesville: University Press of Florida, 2004.

Index

Mary E. Adkins is director of legal writing and appellate advocacy at the University of Florida Levin College of Law. She has been a member of the Florida Bar since 1992 and is a trustee of the Florida Supreme Court Historical Society.

FLORIDA GOVERNMENT AND POLITICS

Series editors, David R. Colburn and Susan A. MacManus

Florida has emerged today as a microcosm of the nation and has become a political bellwether in national elections. The impact of Florida on the presidential
elections of 2000, 2004, and 2008 suggests the magnitude of the state's influence. Of the four largest states in the nation, Florida is the only one that has
moved from one political column to the other in the last three national elections. These developments suggest the vital need to explore the politics of the
Sunshine State in greater detail. Books in this series will explore the myriad
aspects of politics, political science, public policy, history, and government in
Florida.

The 57 Club: My Four Decades in Florida Politics, by Frederick B. Karl (2010)
The Political Education of Buddy MacKay, by Buddy MacKay, with Rick Edmonds
    (2010)
Immigrant Prince: Mel Martinez and the American Dream, by Richard E.
    Fogelsong (2011)
Reubin O'D. Askew and the Golden Age of Florida Politics, by Martin A. Dyckman
    (2011)
*Red Pepper and Gorgeous George: Claude Pepper's Epic Defeat in the 1950
    Democratic Primary*, by James C. Clark (2011)
Inside Bush v. Gore, by Charley Wells (2013)
Conservative Hurricane: How Jeb Bush Remade Florida, Matthew T. Corrigan
    (2014)
The Failure of Term Limits in Florida, by Kathryn A. DePalo (2015)
Jigsaw Puzzle Politics in the Sunshine State, edited by Seth C. McKee (2015)
*Making Modern Florida: How the Spirit of Reform Shaped a New State
    Constitution*, by Mary E. Adkins (2016)